D1616104

UP FROM CONSERVATISM

UP FROM CONSERVATISM

Revitalizing the Right

after a Generation of Decay

EDITED BY ARTHUR MILIKH

CLAREMONT
BOOKS

BOOKS

NEW YORK · LONDON

First American edition published in 2023 by Encounter Books, an activity of Encounter for Culture and Education, Inc., a nonprofit, tax-exempt corporation.
Encounter Books website address: www.encounterbooks.com

Manufactured in the United States and printed on acid-free paper. The paper used in this publication meets the minimum requirements of ANSI/NISO Z39.48—1992 (R 1997) (*Permanence of Paper*).

FIRST AMERICAN EDITION

LIBRARY OF CONGRESS CATALOGING-IN-PIUBLICATION DATA

Names: Milikh, Arthur, 1986– editor.
Title: Up from conservatism : revitalizing the right after a generation of decay / edited by Arthur Milikh.
Description: New York : Encounter Books, 2023. | Includes bibliographical references and index. | Summary: "The Conservative Establishment consensus of the past two generations has almost totally broken down. The right needs to rethink its positions on all the essential questions: race, male/female, religion, the economy, foreign policy, and other major issues. This book hopes to frame the direction of where the right is going" – Provided by publisher.
Identifiers: LCCN 2023010140 (print) | LCCN 2023010141 (ebook) | ISBN 9781641772907 (hardcover) | ISBN 9781641772914 (ebook)
Subjects: LCSH: Conservatism—United States. | United States—Politics and government—2021–
Classification: LCC JC573.2.U6 U7 2023 (print) | LCC JC573.2.U6 (EBOOK) | DDC 320.52097309/052—dc23/eng/20230403
LC record available at https://lccn.loc.gov/2023010140
LC ebook record available at https://lccn.loc.gov/2023010141

1 2 3 4 5 6 7 8 9   20 23

| CONTENTS |

INTRODUCTION

Arthur Milikh

THE GOAL OF THIS VOLUME is to correct the trajectory of the Right after several generations of political losses, moral delusions, and intellectual errors. Only such a correction can alter, if not the trajectory of the whole nation, then at least parts of it. Should the New Right overtake the establishment Right and succeed over the Left, a recognizable America could reemerge through the means outlined here. But this volume is not a dogmatic statement. It is an invitation to join the individual authors in rethinking the proximate causes of our decay, exploring new directions – and new risks – politically, and reassessing what the Right is attempting to save.

The establishment Right's failures over the last generations have been manifold. Some were a result of the belief in the eternal stability of the country, for which patriots can be forgiven. But much of the decay we are experiencing originated in the Right's own ideas, its failure to grasp the nature of the Left, and to arrest the latter's growth. One cannot, however, leave it at the level of intellectual error: fear of the Left, combined with underlying belief in the Left's moral superiority, were causes as well, to say nothing of the establishment elites who really wanted, above all, to belong to the ruling class.

To begin to grasp the magnitude of these failures, Americans should ask themselves the following question: Since the end of the Cold War, what trajectory-altering successes or victories can the Right cite to demonstrate its worth? The depressing answer is that, despite spending billions of dollars supporting its infra-structure, and publishing untold thousands of white papers, the establishment Right has registered no clear gains and many clear losses. Much of the nation was conquered on its watch. While leaders of the establishment Right were busy saluting American symbols – the Founders and the Constitution – the Left strove with great success to end constitutional government in America. The Constitution cannot be said to be governing the nation when there is no real presidency (but rather an intelligence apparatus and an administrative state that operate, more or less, on their own); no real Congress (which delegates its powers away to the administrative state); and no real independence of the states (which, with the aid of the Supreme Court, have largely been rendered mere federal fiefdoms).

In terms of political and moral power, the Left currently rules every consequential sector of society, from the nation's educa-tional institutions (K–12 and higher education), to large parts of the media, corporate America, Big Tech, and the federal admin-istrative apparatus. Although unimaginable to conservatives just fifteen years ago, the Left now seems even to own the top military brass. While the Right boasts about how it has stocked the federal courts with "originalists," the Left has attained nation-altering legal victory after legal victory, entrenching racial preferences, creating gay marriage, and limiting state authority on immigra-tion, among many other things.

The mainstream Right was ripe for such defeats as its domi-nant and proudest intellectual framework was economics. It wanted to believe that a nation is its economy. It sought to moral-ize economics – a rising tide would lift all boats, and the main concern for the common good was increasing wealth. To some degree, of course, this is true in a commercial republic, but a nation can also have free-ish markets *and* tyranny. Over these decades of losing, the establishment Right relegated moral and political questions of enormous importance to the status of "social issues" and treated them as largely insignificant, and even embarrassing, second-order concerns, of relevance only when useful to galvanize the vote.

In this regard, the establishment Right seems to have tacitly accepted its subordinate position in America: we do the economic policy, while the Left governs the culture, controls the moral consensus, and holds the levers of real power. As all the nation's sectors were being assimilated into leftist ideology and redirected to leftist ends, often only economically oriented speedbumps were placed in the way. As a result, the Right could do nothing about the changing cultural norms but complain – or go along. This process reveals the extent to which the Left has the real moral authority, and the ruling power, in society. The Right could not even prevent its core constituency, corporate interests, from going left; nor could it protect its largest electoral block, Southern whites and Evangelical Christians, from being increasingly dominated by and assimilated into leftist morality.

At the same time that it lost its electoral power, the Right grew confused and obsessed with a narrow understanding of freedom, which became about private indulgence and "choice," rather than the robust American conception of political liberty. Intellectually enfeebled, the Right failed to halt our civilizational decline. One cannot defend civilization, or do what is necessary to preserve it, when consumption and private frivolity are the goals. In fact, this view of the nation gives moral energy to the Left, which promises no limits and a good conscience. The Right seems to have forgotten that a nation can easily combine, in the short term at least, both prosperity and moral degeneracy which undermines self-rule.

The New Right is a response to these circumstances. But in truth, this isn't the first New Right. The creation of *National Review* in 1955, the Goldwater insurgency of 1964, and the Reagan Revolution of 1980 were all efforts to shape popular understandings of conservatism and to shift the agenda of the Republican Party. These earlier iterations of the New Right succeeded, in large part, in becoming the mainstream Right. But the end of the Cold War, the demographic transformation wrought by the 1965 Immigration Act, and the new morality coming out of the civil rights revolution have made these earlier versions outdated.

The time calls for another renewal, with new goals, different strategies, and a disposition that fits a changing America. This renewal was accelerated by President Trump nationally, but the need preceded Trump and will outlive him.

A marked change in the New Right is one in attitude, a growing boldness that restores something nearer to real politics: overt contention concerning core questions of the common good. The New Right recognizes the Left as an enemy, not merely an opposing movement, because the Left today promotes a tyrannical conception of justice that is irreconcilable with the American idea of justice.

The establishment Right hoped to be left alone. The New Right understands that this is impossible. The Left is imperious, morally and politically. The Left cannot rest until all minds, institutions, traditions, and laws are assimilated to its project. It has shown its willingness to tear through all of America's accumulated social capital; to tear down all institutions, including churches and families; to humiliate, corner, and dissolve all opposition. It has not hesitated to deploy violent mobs against cities, suburbs, and individual residences, to subvert the rule of law, and to employ eliminationist rhetoric against the America – its monuments, its symbols, its people – that it hates.

The Left's relentless and intensifying assault on America has made many citizens question whether the nation can endure. Millions have tried to move to safety out of blue cities and states, or into suburbs and rural areas; others still hope they will be left alone. But the New Right sees that hiding in the woods is not a viable political strategy. Only a few clever dissidents may be able to swim alongside the shark like suckerfish, and even this will work for only a limited time. There must be a political force that earnestly opposes this tyranny and wields legitimate political power in a way the old Right was allergic to. This is the goal of the New Right.

In this regard, the New Right is a counterrevolutionary and restorative force. It does not seek to preserve the status quo, which is defined by the Left. The New Right has abandoned the soothing illusion that, despite a few hiccups, things are essentially normal and stable in America, and that we can go on down the present trajectory in collegial give-and-take with the Left. Our crisis demands a bolder and sometimes more confrontational approach. Any adequate response must arise from a fearlessness that comes from renewed seriousness about the consequences of inaction and defeat. One already sees this civil courage among younger dissidents, many of whom are new to politics.

The leftist revolution in America has already taken place. As a counterrevolutionary force, the New Right must have a strategy for creating and retaking space for its constituents, breaking and replacing captured institutions, and liberating them from the moral horizons of the Left. The essays contained in this book lay out examples of such thinking and action, steps to be taken, and the arguments required to free minds and vital institutions.

We like to say that one must learn to govern, but a truer expression is that one must learn to rule. Governing has come to mean pulling levers of policy. Ruling requires taking responsibility for the good of your people and defending them against their enemies. Ruling in this sense is inspiring, invigorating, and beautiful to behold. The New Right must become the party of beauty, vitality, strength, truth, high purpose, and fierceness. It must view itself as the guardian and ruthless defender of a sacred thing: our civilization.

THE PESSIMISTIC CASE FOR THE FUTURE

Michael Anton

I WAS ASKED to make the "pessimistic case for the future." I present instead more of a "pessimistic take on the present." The future, while imminent, is obscure. The present, by contrast, is knowable. This is also not so much a "case" replete with exhaustive evidence – there isn't space for that, nor is there a need – as a quick tour through our present hell. No one who thinks "everything is fine" will be persuaded otherwise. Those who see the seriousness of our problems hardly need "proof." Nor have I made any attempt to be evenhanded, much less philosophically detached. My account is perforce one-sided. I hope it is wrong.

TRENDING DOWN FOR TWO GENERATIONS

Think of the fortunes of the United States – if you will, of the whole West – like a stock price chart. There will be a lot of ups and downs, positive and negative spikes. But zoom out and the trendline is clear. In conventional terms, the United States peaked around 1965. One may quibble over that date. Why not the moon landing? Victory in the Second World War or the Cold War? Fine. When do you think our political, moral, and spiritual health were at their peak? When was our power, prestige, wealth, cohesion, competence, and confidence – on balance and in the aggregate – highest? (For instance, GDP was lower and infant mortality higher in 1965, but by those other metrics, we were healthier.)

Whatever date you pick, part of the answer must be: not today, and not recently. The great exception might appear to be the "Reagan Era," which I might amend to the "Reagan-Clinton Era," to capture both our emergence from malaise and our post-Cold War decade or so of unchallenged preeminence. This period was sold to us at the time, and interpreted by its partisans ever since, as the restoration of the American spirit, a burial of the twin albatrosses of Vietnam Syndrome and stagflation. In hindsight, though, it was one of those spikes on the chart. Most, if not all, causes of our pre-Reagan anomie have returned with a vengeance, and are accompanied by many more reasons for concern.

THE CONSTITUTION IS ALL BUT DEAD

We Americans are supposed to govern ourselves via a constitution that rests on a specific understanding of natural right (that right and wrong, good and evil, better and worse exist by nature) and natural rights (that government's job is to secure people's God-given rights to life, liberty, property, etc.). The Constitution specifically declares and delimits the purposes of government and its powers, and it dictates how we the people choose the officers of the state, who are supposed to exercise those powers.

We still choose, sort of, but that hardly matters because the people we nominally elect do not hold real power. And when they do, they often use it for unconstitutional ends. America's real rulers are not the constitutional officers we vote for, and certainly not the American people, whom our understanding of political legitimacy asserts to be sovereign. They are, rather, a network of unelected bureaucrats, revolving-door cabinet and subcabinet officials, corporate-tech-finance senior management, "experts" who set the boundaries of acceptable opinion, and media figures who police those boundaries.[1]

Add to this the routine, repeated violations of our explicitly guaranteed rights – Big Tech censoring free speech, big cities denying the right of self-defense, the government itself violating the right to be secure in one's person, home, papers, and effects, against unreasonable searches and seizures – and it becomes more than a stretch to describe the United States as any longer a "constitutional republic."

THE SECURITY STATE HAS BEEN WEAPONIZED

Arguably the two most alarming spectacles of recent times are the Russia Hoax and the federal government's reaction to January 6. Our intelligence agencies spied not just on American citizens but on a presidential candidate and his senior-most aides, and then, after he won, on government officials. The FBI launched a phony investigation under false pretenses to prevent one candidate from winning the 2016 election and to lay the groundwork for his removal if he did. All of this was later uncovered.[2] The guilty got away with it and the agencies still have their budgets and all their powers. Indeed, the FBI was just given – with Republican votes – a $600 million raise, and will soon be given, also with Republican votes, a new multibillion-dollar headquarters larger than the Pentagon.

As to the second, an unarmed, nonviolent protest (all four deaths were protesters, either directly or indirectly caused by the authorities) resulted in the largest (and still ongoing) manhunt in US history, widespread and ongoing pretrial detention, maximalist demands from prosecutors (up to and including "terrorism enhancements" in sentencing), forced confessions, and draconian sentences for minor crimes.

These same agencies – in particular, the FBI and the Department of Justice – now routinely engage in predawn, no-knock raids and circus arrests before awaiting media (to whom time and place of said arrest have been pre-leaked) against the ruling class's perceived enemies, such as peaceful pro-life demonstrators and those the January 6 Commission wanted to feature in its show trial. These are the kinds of practices that, when Eastern

Bloc Communist tyrannies did them, the US government condemned. Now our government does them itself.

WE HAVE TWO-TRACK "JUSTICE"

How the same offense is treated by our "justice" system depends on who's committed it and, often, for what purpose. At the upper strata, compare the treatment of Hillary Clinton, James Comey, and Andrew McCabe with that of Roger Stone, Paul Manafort, Steve Bannon, Carter Page, and Michael Flynn. Mrs. Clinton illegally hid, and then deleted, her proprietary – and classified – communications from government records. Messrs. Comey and McCabe orchestrated the Russia Hoax and lied about it. None of these three was even charged.

The latter five have all been hounded by the state – some convicted and imprisoned, all at least bankrupted and defamed. Their crimes, to the extent that any were even committed, were all much less serious than those of the regime darlings.

Compare the treatment of the January 6 protesters with the total impunity granted to the Summer 2020 rioters. One example: two lawyers, literally caught throwing Molotov cocktails, were given slaps on the wrist.[3] Meanwhile, Kyle Rittenhouse was charged *with first degree intentional homicide* (one of six charges) for shooting three deranged thugs who were in the process of trying to kill him.[4] All over the country, and especially in Blue precincts, acts of self-defense will get you arrested, jailed, and possibly imprisoned. Meanwhile, in the Black Lives Matter era, so long as the perp is the correct race or acting in a sanctified cause, violence and arson are excused.

WE CAN'T EVEN PUNISH OR DETER NORMAL CRIME

In huge parts of the country, we've stopped trying to fight crime. "Bail reform" lets dangerous criminals out of jail the same day they're caught. Witness the psycho who lunged at New York's Republican gubernatorial candidate with a knife.[5] He was apprehended – and released that day. Granted, in that case, the Feds did rearrest him. But all over the country, thousands of offenders are much luckier.

Bail reform assumes that offenders are caught in the first place. In the "defund the police" era, many are not. Crime has spiked dramatically since 2020 (and had already been rising since the first BLM riots in 2014).[6]

We may try to console ourselves with the observation that we're still nowhere close to the crime peaks of the mid-1970s through the early 1990s.[7] But even with the massive declines that followed, we never even got close to the negligible crime rates of the pre-1960s era. Worse, we appear to have entirely lost the will to try. Worse still, our elites have moved beyond mere unwillingness to fight crime and into an almost positive embrace of leniency. Our cities, which still haven't recovered from being sacked in 2020, face ongoing gunbattles, random attacks, subway pushings, and beatdowns of the elderly that our elected and appointed leaders refuse to do anything about.[8]

WE'RE SO BLINKERED BY IDEOLOGY THAT WE CAN'T – OR WON'T – APPLY OBVIOUS SOLUTIONS TO SIMPLE PROBLEMS

The same way we don't lock up criminals because "racism," there is almost no end to the sensible things we refuse to do, and the stupid things we eagerly do, because of ideology.

The United States is presently in the midst of our worst energy crunch since the 1970s.[9] Instead of expanding supply, we are constricting it. Why? "Climate change." But nuclear would generate energy without carbon emissions. The same people who say no drilling also say no nuclear. Why? Supposedly, because the plants themselves and the waste they generate are "unsafe," though nuclear power has a near-perfect safety record in this country and in nearly all others. (The real reason is to force everyone to don the hairshirt.)

Our drug problem is fueled by Mexican cartels that cross our border with impunity. But we don't secure the border because "no human is illegal." Monkeypox is transmitted at homosexual orgies. We won't close bathhouses because "love is love." But we *will* close churches, gyms, and restaurants over COVID. That's an emergency!

WE PRIORITIZE "DIVERSITY" OVER MISSION AND PERFORMANCE

Ask yourself how long any complex system, much less a whole civilization, can last when it selects people for jobs, including the most demanding and important, on criteria other than merit.

To take just one example, the major airlines recently announced that their pilot corps are too white and male. To "solve" this non-problem, the airlines have announced a diversity push.[10] Now, obviously there are people of all races, and both sexes, capable of flying planes. But flying an airliner is also a complex job requiring a certain level of smarts and a certain cast of mind (calm and thorough). Not everyone has those things. Hence many who seek to become pilots wash out. Once the airlines start selecting pilots based on criteria other than competence at and suitability for the job, what is going to happen? You can guess. Now apply this lesson across our entire society, because it is happening everywhere.

OUR MILITARY DOESN'T WIN

I suppose we should be grateful that the military hasn't – yet – been turned against the populace. But it has been turned into a woke social-justice welfare program, a kind of student union/sociology department with guns. The brass cares more about pronoun usage than fulfilling its mission.[11] Although it's not implausible to think that its mission today is more about pronoun usage than the application of force in the national interest.

The last US military operation that fulfilled all its tactical and strategic objectives was the first Gulf War (1991). Since then, we've engaged in failed humanitarian missions (Somalia, Haiti), failed nation-building missions (Bosnia, Kosovo), and democracy wars that do not produce democracy (Iraq, Afghanistan). We could not even leave Afghanistan without humiliating ourselves.

The military is also, unsurprisingly, incompetent. The Navy crashed four ships in 2017 alone.[12] Last year, a $67 million F-18 Super Hornet was literally swept off the deck of an aircraft carrier.[13] It is not just the Navy; examples abound across the rest of the armed services. And, to be fair, the Navy faces the most significant operational challenges. But given all the failures of the last thirty years, one cannot be comforted even by that valid excuse.

NOTHING WORKS ANYMORE

That heading is an exaggeration, but not by much. And it's not just the military. Overall competence in nearly every field of endeavor has dropped in recent years.

Everyone has stories of things that used to work well, even flawlessly, that no longer do. For me, it's public transportation (especially commuter trains), civil aviation, and ordinary customer service. It's well-nigh impossible now to hire competent people for almost any job. If you're a boss, telling your workers to actually, you know, *do their jobs* is to face mutiny. Insisting on standards is racist, sexist, and oppressive. Enforcing standards is Nazism. The whole country is becoming the DMV.

THE PEOPLE ARE CORRUPT

This is a terrible thing to say, and I wish I didn't have to, but perhaps the above is because the people are corrupt? I don't mean "on the take." I mean simply less capable of functioning as productive adults. Rates of nearly every pathology that saps the human spirit and degrades basic performance are at all-time highs, or close.

People will quibble with this and insist that this or that bad metric is down since – choose your year. But has the United States ever had a widespread *heroin* problem outside jazz clubs? Has our overall obesity rate ever been this high? The ubiquity and vileness of modern porn are surely unprecedented, if for no other reason than the technology to mainline smut twenty-four seven has never before existed. This corruption perhaps explains not just why so many slack off at work (assuming they even show up), but more importantly why our supposedly republican form of government no longer functions as such.

POP CULTURE IS FILTH

I borrow the phrase from John Derbyshire.[14] It would take almost no effort to establish that ours is a tin age. No memorable, much less great, works of art have been produced in decades. A generation ago, we at least used to have decent, wholesome entertainment. *Top Gun: Maverick* aside, now we don't even get that. Replace porn's exposed, interacting genitals with less explicit vice, and you have the ubiquitous streaming that is keeping people on the couch (and getting fatter) all over America. All our media, even – especially – the ads, promote debauchery and degeneracy.

RELIGIOUS FAITH IS ALL BUT DEAD

Some will no doubt bristle at the assertion. Relax, I don't mean you. But as a historical matter, religious faith is today at a low ebb in the United States and across the West. Church attendance is way down, along with genuine belief.[15] This is a disaster spiritually and materially. A moral and religious people is more likely to get and stay married; beget and rear children; hold jobs, even boring but necessary ones; participate in civic life; stay out of trouble; save money and build wealth (however modest); and do all the other things that make for long, happy, productive, fruitful, fulfilling, moral lives.[16] Lack of religion tends to produce the opposite, and hence fuels the dismal trends discussed in this dismal chapter. This lesson is as old as mankind.

MARRIAGE AND OTHER SOCIAL BONDS ARE DESICCATED

People don't get together anymore, or they do much less. Marriage rates are down and the average age of marriages is way up. Divorce may be down from its 1980 peak, but the rate still hovers well above 40 percent.[17] Deep friendships are rare. Even loose associations that bring people together for frivolous fun are uncommon. We are increasingly a nation of atomized loners.

BIRTHRATES HAVE CRATERED

One of the core metrics of the health and confidence of a society is its birthrate. This is not to say that a society must have a birthrate above x (whatever x might be) to be considered healthy. But it is to say that if birthrates are consistently below replacement, that society is in some fundamental way unhealthy. By that metric, not just America, not just the West, but every advanced or developed society is not healthy. There is something about the experience of modernity and prosperity that makes people not want to have children. Nothing bodes more ill for our future than this.

YOUNG PEOPLE FACE DIM PROSPECTS

This is not the place to go into the deep spiritual roots of our anti-natalism. But we should recognize one prosaic cause: kids and houses have gotten really expensive, while career and monetary prospects for younger people have crashed. Therefore, falling birthrates are to some extent a rational response to crummy economic reality.

The ratio of average home prices to average incomes is, in many parts of this country, ten-to-one or worse,[18] making it impossible for young people to buy without a parental subsidy. That's before you even consider the question of school districts – the key deciding factor for actual or would-be parents – which pushes prices up much higher. Adjusted for inflation and purchasing power, salaries are much lower than in the postwar middle-class heyday, when it was possible for the average man to own a home and support a family on one income. Maybe that was always going to be a short-lived Elysium. We're certainly far from it now.

THE MIDDLE CLASS HAS BEEN HOLLOWED OUT

The economic forces squeezing the youth are the same ones that have hollowed out the middle class across the board. Financialization, outsourcing, automation, technification – all these trends and more have reduced a formerly middle-class country into a bifurcated state in which winners increasingly take all and "losers" get scraps. The middle class is shrinking numerically and as a percentage of the population.[19] Plus, the standard of living enjoyed by what's left of our "middle class" is much lower than it was a generation, and especially two generations, ago.

INCOME AND WEALTH INEQUALITY ARE OFF THE CHARTS

Not since the Robber Baron era, and by some metrics not even then, has American wealth been so concentrated at the top and so sparse in the middle and at the bottom.[20] This presents a few problems. First, it's felt to be unfair, which increases resentment among the have-nots. Second, just as Aristotle warned, massive wealth inequality increases the arrogance of the haves, who behave in more and more insolent and high-handed ways. Third, it makes our republic unworkable. The American Constitution needs a thriving, numerically and proportionally large middle class in order to function properly. Without that, its elegant machinery cannot work as designed. The whole apparatus becomes a tool and shield of oligarchy.

WE'RE INCREASINGLY OWNED AND GOVERNED BY FOREIGNERS

And not necessarily even a domestic oligarchy, which would be bad enough. But in our folly, we've allowed foreigners to buy up huge numbers of our key assets: land, houses, companies, infrastructure, and so on. One reason home prices are so high is that we let not just foreign financiers but generals in the Chinese military (no joke) buy up our real estate at will.[21]

Many of the most powerful people in our country – CEOs, high government officials, prestige professors – were born elsewhere. This is one of those things one is allowed to notice only if one approves, a phenomenon I call the "Celebration Parallax."[22] Yet it's reasonable to ask: why should we assume that those born elsewhere have the best interests of the United States or its people at heart when they assume the top jobs in our country? It's obvious what's in it for them. What's in it for us?

CORPORATE POWER IS GREATER THAN IN THE PRE-ANTI-TRUST ERA

We've also delegated many properly political tasks and powers to private corporations. A handful of tech and media monopolies control nearly all public speech. Since they are "private companies," they are not covered by the First Amendment. But try getting your message out without them. Or when the banks won't let you have an account. Or when any other company whose services you need denies you access for political or ideological reasons. We are ruled at least as much by corporate behemoths whose interests and dogmas are identical to the state's as by the state formally understood, and over whose power we have just as much control – which is to say, none.

OUR ECONOMY IS FAKE

This should be one of the bright spots in my little litany. GDP is, after all, way up, both in the aggregate and per capita. And yet. We may leave aside, because already mentioned, the extent to which all those gains have accrued to the top, and/or to foreigners, and also the declining purchasing power, and hence standard of living, of the middle class.

What *is* our economy? Those who benefit from it extol it as an "information" or "service" economy, but it is better described as a "paper" or better still "pixel-and-byte" economy. What about making real stuff and doing real things? That still happens, but the renumeration for providing for human necessities, much less facilitating human flourishing, is paltry – almost insulting. This is hardly an original insight, but the greatest rewards in our system accrue to those who produce the least – who merely manipulate pixels and bytes. None of that answers any real human need or aspiration. Our fake, financialized economy looks and feels jury-rigged and liable to collapse. When it does, what then?

THE UNIVERSITIES HAVE BECOME EVIL

The most important institutions in modern America are the universities, and they are all evil. They are supposed to be repositories of knowledge. They are supposed to inform participatory republicanism by educating citizens capable of self-government. They are supposed to seek, find, and communicate truth.

They do none of this. Instead, they invent and push corrosive lies. They indoctrinate students to hate their country and civilization. They use centuries of accumulated prestige to tear down millennia of civilizational standards and achievement. They are basically satanic temples bent on destroying everything and everyone around them – except, somehow, themselves and their donors.

GRAMMAR AND HIGH SCHOOLS TEACH OUR KIDS TO HATE THEMSELVES AND THEIR COUNTRY

Worse, the universities' corrosive self-hatred has trickled down into primary education. Chris Rufo's heroic efforts notwithstanding, tens of thousands of schools – public and private – teach American children to hate not merely their country but, if they are white, themselves. Aside from being the mark of an insane society, the psychological damage this does to innocent, impressionable children is incalculable and unconscionable.

WE DON'T MERELY TOLERATE BUT CELEBRATE ANTIWHITE RACISM

This may be the most sensitive topic of all, the true third rail that no one on the wrong side is allowed to touch. Elite, establishment opinion in this country has become openly, giddily antiwhite. They get to say it – scream it, really – but if we object, or merely point it out, we are doubly demonized.

(I've refrained from making recommendations throughout this chapter, but here I'll make an exception. You have nothing to lose by calling out their antiwhite racism. They hate you on the basis of your race already. They might hate you a bit more for telling the truth about their hate, but that extra bit is negligible.)

I can't think of another example in history when a country's elites became opposed, on a frankly racial basis, to its majority population and founding stock. It surely bodes ill for our future.

INSANE ENTHUSIASMS LIKE TRANSGENDERISM RECEIVE LITTLE PUSHBACK

We are now required to call women men, and vice versa, and to profess faith in an ever-expanding number of "genders." We're mutilating troubled children with surgeries and damaging them with drugs, often against their parents' wishes. Indeed, some parents are punished for objecting.

I again wrack my brains to think of a … "fad" seems too insubstantial a word … quite so destructive and so obviously contrary to concrete reality that was nonetheless adopted, and then made mandatory, so quickly. We are literally *cutting off children's body parts* in order to placate psychotic far-left activists. And just about every institution in our country – from government, to corporations, to (of course) the universities – have not merely gone along but are driving this barbarity.

If civilization survives the present epoch and recovers its senses – a big "if" – one easy prediction is that the transgender craze will be looked back upon as among the two or three most wantonly cruel mass delusions in human history.

WE HAVE NO SOCIAL COHESION

It should not be surprising, then, that America has close to zero remaining social cohesion. What do we have in common anymore? Not a culture, not patriotism, barely a language. We're divided by race, class, region, religion (among those few who still believe), habits, tastes, and, of course, politics. We seem to agree on nothing. We can't even talk to one another anymore. At best, the United States is just an economic zone filled with atomized consumers. The idea of us coming together on some grand national project is ludicrous. The prospects even of "live and let live" federalism seem vanishing.

THE RULING CLASS HATES THE PEOPLE

At our worst, we hate each other. I could pretend to be even-handed here, but let's face it, that hatred is driven by one side: coastal-credentialed-moneyed-liberal-elites, or whatever you want to call them. We all know who they are.

Red America resents Blue America for outsourcing its jobs and otherwise treating it with contempt. But Blue America hates Red with feverish intensity. We can speculate about the cause another time. The point here is that we have a ruling class who believe half the country, at least, is irredeemable: born evil and deserving of every fresh insult they can throw at it. A ruling class that, to boot, works tirelessly to further degrade social and economic conditions for tens of millions and then enjoys kicking them when they object. It's a kind of sadism practiced by the worst Roman emperors but today spread across millions of credentialed mandarins.

CONSERVATISM IS A FAILURE

Conservatism, both as an intellectual movement and as a set of institutions, was supposed to prevent all this. It didn't. You could even argue that it abetted most of it. Where official conservatism's opposition hasn't been ineffectual, it's been collaborationist.

If conservatism failed to prevent the disease, why should anyone believe it can provide a cure? Illnesses are easier to prevent than cure. What other cures do we have on hand? All I see are the same tired clichés that already brought us to the present morass.

REMORALIZATION NEVER OR RARELY HAPPENS WITHIN THE SAME SOCIETY OR REGIME

There are very few examples of a formerly moral or at least some-what virtuous people becoming dissolute and then remoralizing absent some sort of collapse and reset. Some will point to Britain in the Victorian era. OK, let's stipulate that. Can you think of any others?

What caused the Victorian example? It was, first, a religious movement led by dissenting Protestants and, second, the result of a widely expanding middle class insisting on "middle-class morality." As to religion and the middle class in America, see above.

At any rate, the question before us is: could we replicate the Victorian era's resurgent morality? I for one don't know how. I don't think anyone else does, either.

OUR CIVILIZATION HAS LOST THE WILL TO LIVE

The will to live is (supposedly) an ingrained natural human impulse. We reflexively recoil from physical harm. We instinc-tively defend ourselves from attack. We protect our own.

Or we used to. Today, as noted, our "civilization" lets criminals walk and punishes self-defense. It celebrates destruction, arson, and rioting. It mutilates and sterilizes children. It propagandizes people to despise themselves, their countries, and their histories. It guilt-trips them into having fewer children ("for the planet!") – and then says that, to make up for the birth dearth, they must welcome endless waves of immigration. It brags "we can replace them" – and gaslights and demonizes those who notice and object to being replaced.[23] Above all, it is in the process of transforming itself so fundamentally through demography that, in a few decades at most, it will no longer make sense to call this the same society. Another Celebration Parallax: if you're for that, you can say it; if not, it's a "racist conspiracy theory." Whatever. There seems to be, on one side, intense eagerness to see the project through and, on the other, insufficient will to stop it.

This, then, is the pessimistic case for our present *and* future. Assuming present trends continue is said to be a logical fallacy. But assuming they won't, especially when they've been worsening for two generations, is wishful thinking.

But perhaps there is optimism in pessimism. Is it really pessimistic to predict (or hope) that a rotten system will give way to something better? I don't know what the future holds. But to call "optimistic" the assertion that the present regime has a long time to run presupposes that one favors it.

NOTES

1   Witness, for instance, the reaction to COVID. The government simply declared an emergency and started making diktats and enforcing them by fiat. None of this was passed legislatively and signed by the president, as the Constitution prescribes. Mayors and governors routinely violated enumerated constitutional rights, without paying any price.

2   See Lee Smith, *The Plot against the President: The True Story of How Congressman Devin Nunes Uncovered the Biggest Political Scandal in U.S. History* (New York: Center Street, 2019).

3   See David Thomas, "N.Y. Lawyer Who Threw Molotov Cocktail During George Floyd Protest Sentenced to 15 Months," Reuters, November 18, 2022, https://www.reuters.com/legal/legalindustry/ny-lawyer-who-threw-molotov-cocktail-during-george-floyd-protest-sentenced-15-2022-11-18/.

4   See Todd Richmond, "Explainer: What Charges Did Kyle Rittenhouse Face?" AP News, November 19, 2021.

5   See Rachel Pannett, "Suspect in Attack on GOP Nominee for N.Y. Governor Faces Federal Charges," *Washington Post*, July 24, 2022, https://www.washingtonpost.com/politics/2022/07/24/zeldin-attack-charges-governor-new-york/.

6   See "Reported Violent Crime Rate in the United States from 1990 to 2021," Statista, October 10, 2022, https://www.statista.com/statistics/191219/reported-violent-crime-rate-in-the-usa-since-1990/.

7   See Joseph Kiprop, "The Worst Decades for Crime," WorldAtlas, July 9,

2017, https://www.worldatlas.com/articles/which-decade-had-the-most-crime.html.

8   See Craig Wall, "Chicago Violence: Prosecutors Reject Charges in Deadly Gang-Related Austin Shooting," ABC 7 Chicago, October 4, 2021, https://abc7chicago.com/chicago-shooting-violence-austin-police/11079879/; Larry Celona and David Propper, "Subway Shoves in NYC Exceed Number of Incidents Compared to Last Year," *New York Post*, October 27, 2022, https://nypost.com/2022/10/27/nyc-subway-shoves-exceed-number-of-incidents-compared-to-last-year/; Dion Lim, "70-year-old Woman Brutally Beaten, Kicked in Head by 4 Attackers in San Francisco," ABC 7 Chicago, August 2, 2022, https://abc7chicago.com/san-francisco-attack-asian-woman-beaten-in-sf-attacked-by-four-people-elderly-kicked-head/12093778/.

9   See Leigh Thomas, "World Faces Worst Energy Crisis Since the 1970s, Warns OECD," *Financial Post*, November 22, 2022, https://financialpost.com/news/economy/oecd-outlook-energy-crisis-slowdown.

10 See Robert Silk, "Airlines Making Diversity a Priority," *Travel Weekly*, February 27, 2021, https://www.travelweekly.com/Robert-Silk/Airlines-making-diversity-a-priority.

11 See Adam Kredo, "U.S. Forces Ordered to Stop Using Gender Pronouns to Improve 'Lethality,'" *Washington Free Beacon*, August 31, 2022, https://freebeacon.com/national-security/u-s-forces-ordered-to-stop-using-gender-pronouns-to-improve-lethality/.

12 See Julia Jacobo, Luis Martinez, and Emily Shapiro, "USS McCain the 4th Navy Warship to Crash in Asia This Year," ABC News, August 21, 2017, https://abcnews.go.com/US/uss-mccain-4th-navy-warship-crash-asia-year/story?id=49333429.

13 See Alison Bath, "Navy Super Hornet That Was Blown off Carrier Deck Recovered from Mediterranean," *Stars and Stripes*, https://www.stripes.com/branches/navy/2022-08-08/super-hornet-recovered-navy-6915155.html.

14 John Derbyshire, "Unpleasant Truths," *National Review*, August 2, 2002, https://www.nationalreview.com/2002/08/unpleasant-truths-john-derbyshire/.

15 See Jeffrey M. Jones, "How Religious Are Americans?," Gallup, December 23, 2021, https://news.gallup.com/poll/358364/religious-americans.aspx.

16 See Alex Berezow, "Religious People Really Do Have More Children," American Council on Science and Health, July 20, 2016, https://www.acsh.org/news/2016/07/20/religious-people-really-do-have-more-children; David Briggs, "No Time For Crime: Study Finds More Religious Communities Have Lower Rates Of Black, White and Latino Violence," *HuffPost*, December 4, 2013, https://www.huffpost.com/entry/no-time-

for-crime-study-f_b_4384046; "Religion's Relationship to Happiness, Civic Engagement and Health Around the World," Pew Research Center, January 31, 2019, https://www.pewresearch.org/religion/2019/01/31/religions-relationship-to-happiness-civic-engagement-and-health-around-the-world/; "Highly Religious People Not Distinctive in All Aspects of Everyday Life," Pew Research Center, April 12, 2016, https://www.pewresearch.org/religion/2016/04/12/highly-religious-people-not-distinctive-in-all-aspects-of-everyday-life/.

17 Jason Crowley, "How Many Marriages End in Divorce?," *Survive Divorce*, August 2, 2022, https://www.survivedivorce.com/how-many-marriages-end-in-divorce.

18 "Home Price to Income Ratio (US & UK)," Longtermtrends, accessed November 22, 2022, https://www.longtermtrends.net/home-price-median-annual-income-ratio/.

19 See Juliana Kaplan, "America's Middle Class Has Shrunk Over the Last Half Century as the Economy Rewards Some and Punishes Others," *Business Insider*, April 20, 2022, https://www.businessinsider.com/americas-middle-class-shrinks-as-richest-households-make-more-2022-4?op=1.

20 See Joshua L. Rosenbloom and Gregory W. Stutes, "Reexamining the Distribution of Wealth in 1870" (working paper, NBER Working Paper Series, National Bureau of Economic Research, Cambridge, MA, June 2005), https://www.nber.org/system/files/working_papers/w11482/w11482.pdf; "Wealth Inequality in the United States," Inequality.org, Institute for Policy Studies, https://inequality.org/facts/wealth-inequality/.

21 See "Kyle Bass: Communist China Controls 200 Sq Miles in Texas Next to Major Air Force Base," American Thought Leaders, *Epoch Times*, video, 11:10, May 27, 2021, https://www.youtube.com/watch?v=HPChSpLdELU.

22 See Michael Anton, *The Stakes: America at the Point of No Return* (Washington, DC: Regnery, 2020), 165–67.

23 Michelle Goldberg, "We Can Replace Them," *New York Times*, October 29, 2018, https://www.nytimes.com/2018/10/29/opinion/stacey-abrams-georgia-governor-election-brian-kemp.html.

STRATEGIES AND HEURISTICS FOR CONFRONTING LIBERAL INSTITUTIONS

Richard Hanania

FREDRICK THE GREAT said "he who defends everything, defends nothing." One could similarly say "he who attacks everything, attacks nothing." Any individual, or movement, trying to change the world is going to have limited time, energy, resources, and focus. In the last decade in particular, conservatives have come to feel that practically everything that can reasonably be called an "institution" – from sports journalism to the federal bureaucracy – is against them. It is common to hear conservative commentators complain about big banks, large corporations, medical and trade associations, labor unions, government agencies, universities, and an endless number of other villains leading the country to ruin. While the "world is against us" sound bite is good for fundraising and building a media following, it neither provides clear steps for taking political action, nor allows one to intelligently differentiate between worthy and unworthy targets.

This essay tries to provide practical guidance for thinking about the problem of liberal institutions. In broad terms, it proposes three suggestions: that conservatives focus on institutions that are the most important and the most malleable; that they distinguish between the redeemable and irredeemable; and that they think carefully about disrupting systems of liberal patronage and ways to create their own self-sustaining systems that reflect their beliefs and values. This essay is not an all-encompassing guide to taking the country back. Rather, it introduces considerations and heuristics that conservatives should keep in mind as they engage in political activism. It also highlights the most important issues about which there should be no disagreement within the movement.

IMPORTANCE AND MALLEABILITY

Conservatives should put their energies into fighting to take over – or, in some cases, denigrating and destroying – those institutions that are most important and most influenced by leftist politics. This must be the primary goal. At the same time, every movement must understand the limits of what it can accomplish in order to direct its resources effectively. Conservatives have focused on the education system and the media as obvious foundations of left-wing power. Yet that leaves open questions regarding where and how to seek changes in these areas.

Institutions, or parts of institutions, that are trivial, or that are not subject to political pressure, can be largely ignored. While it is simple to say that importance and malleability are key concepts to keep in mind, conservatives rarely approach their situation this way. For example, they incessantly talk about radical universities. Yet how much does it matter if a sociology professor making $60,000 a year at a state school is conservative or liberal? Steven Teles has written about how the conservative legal movement focused its limited resources and energy on changing the top law schools in the country, finding those that were lower ranked could be counted on to follow the lead of the most prestigious institutions anyway. Increasing conservative representation at top schools has created enough plausible candidates for judgeships and executive branch positions for a Republican administration to rely on.

For academic fields other than law, one probably does not have to even worry about the top schools. Major court decisions and federal regulations are justified by appeals to expertise. As opinions regarding the concept of expertise itself become more polarized, however, we find a "conservative" and a "liberal" form of each science, whether in epidemiology, economics, psychology, or a wide variety of other fields. Which experts are listened to by decision-makers depends ultimately on political power; it doesn't matter if conservatives are outnumbered among the expert community as a whole. What is more important is having a critical mass that can fill positions of power and influence, and ensuring that there is enough political pressure to appoint the right people in places where they can make a difference.

This does not mean that nothing can or should be done about the universities. Although they often seem to be completely autonomous, the existence of higher education in the end depends on the taxpayer. In many states, governors appoint the members of the board of regents, which runs the university system. The taxpayer ultimately provides the funding, and state legislators have the power to condition that money on political neutrality. This is simply the inverse of what liberals do through civil rights law and other kinds of regulation. There is nothing preventing any state from cutting college bureaucracy at public schools by legislative fiat, or deciding that fields like women's studies should not be taught at public expense.

What about the media? Conservatives have been complaining about the biases of institutions like NBC, CBS, and the *New York Times* for generations. Except to the extent that it has inspired conservative news organizations as a counterbalance, that complaining has not done much good, for the obvious reason that there are no realistic levers to pull in order to make these outlets report in a more balanced manner. Nonetheless, in recent years we see a shift away from the legacy media and a rise in the importance of social media, particularly Twitter. Trying to make the *New York Times* less biased is probably hopeless, but Elon

Musk's purchase of Twitter, as of this writing, seems like it may create a world where we no longer have to play along with the delusions of so-called "trans" individuals, for example, to have access to the public square.

Musk has provided a proof of concept. Few can afford to spend tens of billions to buy a company, but publicly traded firms are open to direct influence if enough money is spent. This is the idea behind "shareholder activism" on the Left, which has allowed it to exercise influence over major oil and gas companies. This may not work, and it may not be sufficient to achieve balance in the marketplace of ideas. But there is no perfect solution. As seen in the *Dobbs* decision and the subsequent banning of abortion across wide swaths of the country, a focused movement on the Right can achieve political goals in the face of unrelenting media hostility.

Like the media, the civil rights regime is a major source of liberal influence and power. The federal government forces private institutions to classify individuals according to race and sex, to prefer protected groups, that is non-whites and women, over others, and even to regulate social life. There are a handful of government agencies that are most responsible for enforcing compliance with this regime – the Equal Employment Opportunity Commission (EEOC), the Office of Federal Contract Compliance Programs (OFCCP) in the Department of Labor, and the Office of Civil Rights in the Department of Education. While the process of how one gets from civil rights law to wokeness is somewhat complex, the solution to the problems posed by these agencies is not. Congress needs to defund them, or at the very least tie their hands by specifying that discrimination means intentional discrimination, not disparate impact or acting upon the basis of sex stereotypes. Conservative organizations have succeeded in creating unofficial litmus tests on guns and abortion for all Republican-appointed judges. Having the correct views on civil rights issues needs to be seen as similarly important.

REDEEMABLE AND IRREDEEMABLE

Some institutions are liberal because of the pressures that they face. Others are liberal for reasons rooted in their mission, the people they attract, or other factors. They are destined to be hostile to everything conservatives believe. We can call these, respectively, redeemable and irredeemable institutions. Those that are redeemable should be pressured, taken over, or reformed. One should not see hurting them as a goal in and of itself. This is in contrast to irredeemable institutions, which conservatives should work to isolate and reduce in status and power. The aforementioned civil rights bureaucracy is one example of the latter.

Corporations, in contrast, fall into the redeemable category. Business may be, as some conservatives argue, indifferent to the public good or national interest, but it is not inherently hostile to these things. Lenin's famous quotation about capitalists selling communists the rope they would hang them with illustrates the point that merchants often do not care who they trade with or about the larger social influence of their work. The growth of woke capital can be explained by a combination of the Environmental, Social, and Governance (ESG) movement, civil rights law, and the pressures that corporations face from their own employees, the media, and left-wing consumers and public interest firms. The answer here is not to mindlessly seek to hurt business but to find ways to incentivize it to behave in better ways. Thus, something like an across-the-board hike in the highest-level income or corporate tax rate – on the grounds that it "hurts our enemies" – makes little sense, since every company or individual, whether they are left-wing, right-wing, or neutral in their behavior, suffers in the exact same way. Recently, there has been a push to use antitrust law to attack Big Tech, which would do nothing about the censorship issue most conservatives care about, or, if anything, make it worse by putting more regulatory power into the hands of left-wing attorneys. In contrast, the recent targeting of tax benefits received by Disney in Florida applies direct pressure on a corporation that has wronged conservatives, and it will hopefully send a message and incentivize better behavior in the future. Conservative states have gone after the ESG movement by blacklisting firms that have divested from energy companies. As it turns out, Big Oil has more power within the conservative coalition than antiwokeism, even if the latter is what delivers the votes. Nonetheless, state pensions and government contracting are sources of leverage that can be used for purposes other than energy policy.

The major problem with attempts to regulate corporate behavior and speech is that liberal judges will often toss them out as unconstitutional. Suddenly, when it is conservatives that want to tell private institutions what to do, "living constitutionalists" become free speech absolutists. Unfortunately, there seems to be no better answer here than winning more elections and appointing the right judges. This implies putting an emphasis on electability when choosing candidates for the Senate, given that practically all Republican senators support conservative judges. Particularly in that body, the important thing is to win as many seats as possible, not to find ideal candidates.

Irredeemable institutions are generally those with ties to government or that have formed for a left-wing purpose. Practically all identity politics groups fall into the latter category, even when they identify with the Right. Take the Log Cabin Republicans, an organization that advocates for gay rights within the broader conservative movement. At first glance, there may seem to be nothing wrong with this from the perspective of conservatives who think that homosexuals should be able to arrange their private lives as they see fit. A look at the Log Cabin Republican website, however, shows that the organization favors antidiscrimination laws for LGBT individuals, a ban on conversion therapy, and "additions to existing civil rights, anti-bullying, and housing bills to include both sexual orientation and gender identity as legally protected groups." In other words, they are Republicans, but break with conservatives in supporting social engineering in situations where so-called "gay rights" conflict with free speech, religious liberty, or freedom of association. A movement can welcome identity groups if they are willing to join on the terms set by the movement itself. Yet this rarely happens; usually, individuals form organizations centered around race, gender, or sexual orientation because they want special privileges from the government. Conservativism, with its embrace of individual freedom and national unity, will necessarily compromise its entire purpose by accepting such groups.

More controversially, labor unions are another kind of irredeemable institution. Police and firefighters, which disproportionately attract high testosterone men, may be an exception, and they should be treated as such. As a general matter, however, labor unions exist to gain special privileges for their own members, even if that means restricting the freedom and hurting the economic prospects of others. They cannot exist without government support, and it is no coincidence that early American labor unions were closely tied to the communist movement and that their successors have enthusiastically embraced wokeness and Covid hysteria.

In addition to the purposes for which an institution was created and the functions it serves, conservatives must be deeply conscious about the role of sex differences between men and women. A decade ago, educated observers on both the Left and the Right believed that demographics was destiny, and that an increasing nonwhite population meant that conservatism was doomed. But this narrative no longer seems plausible. Among the biggest political stories in recent years is the apparent Hispanic shift toward the GOP. Immigration seems to be less of an existential threat to the Right than it was even a few years ago. Yet while racial determinism has fallen out of fashion, massive gaps have opened up along the lines of sex. College-educated women of every race have proved to be the most eager and enthusiastic devotees of political correctness.

Conservatives have for decades, in alliance with moderate

liberals, sought to "take back the academy," just as they have tried to do with elementary and secondary schools. But what if the academy, by its very nature, is a feminized and liberal institution that attracts people who are naturally going to be drawn to left-ism? Often, we think about institutions being "right" or "left" because of some decision made by its leadership at some point in time. Yet the way in which a profession, business, or bureaucracy takes its political character is often more of an organic process. Nobody decided, for example, that police officers would support Republicans. Rather, a profession that attracted a lot of high testosterone men who wanted to stop crime and protect the innocent was always going to be skeptical of the Left's agenda.

Higher education has the opposite tendency. Women, despite scoring lower on standardized tests, now make up around 60 percent of all college graduates. Contemporary education inherently measures conformity, awards arbitrary credentials, and teaches ideas and concepts that are rarely if ever tested against reality. Women – being inherently more risk averse, agreeable, and deferential to authority – naturally thrive in such an environment. As university governance has moved out of the hands of professors and into the hands of administrators, who are even more feminized than academics, the problem has gotten worse. The main answer, then, is not to necessarily reform the university system to make it more agreeable to conservatism, but to reduce the status and influence of higher education, while depriving the academy – or at least the parts of it that are inherently hostile – of resources to the greatest extent possible.

Tennessee, for example, is currently considering reforms that will provide more funding for students majoring in science and medical fields and less to those in the social sciences and humanities. This would be a good step, as many social science and humanities professors are no more than government-funded political activists. States should also follow the lead of Maryland, which under Governor Hogan recently stopped requiring college degrees for some kinds of government employment. There is a synergy between the fight against credentialism and reforming civil rights law, as standardized tests are an alternative to degrees as a way of judging talent. In addition to enacting legal reforms, conservatives should continue their propaganda campaign against the universities and what they have become, since polls suggest that there has been a payoff to this effort so far.

SELF-SUSTAINING SYSTEMS

The Left has excelled at creating self-sustaining systems that ensure it stays in power. For example, Democrats win elections, so they create public sector unions. These unions in turn take money from their members and put it back into Democratic election efforts, encourage their members to support liberal causes, and, in the case of the teachers' unions, indoctrinate young people to adopt left-wing ideas. The federal government similarly provides grants to activist organizations and so-called "public interest firms," which in turn seek to increase state power.

Conservatives need to find ways to break these cycles. In 2010, Scott Walker pushed through reforms in Wisconsin that reduced the power of public sector unions to engage in collective bargaining and made dues optional for workers. Partly as a result, the percentage of the state labor force belonging to a union plummeted by over a third in the next decade. In 2009, the largest teacher's union in the state had seventeen lobbyists and spent $2.5 million influencing state government. Ten years later, it was down to two lobbyists and a budget of $71,000. In the meantime, the state has trended red and, although it is difficult to prove a direct connection between the war on organized labor and later Republican victories, the Walker administration does seem to have provided an example of the successful use of state power to achieve conservative ends.

A more ambitious goal for conservatives is to create their own self-sustaining systems that keep them in positions of power and influence. For the party that believes in small government and individual liberty, this is inherently more difficult than it is for its political opponents. Nonetheless, there are hints of a new strategy emerging, in which Republicans funnel resources away from public education and to constituencies that can be expected to be more sympathetic to conservative ideas and values. Recently, Arizona created a universal school voucher program that will provide money directly to parents who check out of the public school system. The effect of this scheme – as many on the Left realize – means less money for public education, and more for parents. Thus, resources move from an institution inherently hostile to conservative values to the family, which is the basic building block of a healthy society.

In the short term, Arizona Republicans may well suffer at the ballot box for this. Political scientists talk about "thermostatic public opinion," meaning that voters tend to punish either party when it seems to be doing anything that diverges too far from the status quo. But changing the status quo creates a new one, and entitlements are rarely taken away. It simply requires leadership to take the first steps toward shaping a new reality. Passing Obamacare was a tough slog that hurt Democrats for years, but today repealing it is unthinkable, to say nothing of Social Security or Medicare. Not every conservative attempt to fight the Left will have such dire political costs, but the job of activists should be to support politicians willing to take some risks and ultimately pay a price for their beliefs. Attacking the public education system should not pit libertarians against conservatives more accepting of state intervention, as voucher programs involve taking money away from harmful government institutions and transferring to where it can do more good, while removing a built-in advantage for the Left.

HOLDING POLITICIANS ACCOUNTABLE

Since the rise of the regulatory state in the middle of the twentieth century, federal elections have come to matter less and less. Congress rarely legislates on the most important or hot-button issues, and unaccountable bureaucracies and the judiciary make many of the most fundamental decisions about public policy. It may therefore seem as if politicians are powerless, and we should expect little more from them than to make the right noises about the unfairness of the liberal dominance of institutions.

Yet just because conservatives have not used their power wisely does not mean they are powerless. Politicians have gotten away with shirking their responsibilities by deflecting blame, while conservative voters and even activists have been more or less happy to play along so far.

What sounds like a weakness of the American Right actually makes the case for optimism. In a very deep way, conservatives have not yet begun to fight. It is true that they've cut taxes, appointed some judges, and, when in power, erected small speed-bumps on the path to becoming an identity-obsessed social democracy. But the structural strengths of liberalism – the non-profit complex, organized labor, civil rights law and the bureaucracy that depends on it, the education system – have mostly been left untouched. The last days of the Trump administration gave a glimpse of what is possible. In September 2020, the president issued an executive order banning critical race theory in government training. The next month, he signed another executive order that would have made around 90 percent of the federal bureaucracy easier to fire. A few months later, there was talk of the Department of Justice doing away with the "disparate impact" standard in its interpretation of the Civil Rights Act.

The first two of these initiatives were of course undone by the Biden administration, while the third was never enacted. Yet these were exactly the kinds of policies that should have been put forward at the start of a presidency rather than at its end. Trump should get credit for acting, but he ultimately moved too late. And on some things he never moved at all. The executive branch requires federal contractors to all have affirmative action programs, and this reaches about a third of the private sector workforce. Ronald Reagan considered a new executive order that would have undone this, but he was thwarted by a coalition of Democrats and moderate Republicans in Congress. Being more easily able to fire federal employees would be such a radical change that it would render many points of this essay moot, and would require an entirely new analysis. Right now, for example, there is no point in trying to reform the Department of Education, so it would be best to defund it rather than use it for conservative ends. If a Republican administration could restaff the agency, however, this would open up new possibilities.

Conservatives elected a man who was temperamentally suited to adopt policies to strip power from their enemies, but he felt little pressure from an activist and intellectual class that had not yet thought carefully enough about how to use government for its own ideological goals. This can only be fixed by doing the unglamorous work of building the kinds of institutions that hold politicians accountable on the issues they care about. In certain areas – guns, abortion, taxes – conservatives have already done this and so have created litmus tests for Republican politicians hoping to advance their careers. It is the job of activists to make sure civil rights law, school choice, defunding university bureaucracies, and giving the president greater control over the federal workforce are added to this list.

In the end, the American Right should be thankful for what has happened to liberalism, because the last few years have at least clarified the attitude one should take towards it. A decade ago, there was some debate about how bad things were. Many conservatives could argue that one could work through and improve biased institutions. Who can still say that with a straight face after observing the public health community argue for locking people in their homes and only letting them out for Black Lives Matter protests? After seeing our cities burn down in the memory of criminals who, while they lived, were nothing but a blight on the rest of society? After critical race theory, and teaching transgenderism to toddlers while forcing them to adopt dress codes comparable to what Islamic fundamentalists only impose on adult women in order to protect against a disease that poses practically no threat to the young? And while this is happening, we hear more and more certainty from failed institutions, as they deny any ideological content to what they are doing and instead speak confidently about themselves as the defenders of "democracy," "expertise," and "the Science." No longer does the Right have any basis for questioning whether there are institutions that deserve to be destroyed. Building a united front on that question has allowed conservatives to turn their focus on what to do next.

RECOVERING
THE REAL FOUNDING
Escaping the Destructive Myth of the "Propositional Nation"

Carson Holloway

IF CONSERVATISM MUST be rooted in the past, American conservatism must be guided, at least in part, by the American Founding. But much of modern American conservatism has been based on foolish and self-defeating appeals to the Founders. Too many American conservatives have misunderstood and misrepresented the Founding and therefore have misled themselves, the movement, and the nation about what is necessary for a strong and healthy society.

And no error has had quite the effect of claiming, on the authority of the Founders, that we are a propositional nation. The propositional nation myth has been flogged ceaselessly on the establishment right for decades – by the most prominent opinion columnists, think tank scholars, and elected officials. To take one of the most famous though representative examples, former Speaker of the House Paul Ryan, claiming to speak for what the "Founders envisioned," has declared that "America is the only nation founded on an idea – not an identity."[1]

On this view, America's true national identity can be summed up by its commitment to the truths articulated in the second paragraph of the Declaration of Independence: that all men are created equal, and that they are endowed by their Creator with the inalienable rights to life, liberty, and the pursuit of happiness. Any politics of the Right should be anchored primarily in this understanding of America. Anything outside of it is impure.

Despite its popularity, propositional-nation conservatism is an error. It offers a partial and therefore a distorted understanding of the American Founding. It overemphasizes the political and ideological identity of the country at the expense of its more concrete, historical, and national identity. It elevates adherence to abstract principles at the expense of loyalty to our nation and to our fellow citizens. It is too preoccupied with equality and rights while neglecting other things that are also necessary for a strong and healthy nation.

Propositional-nation conservatism, moreover, is a source of political failure for the Right – indeed, of the kind of failures that threaten the security of our civilization. Its proponents cannot think seriously – as did the Founders, whom they claim to follow – about the national interest in foreign, economic, and immigration policy. They cannot preserve the moral, religious, and cultural inheritance necessary to sustain a free and decent society. And they cannot rally American voters to a political movement capable of depriving the Left of political power and therefore thwarting its ambition to transform the country into something very different from the one we inherited.

A MORE COMPLETE VIEW OF THE FOUNDING

Like most political errors, the claim that America is a propositional nation is based on a partial truth. Nobody can deny that the political creed expressed in the Declaration of Independence is a key element of America's national identity. Repudiate the doctrine of natural equality and natural rights and you would no longer have the same country. In a way, then, propositional-nation conservatives like Paul Ryan are not simply wrong when they say that "America is more than a country – it's an idea."[2] The error lies in equating America's propositional commitments with the country's identity, and in thinking that the principles of the "creed" are a complete list of what is necessary to a strong and healthy nation.

Accordingly, the Right must be able to correct Ryan by reminding us of the equally essential and converse truth: that America is not just an idea but also a particular country – with particular interests, a particular history, and a particular character, all of which are worth preserving. In making this claim, the Right will not be jettisoning but preserving the full political inheritance of the Founding. The Founders did not intend to establish a purely propositional nation, because they knew that there is more to America's identity than the Declaration's political creed and that that there is more to a strong nation than just respect for equality and rights.

The creed expressed in the Declaration's second paragraph is made up of universal truths and therefore has undeniable cosmopolitan overtones. As a result, those who embrace proposition-al-nation conservatism tend to think that nationalism is a betrayal of the principles of our Founding. After all, nationalism involves dedication to a particular country, while the principles of the Declaration seem to dedicate us instead to universal principles of justice. Thus, for example, Jennifer Rubin's announcement in the *Washington Post* that "Nationalism is antithetical to America's founding creed."[3]

In fact, however, America's Founders thought and acted as nationalists even as they at the same time honestly believed in the principles of the Declaration. Those principles obviously condemn the imperialistic and destructive forms of nationalism that emerged in twentieth-century Europe. But one can believe in the equality of human beings in their natural rights and at the same time embrace a moderate and just nationalism. There is no contradiction in accepting universal standards of justice and at the same time believing that nations – particular political communities – are an essential element of human life and that people owe a special loyalty to the nation to which they belong. This is certainly how the Founders thought. They cherished the idea of America as an independent nation and were deeply concerned with its national interest and its national honor.

The Founders' nationalism has three main elements. First, they held that sound foreign policy is not directed at universal aims but should instead seek to promote the national interest. As Alexander Hamilton observed, nations' pursuit of "their own interest, as far as justice and good faith permit, is and ought to be" the "prevailing policy" of nations in foreign affairs. After all, governments are "only trustees for the happiness and interest of their nation," and thus are duty bound to look out for their own country first and foremost.[4] Sharing Hamilton's view, George Washington used his Farewell Address to warn his fellow citizens to be on guard against passionate attachments to or antipathies for foreign nations, since such feelings might well lead them to "betray or sacrifice the interests of their own country."[5] The founders' nationalism thus has little in common with contemporary claims from propositional-nation conservatives that American foreign policy should be in the service of universal goods, to say nothing of suggestions on the Left that America is a morally impure nation, stained by injustice, whose interests should therefore be subordinated to those of other nations.

In the second place, the Founders were also economic nationalists. For them, the point of national economic policy was not merely to establish a system of free economic exchange at home and abroad. They held that the government should take certain substantive steps to promote American prosperity: They understood that the country is more than just its economy, and the latter should be regulated in the interests of the former.[6] This is why the Constitution includes powers to regulate commerce among the states and with foreign nations, and to lay taxes with a view to the "general welfare." Those powers were included so that they might be exercised to make the nation powerful and secure, prosperous and great.

Economic nationalism is most famously associated with Alexander Hamilton, though it is not limited to his work alone. As the nation's first secretary of the treasury, Hamilton, in his *Report on Manufactures*, urged a policy of promoting American manufacturing. According to Hamilton, national "independence and security" are objectives of all governments, which require America to "possess within itself all the essentials of national supply," including "the means of *subsistence, habitation, clothing*, and *defense*."[7] Hamilton's view on this question was not idiosyncratic. He wrote his *Report* at the request of the House of Representatives, which had sought his advice on "the means of promoting such" manufactures as would make the country "independent" of "foreign nations for military and other essential supplies."[8] Later, even Thomas Jefferson, Hamilton's greatest critic, admitted that experience had taught him that "manufactures are now as necessary to our independence as to our comfort."[9]

Finally, the Founders valued America as a nation with a concrete historic identity that went beyond mere adherence to the truths put forward in the Declaration. One of the most well-known statements of this fuller conception of America's national identity was provided by John Jay in *Federalist* 2. Americans, Jay suggested, were "one united people," not only by being "attached to the same principles of government" but also by being "descended from the same ancestors, speaking the same language, professing the same religion," and "very similar in their manners and customs."[10] Similarly, George Washington's Farewell Address indicated that America's national identity rested not only shared "political principles" but also the possession of "the same religion, manners, [and] habits."[11]

These passages show that the leading Founders were far from embracing the simplistic moralism of the assertion, so common in recent years, that "diversity is our greatest strength." They well understood that a certain unity is necessary to a nation's security and tranquility. Linguistic, religious, and ethnic commonalities, they believed, are politically advantageous because they serve as a bond of union. Conversely, divisions along ethnic, religious, and linguistic lines are an invitation to faction and political disintegration.[12]

Moreover, as Jay's and Washington's attention to "manners," "customs," and "habits" suggests, the Founders also believed that America possessed a certain moral character that was worthy of preservation. This task was understood to be primarily entrusted to the state governments in the exercise of the capacious powers reserved to them under the Tenth Amendment. Hence the long-established understanding in American constitutionalism that the states possess what are called "police powers" – powers to regulate in the interests of the public health, public welfare, and public morals.

The Founders thought it utterly uncontroversial that the states would exercise these powers to uphold traditional standards of morality, particularly with regard to the family. They believed in no general "right of privacy" that protected sexual irregularity. They believed in no general "freedom of expression" that included a right to promote obscenity. On the contrary, such acts were considered not only immoral but also offenses that could be punished by law.[13]

Washington and Jay also remind us that the Founders viewed America's religion as an important component of the nation's identity and therefore as a proper object of the government's solicitude. They respected religious liberty, but this respect did not entail indifference to whether religion would flourish or languish. They understood a vital religiosity to be necessary to the preservation of a free and just society. Washington's Farewell Address called "religion and morality" the "indispensable supports" of all the "habits which lead to political prosperity." And, Washington cautioned, "reason and experience both forbid us to expect that National morality can prevail in exclusion of religious principle."[14] Accordingly, as president, Washington used his official position to encourage religious observance. His 1789 Thanksgiving Proclamation called on his fellow citizens to set aside a day for "the service of that Great and Glorious Being, who is the author of all the good that was, that is, or that will be."[15]

For the Founders, civilization was a hard-won achievement that could only be preserved by continually renewed exertions. Unlike many of our contemporaries, they were not so naïve as to believe in the natural goodness and innocence of human beings. Quite the contrary. They understood, rather, that the cultivation of the virtues necessary for a free and good society requires a wholesome fear of human and divine punishments.

To sum up, the Founders had a much more robust understanding of the nation's identity than is suggested by the claim that America is merely a "propositional nation." They therefore had a more expansive understanding of the purposes of government than is suggested by the claim that the creed alone (protection of equality and of individual rights) sums up the purpose of American politics. The Founders believed in the nation and sought to use the government's authority to make the nation strong – morally, religiously, economically, and in relation to foreign nations.

THE BAD CONSEQUENCES OF PROPOSITIONAL-NATION CONSERVATISM

Propositional-nation conservatism is defective not only because it distorts our understanding of the Founding but also because it distorts our understanding of what is required for the health of our country today. The idea that America is simply a creedal nation, and that its well-being can be understood in terms of its continued commitment to the universal principles of the Declaration, has led to much superficiality in our public discourse, the mishandling of important public questions, and a great deal of damage in domestic and foreign policy.

Propositional-nation conservatives have commonly condemned as "isolationism" any suggestion that American foreign policy should be guided by America's national interests. Those who resort to this kind of dishonest argument never acknowledge that a policy of national interest routinely involves cooperation with other countries in matters of mutual concern.

To merely question the continued usefulness of American participation in NATO provokes ire from propositional-nation conservatives, as if such a view is beyond the pale of America's foreign policy traditions. They forget that no less a figure than George Washington taught in his Farewell Address that it is "our true policy to steer clear of permanent alliances with any portion of the foreign world."[16] It has also become common for some conservatives, acting contrary to Washington's advice, to foster passionate attachments to some countries (like Ukraine or Israel) and passionate hatreds of other countries (like Russia or China). Here and in similar cases a reflexive moralism that is divorced from our real traditions is used to stop rational debate about the advantages and disadvantages of our present security arrangements.

Propositional-nation conservatism has led important conservative leaders to treat the worldwide promotion of freedom as the core purpose of American foreign policy. Thus, for example, President George W. Bush, in his Second Inaugural Address, famously asserted that the goal of American foreign policy is "ending tyranny in our world" – an insanely utopian aim that has no basis in the Founders' realistic, national-interest based approach to foreign policy.[17] Such aspirations also overlook the lesson that the Founders learned by observing the French Revolution in real time: that radical movements to overthrow existing governments and establish democracy often end in chaos, terror, and despotism.

Propositional-nation conservatives also argue as if America was founded to be part of a global system of free-trade capitalism instead of an independent nation with a free economy of its own. In the 1990s, such conservatives denounced Patrick Buchanan as "left wing" for proposing tariffs to protect American industry.[18] Similarly, when President Donald Trump actually imposed such tariffs, some responded by calling the policy "socialism."[19] For these critics, great figures like Alexander Hamilton would also have to be categorized as left-wingers and socialists. Here again, the intellectually simplistic moralism of propositional-nation conservatism is expressed in slogans that frustrate a serious, pragmatic debate about what policies are needed in present circumstances to make the nation strong and prosperous in the long term.

The myth of the propositional nation has also undermined our country's ability to deliberate seriously about immigration policy. If someone proposes that immigration should be limited, the default response from the Left will be that any such suggestion is a "nativist" betrayal of the universal principles of the nation's Founding. Remarkably, however, this cosmopolitan moralism is commonly echoed by many who claim to be conservatives. Nevertheless, none of the Founders thought that anyone has a natural right to gain admittance to some foreign political community. On their view, because political communities are constituted by consent, the members of any given community have a perfectly legitimate right to control what newcomers (from where and how many) are admitted. They understood that immigration should be regulated in pursuit of the national interest (a principle that implies that acceptance of immigration is not a sacred duty but that immigration could be reduced to zero if the national interest requires it). This is why, for example, Hamilton and Jefferson warned about the dangers of admitting to citizenship immigrants who were not habituated to the "temperate love of liberty so essential to real republicanism."[20] Such statesmen would never have risked the long-term character of the regime for the sake of the temporary economic gains that might flow from admitting large numbers of low-wage workers.

Finally, excessive preoccupation with America's creedal identity has fostered a conservatism that is largely supine on "culture war" issues. As we have seen, the Founders held that traditional morality and religion are essential to America's identity and to a healthy and decent society. In contrast, today's left views traditional morality and religion as sources of oppression that must be marginalized if not eliminated. Despite paying a good deal of lip service to "traditional values," contemporary conservatism has not been capable of preserving America's traditional religious and moral standards. It has been disarmed by its preoccupation with the "creed." After all, it is possible for traditional religion and morality to be eroded without any direct attack on equality or natural rights.[21] Propositional-nation conservatives cannot summon much energy in defending the nation's traditional moral and religious identity because they cannot see that anything critical is at stake. Thus, marriage has been redefined, public education has been used to indoctrinate the young in radical sexual ideologies, and religion has been marginalized – all while propositional-nation conservatives have been unaware that the nation's character itself is being transformed.

Propositional-nation conservatives think the nation was founded on the idea of freedom. In a sense they are correct. But they have erred in letting the country be hijacked by novel and radical notions of freedom that have nothing in common with the Founding. The Founders wanted freedom understood as secure possession of the rights to life, liberty, and property – the freedom to enjoy these goods under the rule of law, without fear of arbitrary government. They understood such freedom also as a freedom to live according to the moral standards and religious beliefs that they had inherited from the previous developments of Western civilization. They were not champions of a radical freedom understood as unlimited liberation from the claims of a traditional morality that is rooted in religion and human nature. They probably never thought of such a thing, and if they had been presented with it they would have warned that it could only lead to disaster. But by learning only a partial account of the Founding, today's conservatives have lost the ability to articulate what is at stake in the Left's contemporary war on tradition, nature, and religion.

MOVING ON FROM PAST ERRORS

Finally, we should observe that propositional-nation conservatism has been bad politics. Excessive preoccupation with the Declaration's creed – with equality and rights – undermines American conservatism's ability to compete electorally with the Left. The Left has an agenda that appeals to the self-interest and the moral imagination of many voters. They appeal to their self-interest by lavishing them with public money. They appeal to their moral imagination by contending that such payments are a righteous remedy for various social wrongs, and by promising a progressive liberation from traditional social restraints, which they paint as forms of oppression, and from various social inequalities, which they paint as injustices.

Propositional-nation conservatism can offer no compelling appeal to self-interest and the moral imagination that can counter the Left's. It fails to appeal directly to self-interest because it offers policies that are based on abstract principles, like global free trade or, even worse, policies that seem to demand altruistic self-sacrifice of the nation's interests, such as whatever foreign adventure is justified by "American exceptionalism." And it fails to appeal to the moral imagination because it limits itself to procedural (although indeed important) principles like rights and equality instead of offering a spirited defense of the nation and of the moral and religious way of life that we are blessed to have inherited from our noble ancestors.

To escape this predicament, we need a Right that can offer a substantive view of the common good that can compete with the Left's by appealing to self-interest and the moral imagination. Such a vision can be found in the nationalist traditionalism of the Founders. A nationalist conservatism appeals to the self-interest of voters by promoting policies that aim to make the nation more powerful and more prosperous – and that accordingly benefit each of us and all of us together. Such a conservatism would also appeal to the moral imagination by defending the country's traditional identity, now under assault. It would present itself as a patriotism that loves and wants to preserve the country we have inherited – its way of life – and not just some of the abstract principles to which it has been dedicated. This is the way of the future for the Right – if there is going to be any future at all.

NOTES

1   Paul Ryan, "Speech on the State of American Politics," text of speech delivered at the Republican National Convention, Tampa, FL, March 23, 2016, https://time.com/4269260/
paul-ryan-speech-donald-trump-politics-transcript/.

2   Paul Ryan (@SpeakerRyan), "America is more than a country – it's an idea," Twitter, July 4, 2018, 10:03 a.m., https://twitter.com/speakerryan/status/1014509887114522630?lang=en.

3   Jennifer Rubin, "Three Interpretations of Trump's 'Nationalist' Rhetoric," *Washington Post*, October 24, 2018, https://www.washingtonpost.com/news/opinions/wp/2018/10/24/
three-interpretations-of-trumps-nationalist-rhetoric/.

4   Alexander Hamilton, *The Political Writings of Alexander Hamilton*, ed. Carson Holloway and Bradford P. Wilson (New York: Cambridge University Press, 2017), 2: 206.

5   George Washington, *George Washington: Writings*, ed. John H. Rhodehamel (New York: Library of America, 1997), 973.

6   See Arthur Milikh, "Trump and *The Federalist* on National Greatness in a Commercial Republic," in *Trump and Political Philosophy: Leadership, Statesmanship, and Political Philosophy*, ed. Angel Jaramillo Torres and Marc Benjamin Sable (New York: Palgrave Macmillan, 2018), 195–210.

7   Alexander Hamilton, *Alexander Hamilton: Writings*, ed. Joanne Freeman (New York: Library of America, 2001), 692 (emphasis in original).

8   Hamilton, *Writings*, 647.

9   Thomas Jefferson, *The Papers of Thomas Jefferson, Retirement Series*, ed. J. Jefferson Looney (Princeton, NJ: Princeton University Press, 2012), 9: 333–37.

10 Alexander Hamilton, James Madison, and John Jay, *The Federalist*, ed. George W. Carey and James McClellan (Indianapolis: Liberty Fund, 2001), 6.

11 Washington, *Writings*, 965.

12 Some scholars contend that Jay and Washington exaggerated the young
    nation's homogeneity. After all, there were religious differences within the
    Founding generation and important differences in culture between the
    North and the South. Moreover, the country was not exclusively of one
    ethnicity. Jay and Washington nevertheless had a point: Founding-genera-
    tion Americans were predominantly Christian, predominantly British,
    and predominantly English-speaking. More to the point, Jay and Washing-
    ton's arguments show that the Founders did not uncritically celebrate
    diversity but instead valued such unity as the nation's historical develop-
    ment had afforded it at the time, and that they did not understand the
    nation as based only on shared affirmation of the political creed put for-
    ward in the Declaration.

13 On these issues, see Thomas G. West's illuminating discussion in *The Politi-
    cal Theory of the American Founding: Natural Rights, Public Policy, and the
    Moral Conditions of Freedom* (New York: Cambridge University Press,
    2017), 219–43.

14 George Washington, *Writings*, 971.

15 George Washington, *The Papers of George Washington: Presidential Series*,
    ed. Dorothy Twohig (Charlottesville: University Press of Virginia, 1993),
    4: 131–32.

16 George Washington, *Writings*, 975.

17 George W. Bush, "Second Inaugural Address," text of speech delivered at
    the Capitol, Washington, DC, January 20, 2005, https://www.npr.org/
    templates/story/story.php?storyId=4460172.

18 Paul Bluestein, "Pat Buchanan . . . Liberal?" *Washington Post*, February 23,
    1996, https://www.washingtonpost.com/archive/business/1996/02/23/
    patrick-buchanan-liberal/7bc9cfe9-5629-4cbb-b293-fba113ac6280/.

19 Matthew DeBord, "Trump's National Security Tariffs on Autos Would be
    Socialism at its Worst: Here's Why They're Bad for America," *Business
    Insider*, February 21, 2019, https://www.businessinsider.com/
    trumps-national-security-tariffs-auto-imports-socialism-2019-2.

20 See Hamilton, *Political Writings*, 2: 499–502.

21 There is an instructive exception to this tendency. The Right has been ener-
    getic and successful in rolling back the permissive abortion regime estab-
    lished by the Left through *Roe* v. *Wade*. The one issue on which the Right
    could successfully counter the Left's attack on traditional morality is the
    one that can be presented as an assault on a right – the right to life. This
    example also reminds us that continued attention to the natural rights pro-
    claimed in the Declaration is a necessary element of a successful Right,
    even if rights and equality *alone* cannot be the basis of the whole concep-
    tion of the common good that the Right requires.

REDISCOVERING A GENUINE AMERICAN NARRATIVE

John Fonte

THE ACCLAIMED BRITISH HISTORIAN Paul Johnson observed that "The creation of the United States of America is the greatest of all human adventures." America's story is one "of difficulties overcome by skill, faith, and strength of purpose, and courage and persistence." It is the story of "human achievement without parallel." Americans, Johnson remarked, "thrown together by fate in that swirling maelstrom of history," are "the most remarkable people the world has ever seen."[1]

Needless to say, this sentiment is rarely, if ever, expressed today in elite circles. It is either forgotten or openly opposed in almost all corners. That is because the entirety of the American story or "narrative" is interpreted for Americans by the progressive Left, even if only indirectly. They own the national narrative; nearly every single institution propounds their version; even many conservatives hum their tune.

A microcosm of this narrative is expressed by the leading organization of professors of American history who proclaim: "The best historical inquiry acknowledges and interrogates systems of oppression–racial, ethnic, gender, class–and openly addresses the myriad injustices that these systems have perpetuated through the past and into the present." America is "a nation built on slavery, exploitation, and exclusion ... Critical race theory provides a lens through which we can examine and understand systemic racism and its many consequences."[2]

This narrative tells us that from the beginning to the present day, America is permeated by oppression. The great meaning of America, we are told, comes from liberating so-called oppressed groups and taming the power of privileged groups. Thus, our history is one of liberation: first of blacks, then of women, then of gays, and now of the transgendered. The core narrative concerns itself with the continued expansion of the rights of marginalized groups, and the American way of life is legitimate only insofar as this takes place.

Not only is this narrative false; it will take us further down the path of national self-destruction. No nation that despises itself can survive. In the next leg of conservative counterrevolutionary action, this false narrative must be replaced.

THE PROGRESSIVE NARRATIVE BEGETS THE PROGRESSIVE CITIZEN

All nations have narratives that serve to educate their citizens about themselves. Through these, nations try to create certain human types: ancient Sparta venerated the soldier; Renaissance rulers lionized the humanist scholar; the Communist regimes exalted the party militant; other societies have extolled the priest, the businessman, the saint, or the scientist. On the surface, the Left hopes to create engaged global citizens, while the inner, darker teaching is that these citizens will be set against their native country.

The core of the oppression narrative is a focus, ironically, on the *superiority* of "marginalized" racial, ethnic, and gender groups, which gives them special privileges. These privileges are superior to those of common American citizenship, as is seen in the institutionalization of this narrative in the federal government and the bulk of civil society.

A public-private progressive regime has created an almost

medieval two-tiered racial–gender hierarchy in which the so-called "underserved" are provided with what is effectively superior status over other American citizens.[3] In practice, nonprivileged white and Asian Americans are discriminated against.[4] The "underserved" are awarded legal superiority in employment and admission to higher education. They are the first hired and the last fired. Criticism of them is often characterized as "hate speech," which cripples spirited debate and the give-and-take of democratic deliberation in a free society.[5]

All narratives – Diderot's *Encyclopedie*, the *Communist Manifesto*, Critical Race Theory, the 1619 Project – have adversaries, enemies, and villains (ancien regime, bourgeoise, white supremacists), either spiritually and intellectually and/or in terms of material power. The villains of the progressive narrative are America itself and the citizens who are still attached to its traditions. The establishment Right's role in this has been to basically concede the Left's narrative – namely, that the primary meaning of the American story is the continuous expansion of the rights of previously marginalized groups.[6] By design, whites are made to feel guilty and nonwhites resentful and bitter.

Clearly, the increasing predominance of the progressive narrative will not yield harmony and reconciliation, but intensification of what has been called a "cold civil war."[7] Significantly, the progressive narrative is promoted by powerful forces through billions of dollars, physical intimidation, and moral blackmail.[8] It is clear that this narrative has impacted America's young. A Pew study revealed that among eighteen- to twenty-nine-year-old Democrat-leaning citizens, 55 percent believed "other countries are better than America." A mere 5 percent believed "America stands above all other countries."[9]

TOWARD A GENUINE AMERICAN NARRATIVE: AMERICAN CIVILIZATION

As noted above, the story of America, "a human achievement without parallel," is one of the most remarkable in world history. From thirteen English settler colonies huddled on the coast of North America to a world power. We Americans built a civilization in the woods. We settled a continent. What other nation has such a past?

More than any other nation, and unlike France or Russia, America made the various strands of modernity stable. One cannot build a civilization like ours without widespread religious faith, on the one hand, and the habits of reason, on the other. The ideas and practice of English law, institutions, customs, religious organizations, property, individual rights, and government (representative assemblies, local sheriffs, jury trials, etc.,) predominated. Most significantly, the "lived experience" of these English colonists included developing the habit of self-rule through elected colonial legislatures that often challenged royal governors. While European nations like France were either destroying themselves or being ruled by kings and despots, Americans were ruling themselves, at the same time that basic personal safety (let alone consensual government) did not exist in vast regions of Africa, Asia, and the Middle East.

Despite contemporary desires to see ourselves as the superiors of the original settlers, in many ways we are not. We no longer have the kind of industriousness, discipline, and belief to achieve what they did. We do not have the habits of character and soul; nor do we have their education. Many arrogantly believe that we are in a postreligious era. This is a mistake, for what replaces this faith and the inner strength it provided are not wisdom, but ersatz religions like woke ideology, a naïve yet arrogant utopianism, and solipsism and self-indulgence.

These original settlers stood at the beginning of what became the world's foremost military. It was also the beginning of the greatest economy that provided for the hitherto unseen prosperity for the greatest number of people that the world has ever known. Through a determined policy of Americanization, combined with immigration restrictions, we patriotically assimilated millions of people from many different and conflicting cultures, something no other nation has accomplished as well. We no longer seem capable of doing this.

Our achievements in modern science are second to none; they are also gifts that we gave to the world. There was little or no science in the modern era coming from Asia, Africa, and Latin America, though they are the beneficiaries of these discoveries. We invented the telegraph, the telephone, the phonograph, the first practical typewriter, the first passenger elevator, the lightening rod, the light bulb, the domestic refrigerator, refrigerated railroad cars, indoor plumbing, air conditioning, television, the submarine, the airplane, the rocket, the first software operating system, the minicomputer, and the internet. Along the way, we conquered yellow fever and polio. We also are alone in putting a man on the moon. Who at this point understands the genius that went into this, and the generations spent building up knowledge, the many failed experiments, the money invested, the talent culled from a young age? Do we understand the enormous debt that we owe to those Americans who have gone before us? Simply put, we built American civilization and led the modern era.

Our task now is to be the ruthless guardians of that civilization and of the things that made American civilization possible: excellence, merit, opportunity, inventiveness, national self-confidence, national sovereignty, political and economic freedom, belief in an objective standard inherent in nature and in Christianity and Judaism, and in a spiritedness in defense of our principles, our Constitution, our culture, and our nation.

This is our patrimony. The central question is this: will we embrace it, defend it, and improve it, against today's attacks from those who claim America is "systemically" flawed, who place race and gender above our common American citizenship, and who seek to deconstruct and fundamentally transform our nation? At the end of the day, parts of the ruling Left probably know their narrative is essentially false. But they push ahead because they stand to gain ever-increasing power through its promulgation.

The progressive narrative seeks to delegitimize the Founders and therewith historical America. This is a hill on which the American Right must fight. Without apology we should proclaim the undeniable fact that the creation of the United States of America was one of the great achievements in world history.[10]

SLAVERY, AMERICAN INDIANS, AND RACIAL DISCRIMINATION

What about slavery, "stolen" Indian land, and racial discrimination, which prevents some fair-minded Americans from embracing our past? The legacy Right often treats these issues with an apologetic tone, having internalized some of the guilt-ridden tenets of the progressive narrative.

What is needed, however, is not apology but accuracy. Chattel slavery has existed everywhere, and it exists today. In Mauritania and Sudan, the ownership of slaves and the buying and selling of human beings are still widespread, despite (mainly toothless) legal prohibitions. In 2017, CNN reported ongoing public slave auctions in Libya.[11] Westerners and non-Westerners, Middle Easterners, Asians, and Africans have owned slaves and participated in the slave trade. Why doesn't the Left turn its ire on them? It is because the progressive Left's primary enemy is not found in foreign lands. Instead, the major focus of their enmity is directed at fellow Americans who resist the progressive agenda, who "cling to guns or religion or antipathy toward people who aren't like them or anti-immigrant sentiment," as a famous American once said.[12]

It is also patently absurd to say that our Founders embraced slavery. Both the active opponents of slavery (Hamilton, Adams,

Jay, Franklin) and the slave owners among them (Washington, Jefferson, Madison) recognized the injustice of the institution and sought, in Lincoln's words, its "ultimate extinction." It was not politically or economically possible to immediately abolish slavery, or the republic would not have survived its birth pangs. As Washington wrote, "there is not a man living who wishes more sincerely than I do, to see a plan adopted for the abolition of it [slavery]."[13] It is dishonest to think that men who would speak in such terms were adherents of slavery. Moreover, and perhaps most importantly, not a single Founder thought that the presence of slaves on American soil was a good thing.

Abolition was finally achieved in a bloody civil war that decimated 2 percent of the population, the equivalent today of more than six and a half million deaths in combat. Put otherwise, hundreds of thousands of white male farm boys, clerks, and tradesmen gave their lives to end black slavery in America and to preserve our union.

Almost sixty years ago, the 1964 Civil Rights Act was passed to end racial discrimination. Ironically, as Christopher Caldwell explains, the unintended consequences of the act has resulted in the contemporary racial-gender preference regime described earlier.[14] Nevertheless, at the time, the act was embraced by many Americans in good faith, Americans who sought to diminish prejudice and promote fairness in employment and education. Moreover, since the legislation's passage, trillions of dollars have been spent and Americans of all walks of life have worked (in effect, they have done everything realistically feasible) to achieve these ends. Furthermore, America was the first predominately white nation to twice elect a black president. Opposition to his presidency was based on policy not on race. To claim that racism is systemic and pervasive among the American people today is both slanderous and ludicrous.

Yet the progressive Left asserts that America has always been and remains "systemically racist." This falsehood had been vigorously rebutted. Consciously contradicting the progressive Left,

Professor Shelby Steele has retorted with the following statement: "Today we're in freedom. Racism is not there.... We're so free, we don't know what to do with it."[15]

Likewise, relations between American settlers and American Indians should be viewed accurately. Stolen land? The Iroquois stole the land of the Algonquians; the Lakota stole the land of Cheyenne, who had in turn stolen the land of the Kiowa. The Pawnees fought alongside the US Army against other Indians. Besides the well-known massacre at Wounded Knee we should also learn of the Sioux massacring hundreds of white settlers (men, women, and children) in the Dakota War of 1862; of the Salt Creek Massacre of settlers in 1871; of the massacre of settlers by the Apache at Cooks Canyon; and of the well-documented Iroquois practice of the torture of helpless prisoners of all ages and sexes and their custom of cannibalism.[16] Again, the story is a complicated one: let us examine it accurately, warts and all.

On the questions of slavery, American Indians, and racial discrimination, the progressive narrative is not a historically accurate project designed to address past wrongs, but a weaponized movement to deconstruct and replace American civilization. If historic America is to survive, the Right must realize that the progressive narrative is operating in bad faith. It is essentially a strategy for achieving power.

The Czech dissident Milan Kundera, wrote, "The first step in liquidating a people is to erase its memory. Destroy its books, its culture, its history. Then have somebody write new books, manufacture a new culture, invent a new history. Before long the nation will begin to forget what it is and what it was."[17]

Concepts such as Critical Race Theory, the 1619 Project, Queer theory, so-called DEI ("Diversity, Equity, and Inclusion") are weapons "to manufacture a new culture" and "invent a new history." The telos, the ultimate end goal of the progressive project, is the deconstruction of the American nation and its reconstruction along a resentment-based racial-gender-identity regime.

FORGING THE COUNTERNARRATIVE

At the end of the day, our task is to forge a counternarrative. This mission will require not a conservative disposition or mindset, but a counterrevolutionary one, a mindset that refuses to play our assigned subordinate role in acquiescing to a "consensus" mostly dominated by the progressive cultural leviathan.[18] Instead, we must create a powerful *alternative* vision of American civilization that seizes the moral high ground in appealing to most Americans. Because the adversary is fully entrenched, what is needed is a fighting faith. This ultimately means doing what every successful narrative has always done – identifying and defeating a specifically named adversary. Fortunately, in building an alternative vision, we have plenty of raw material that could be shaped into a formidable and morally attractive counternarrative.[19]

Our single most important advantage is that most Americans, like most people throughout human history, prefer a national story that affirms rather than denigrates their own country.

As noted at the beginning, the progressive Left owns the national narrative. Progressives dominate our major institutions – the universities, schools, media, entertainment, and corporations. Therefore, resistance to this false narrative and the rediscovery of a genuine American narrative must come from remaining sectors of patriotic strength such as democratically elected officials. Publicly funded universities and public K–12 education are not private fiefdoms run by unaccountable ideologues and bureaucrats, but public trusts.

At the state and local level, elected governors, state legislators, and school boards should not hesitate to repudiate, renounce, and defund a pedagogy of woke indoctrination that denigrates our country and mandate instead history-civics K–12 curricula, textbooks, educational materials, and the like, all of which affirm American civilization.

At the federal level, the US Congress should prohibit any federal funds in education to support projects (e.g., curricula, teacher training in K–12, freshmen orientation in colleges) that promote DEI ("diversity, equity, and inclusion") and divisive concepts such as the idea that America is "systemically racist." A new presidential administration should supplant the current Department of Education's woke criteria for funding federal grants in history/civics education with positive and accurate guidelines for framing our nation's past and the rights and responsibilities of American citizenship.

In addition, a new presidential administration should be prepared for the 250th birthday of the United States in 2026 by launching a major cultural renewal project whose goal is to eradicate the progressive narrative. This would mean uprooting and displacing this narrative from federal government agencies including the Smithsonian Institution, the National Park Service, the National Archives, the National Endowment for the Humanities, and the National Endowment for the Arts.

This would also mean having a president using the bully pulpit without hesitation and with gusto to excoriate the Mellon Foundation's thoroughly woke "Monuments Project" and lambasting the private philanthropic institutions that have seized ideological control of Jefferson's Monticello and Madison's Montpelier.

The main point is the realization that the progressive Left has weaponized the American narrative and turned it against the American nation. We are not involved in an academic argument among intellectuals, but a life and death regime struggle over the American way of life.

No political society will endure if its core principles, its story, and its self-perception consist of resentment, guilt, embarrassment, and anger. This will destroy the America we love. No political community that, at worst, denigrates and, at best, problematizes patriotism, will long endure.

Our end goal is to improve, perpetuate, and transmit our way of life – American civilization – to future generations of Americans. To accomplish this end, we must seize the moral high ground with unapologetic love of country and delegitimize and thoroughly defeat those who would "fundamentally transform" our nation.

NOTES

1   Paul Johnson, *A History of the American People*, (New York: HarperCollins, 1997), xv, 3, 697.
2   Organization of American Historians, "Statement on White House Conference on American History," September 25, 2020.
3   Christopher Caldwell, *The Age of Entitlement: America Since the Sixties* (New York: Simon & Schuster, 2020).
4   Wil Jones and Claire Raynes, "Meeting the Moment by Looking Inward," Rockefeller Foundation, June 17, 2020, https://www.rockefellerfoundation. org/blog/meeting-the-moment-by-looking-inward/; "Diversity, Equity, and Inclusion," Ford Foundation, accessed December 13, 2022, https:// www.fordfoundation.org/about/people/diversity-equity-and-inclusion/; "About," Harvard Office for Equity, Diversity, Inclusion & Belonging, accessed December 13, 2022, https://edib.harvard.edu/about; Prasad Krishnamurthy, "Harvard's Cult of Personality," *The Hill*, October 26, 2022, https://thehill.com/opinion/education/3704542-harvards-cult-of-personality/; SFFA v. Harvard, *980 f.3d 157* (1st Cir. 2014), https://students forfairadmissions.org/wp-content/uploads/2014/11/SFFA-v.-Harvard-Complaint.pdf; Peter Salovey, "Building a Stronger and More Inclusive Yale," Yale University, Office of the President, October 14, 2020, https:// president.yale.edu/president/statements/building-stronger-and-more-inclusive-yale; Joseph R. Biden Jr., "Executive Order on Diversity, Equity, Inclusion, and Accessibility in the Federal Workforce," White House, June 25, 2021, https://www.whitehouse.gov/briefing-room/presidential-actions/2021/06/25/executive-order-on-diversity-equity-inclusion-and-accessibility-in-the-federal-workforce/; Office of the Spokesperson, "Announcement of the Finalization of the State Department's Five-year Diversity, Equity, Inclusion, and Accessibility (DEIA) Strategic Plan," U.S. Department of State, September 13, 2022, https://www.state.gov/ announcement-of-the-finalization-of-the-state-departments-five-year-diversity-equity-inclusion-and-accessibility-deia-strategic-plan/.
5   Heather Mac Donald, *The Diversity Delusion*: (New York: St. Martin Press, 2018); Peter W. Wood, *Diversity Rules* (New York: Encounter Books, 2019); Peter W. Wood, *Diversity: The Invention of a Concept* (New York: Encounter Books, 2003).

6   For example, in response to the George Floyd riots, some on the legacy
    Right responded that racism remained a major problem in America and
    that "systemic change is necessary." See, e.g., Condoleezza Rice, "This
    Moment Cries Out for Us to Confront Race in America," *Washington Post*,
    June 4, 2020, https://www.washingtonpost.com/opinions/2020/06/04/
    condoleezza-rice-moment-confront-race-america/.

7   Angelo M. Codevilla, "The Cold Civil War," *Claremont Review of Books*,
    Spring 2017, https://claremontreviewofbooks.com/the-cold-civil-war/.

8   In this vein, Stephen Heintz, head of the $1.46 billion Rockefeller Brothers
    Fund, promised to be a good ally to the George Floyd protestors in June
    2020 by establishing a "racial justice initiative" that would support orga-
    nizations (like Black Lives Matter) that "challenge the dominant normative
    value of whiteness." Overall, American corporations have committed
    around $50 billion to "antiracism" projects, including the violence-prone
    BLM.

9   Katherine Schaeffer, "On July Fourth, How Americans See Their Country
    and Their Democracy," Pew Research Center, June 30, 2022, https://www.
    pewresearch.org/fact-tank/2022/06/30/how-americans-see-their-country-
    and-their-democracy/. In addition, a Quinnipic poll revealed that among
    all eighteeen- to thirty-four-year-olds, if the United States was invaded,
    48 percent would "leave the country" and 45 percent would "stay and
    fight." See Quinnipiac, "Vast Majority Of Americans Say Ban Russian Oil,
    Quinnipiac University National Poll Finds; Nearly 8 In 10 Support U.S.
    Military Response if Putin Attacks A NATO Country," Quinnipiac Univer-
    sity, March 7, 2022, https://poll.qu.edu/poll-release?releaseid=3838.

10 Harry V. Jaffa, *A New Birth of Freedom* (Lanham, MD: Roman & Little-
    field, 2004).

11 Nima Elbagir et al., "People for Sale: Where Lives Are Auctioned for $400,"
    CNN, November 15, 2017, https://www.cnn.com/2017/11/14/africa/libya-
    migrant-auctions/index.html.

12 Janell Ross, "Obama Revives His 'Cling to Guns or Religion' Analysis,"
    Washington Post, December 21, 2015, https://www.washingtonpost.com/
    news/the-fix/wp/2015/12/21/obama-dusts-off-his-cling-to-guns-or-
    religion-idea-for-donald-trump/.

13 Thomas G. West, *Vindicating the Founders: Race, Sex, Class, and Justice in
    the Origins of America* (Lanham, MD: Roman & Littlefield, 1997);
    Thomas G. West, *The Political Theory of the American Founding* (New York:
    Cambridge University Press, 2017). See also Arthur Milikh, "1776, not
    1619," *City Journal*, October 29, 2019, https://www.city-journal.org/
    new-york-times-1619-project.

14 See, Christopher Caldwell, *Age of Entitlement*.

15 Glenn Loury, "Are We Ready to Abandon Racial Solidarity?" Substack,

November 22, 2022, https://glennloury.substack.com/p/are-we-
ready-to-abandon-racial-solidarity.

16 Gary C. Anderson, *Massacre in Minnesota: The Dakota War of 1862, The
Most Violent Ethnic Conflict in American History* (Norman: University of
Oklahoma Press, 2019); Vern Raven and Kathryn Howard, "The Salt Creek
Massacre," Mansfield Historical Museum and Heritage Center, accessed
December 14, 2022, https://www.mansfieldtexas.gov/1370/The-Salt-
Creek-Massacre; Jay W. Sharp, "Cooke's Canyon: Journey of Death,"
DesertUSA, accessed December 14, 2022, https://www.desertusa.com/
desert-new-mexico/cookes-canyon.html; Jeffery P. Blick, "The Iroquois
Practice of Genocidal Warfare (1534–1787)," *Journal of Genocide Research*
3, no. 3 (November 2001).

17 Milan Kundera, *The Book of Laughter and Forgetting* (New York: Harper
Perennial Modern Classics, 1980).

18 Acceptance by some conservative intellectuals of a Left-dominated "consensus" in the "Educating for American Democracy" project highlights
this problem. See Educating for American Democracy, "Excellence in History and Civics for All Learners," iCivics, March 2, 2021, https://www.
educatingforamericandemocracy.org/wp-content/uploads/2021/02/
Educating-for-American-Democracy-Report-Excellence-in-History-and-
Civics-for-All-Learners.pdf. See also John Fonte, "No Compromise with
the Woke Revolution," *American Mind*, October 13, 2022, https://
americanmind.org/features/florida-versus-davos/no-compromise-
with-the-woke-revolution/.

19 The material available includes arguments from the National Association
of Scholars (American Birthright.) It includes material from the Presidential 1776 Commission. Robert Woodson's mostly African American history 1776 Unites project, the civic education curriculum of Florida, and
American Achievement Testing (AAT) will ultimately challenge the progressive College Board's Advance Placement US History (APUSH)
courses in American high schools. The material also includes work by the
Intercollegiate Studies Institute (ISI) (*A Student's Guide to US History* and
A Student's Guide to American Political Thought), Hillsdale College, the
Ashbrook Center; William Bennett's *America: The Last Best Hope*, and the
work of major scholars past and present (Harry Jaffa, Bernard Bailyn, Wil-
fred McClay, et.al.). Indeed, Professor McClay has written a masterful
textbook that contains the seeds of a true and inspiring American narrative: *Land of Hope: An Invitation to America's Story*. In short, there is a treasure trove of *matter* in which to *form* a compelling narrative.

RACE AND THE CONSERVATIVE CONSCIENCE

David Azerrad

For all the profound disagreements between the conservative establishment and those of us on the emerging new Right, we broadly agree on what to do about the most contentious issue in America: race – by which we mean, as everyone else does, black people. We both reject invidious discrimination (including so-called "affirmative action") and believe desirable positions should generally be awarded on the basis of merit and competence. We both expect the government to secure the rights of all Americans equally, regardless of race. And, of course, we both think that our fellow black citizens should be treated with courtesy in everyday life (the days in which a grown man was called "boy" – or worse – are, in any case, long gone).

Equal rights under equal laws with no special treatment should be the bedrock of American justice. Nothing less, nothing more – *come what may of life outcomes*. That last qualifier is the real holdup. Conservatives claim to believe in colorblindness but they in truth do not have the stomach to accept the outcomes it produces. They tirelessly quote that one line from the "I Have a Dream" speech but feel uneasy when they end up without enough people of a particular skin color after having judged people by the content of their character.

Quoting Martin Luther King Jr. is easy; defending actual colorblind practices is hard because they produce disparities. These disparities almost always cut against black people and, according to the reigning critical race orthodoxy, are evidence of racism. To quote America's leading charlatan on racial questions, Ibram X. Kendi: "when I see disparities, I see racism."[1] Our laws are "racist" because they send too many black criminals to jail. The SAT is "racist" because blacks score lower than whites – and Asians and Hispanics. Good health itself is now "racist" because the black obesity rate is higher than anyone else's. In short, all standards, norms, laws, and codes of conduct are "racist" because blacks have a harder time complying with them.

Many Americans, in particular, those of the older generation, have difficulty grasping just how far left the elites and the civil rights regime have gone on race. What they would think is the ideal of nonracism – that is, color-blindness – is now denounced as racist.[2] Racism used to be defined in terms of the malicious intent to discriminate. It is now strictly about outcomes. Opposing "racism" today thus *requires* discriminating on the basis of race. According to this logic, it is racist to treat Americans of all races equally.

This puts conservatives in a bind. They can either give up on their commitment to impartial justice and excellence – to say nothing of basic competence – or resign themselves to being "racists." This, in truth, is a false choice. The new Right clearly sees what establishment conservatives are reluctant to accept: nothing we could say or do would ever absolve us in the eyes of the Left and the ruling class whose opinions are shaped by it. No amount of black outreach, Juneteenth celebrations, or expressions of sympathy for George Floyd will ever get them to stop calling us racists. Politics for them is a struggle against racism and, to a lesser extent, misogyny, homophobia, and transphobia. Their political movement thus *requires* the existence of racists. When they do not exist, they must be manufactured.

As the ultimate arbiters of all racial controversies, those on the Left occupy the moral high ground in American politics. The accusation of racism, however unfounded, is their most powerful political weapon. They would have to be crazy to give it up.

But we on the Right would have to be even crazier to think we can beat them at their own game. The game is rigged. Democrats may well be the real racists but we don't get to decide who the real racists are. Their allies in the media do. More importantly, why should we care who the real racists are? Why must we accept the Left's central piety as our own?

The only way forward for any Right worthy of its name is apostasy: we must abandon the church of antiracism. We must refuse to play by the Left's racial rules. Absent overwhelming force, it is simply not possible to defeat an enemy if you fight him on his own terms. But in contemporary America, it is the Left's pieties that are authoritative – not ours. No one gets canceled for offending the Right. Only the most clueless of Boomers still believe that accusations of socialism carry any weight in contemporary America.

We must therefore reject the idea that American politics is a competition to show who can better help blacks and who can denounce racism more loudly. We need to free our minds once and for all from the fear of being called racists. We may well have the best policy ideas and know how to own the libs, but none of it will matter unless we fundamentally rethink our approach to race.

NEUTRALIZING THE LEFT

The first step is to gain clarity on what the Right's goals on race should be. For too many conservatives, the goal is to outdo progressives in displays of compassion for blacks in order to win them over to the Republican Party in a futile quest to prove that "we're not racists – Democrats are!" Hence the conservative obsession with showing how their policies – from school choice to enterprise zones to occupational licensing reform – benefit black people. Conservatives have been doing this for decades, yet blacks continue to vote monolithically for the Democratic Party and progressives have only ramped up their hysterical accusations of racism.

A more sensible way for the Right would instead be to set our sights on two achievable goals that would benefit us, our fellow black citizens, and the country as a whole. The first is to neutralize the Left's moral advantage by refusing to bow before the altar of antiracism.

We must learn to shrug off accusations of racism. Tucker Carlson's impious laugh may well be what drives his critics most mad. We must defend fellow conservatives who get smeared with this defamatory charge. No more senseless sacrifices to Moloch. In a sane world, conservatives would be much more outraged at Americans who sell out their country to China or harm their families than at those who casually dropped the n-word twenty years ago at a frat party.

Systemic antiblack racism has long been dead in America, and racism is low on the list of problems confronting black America. There is no reason why the Right should continue to recognize antiblack racism as the one unforgiveable offense worthy of cancelation in 2023. This does not mean, of course, that we should embrace or celebrate racism. But there is no reason to accept the Left's demonization of racism as the one unforgivable sin when real, malicious antiblack racism is dead beyond resuscitation. Such a claim will sound preposterous to someone whose knowledge of America comes from the *New York Times* and *CNN*, but no one who has spent time within the conservative movement or traveled across the country – especially in the South, once the hotbed of segregation – would believe that Jim Crow is about to make a comeback.

Real racism – the belief that humanity is divided into superior and inferior races and that the latter exist to serve the former who may do with them as they see fit – can still be found, but only in the most obscure corners of the internet. Almost all of what gets called racist today is, at most, tasteless and, more often than not, merely the stating of indisputable facts that contradict the narrative or the application of impartial norms that have a "disparate impact" on blacks. It is not racist to notice that blacks commit the majority of violent crimes in America, no more than it is to incarcerate convicted black criminals. Criminal justice is not the new Jim Crow.

The following thought exercise might be helpful for conservatives: would you rather your child be a racist *as the term is understood today* – someone who speaks indelicately about racial questions without, however, harming anyone – or a meth addict? Or a pornographer? Or an adulterer? Or a murderer? No conservatism worthy of its name can continue to make racism as defined by the Left – that is, noticing what we are not supposed to notice – the *summum malum* and the lone cause of social ostracism in America a century and a half after the last slave was freed and close to sixty years after private discrimination was outlawed across the land (except, of course, if it benefits the "formerly oppressed").

The Left's power over the Right is based not only on the justifiable fear of being canceled for "racism" but also on the extent to which it has successfully imbedded some of its core doctrines into the conservative mind. Conservatives are torn between two incompatible understandings of justice. They claim to be dedicated to justice understood as equality under the law and meritocracy. But the competing claim of social justice – equal outcomes for blacks – tugs at them. The black-white disparities weigh on their conscience, even when they fully know they result from the just application of equal standards.

To a certain extent, conservatives have bought into the reigning moral framework of the Left, which makes black representation in all realms of life the measure of justice. It is this conception of justice that is most honored in elite American society today. Ambitious conservatives generally want to fit in with their college-educated peers in Manhattan, DC, San Francisco, and the other blue metropolises where they reside. At first, they simply do not challenge the prejudice in favor of black people. Then they start to accept it in part. Eventually, they come to feel good about themselves for embodying it. Let's be honest: most prominent conservatives would rather be photographed helping inner city black kids than helping Appalachian white kids.

To truly neutralize the Left's moral advantage, the Right will also need to develop a clean conscience on race. Conservatives – to say nothing of the rest of America – need to rid themselves of what guilt they still feel over America's past mistreatment of blacks. Slavery was a cruel institution and a great misfortune. It was in no way unique to America. And it ended a long time ago. It surely does not constitute the country's original sin. Nations do not commit original sins – that is, they do not contract inexpiable moral debts. They can commit crimes that may demand restitution or compensation. America arguably owed some form of compensation to the freed slaves at the end of the Civil War, but it does not owe their descendants 158 years later anything more than it owes its white, brown, or other citizens. Anyone involved in slavery has long since been dead. Justice demands we treat one another equally – not that we punish one race in perpetuity for the crimes of its ancestors, and reward another in perpetuity for the suffering of its ancestors. Innocence and victimhood are not inheritable biological categories.

Racial injustice, of course, did not end with the emancipation of the last slave. It took another century to end segregation, secure the black right to vote, and overcome the worst vestiges of racism. But, in the end, America did the right thing. And it has spent the last six decades since then reckoning with the past. We have not one but two black national holidays (MLK Day and now Juneteenth). We devote an entire month to black history. King has a monument on the mall, next to those of our greatest presidents. Our schools probably spend more time teaching America's past racial injustices than any other discrete topic. America has become one never-ending truth and reconciliation commission that only serves to cultivate victimhood and hatred in blacks and guilt in whites. It is time to move on.

Lastly, conservatives will need to root out from their souls the pathological pity for blacks, masquerading as compassion, that is the norm in contemporary America. For all the talk of dignity and equality, America treats its black citizens as if they were children who need to be coddled and sheltered from the harshness of the world. This is most obvious in the widespread embrace of affirmative action (the lowering of standards to advance blacks) and the general reluctance to speak certain blunt but necessary truths about the pathologies plaguing black America – in particular, violent crime, fatherlessness, low academic achievement, nihilistic alienation, and the cult of victimhood.

During the civil war, Frederick Douglass took up the thorny question of what to do with the freed slaves after emancipation. His manly answer was in keeping with the best of the American tradition: "do nothing with them; mind your business, and let them mind theirs." His justification was even more compelling: "The great majority of human duties are of this negative character. If men were born in need of crutches, instead of having legs, the fact would be otherwise."[3] Even after emerging from the degraded condition of slavery, blacks remained men who could stand on their own feet. Today, the consensus seems to be that they need crutches in perpetuity.

JUSTICE AND MERITOCRACY

The second goal for the Right is to defend, with uncompromising resolve, the rule of law and meritocracy. The Right needs to accept that the impartial enforcement of just laws and meritocratic standards of admissions, hiring, and promotion will not produce prisons, C-suites, faculty lounges, and incoming freshmen classes that "reflect our diversity." There is no reason to expect equal outcomes between the races – no more than there is to expect it between the sexes, religions, regions, or any other segments of the population. Diversity, as its very name indicates, does not mean homogeneity.

In some elite and highly technical sectors in which there are almost no qualified blacks, color-blindness will mean no blacks. This truth makes conservatives very uncomfortable. We need to dislodge from the conservative mind the firmly embedded belief, imbibed from the Left, that an organization or gathering without black people is somehow morally suspect. The absence of black bodies, to use Ta-Nehisi Coates's preferred nomenclature, is not proof of discrimination. Proof of discrimination is the explicit intent to keep black people out. Period. There is no such thing as unintentional discrimination. To put it differently, color-blindness doesn't stop at the selection stage. It should extend to outcomes too. If you don't see color when selecting, then you should not see color when looking at your workforce or student body either. The goal of conservatism is not to close racial gaps. For a variety of reasons, some more complex than others, this is not possible. The only way to bring about racial equity would be through tyrannical measures along the lines of Kendi's proposed Department of Antiracism which would grant the state complete jurisdiction over the mind and property of the American people.

If conservatives become capable of not only defending norms of civilized conduct but reimposing them on the country (or, at least, parts of it), that will do more to help blacks than any First Step Act or reparations check. What black Americans are most in need of is law enforcement, rigorous school standards, strong families, and the end of white America's condescending and infantilizing pity toward them. That will not solve all their problems, but it is the prerequisite to allowing black Americans to do what only they can do: help themselves. As the black economist Glenn Loury has explained: "We must accept responsibility for the way we raise our children, and how we conduct ourselves, what we do with our time, for the nature of our family life, for the foundation of the development of our full reach of our human potential."[4]

It is important to stress that the overarching goal for the Right should not be to "solve the racial problem" but to prevent it from destroying the country. It may well be that the problem cannot be solved – at least, not in the way most of us hope. Too many Americans have been seduced by MLK's utopian dreams of brotherhood – for understandable reasons. But given our ugly past, the frenzied wokeness of our present, and the deeply entrenched civil rights regime that mandates wokeness, that dream is unattainable.

Even in times of war, Americans have never united in "a beautiful symphony of brotherhood."[5] We surely will not do so when it comes to the most divisive issue in our country's history. While the causes are complex and deep-rooted, it is worth noting that blacks themselves evince little interest in becoming fully racially integrated with whites in all realms. HBCUs have lost their raison d'être, and yet they continue to attract students. In a vast commercial modern republic, people are free to choose to retain elements of a distinctive cultural identity. America is not Sparta.

To give up on the pipe dream of completely going beyond race does not imply resigning oneself to an America torn apart by racial strife. We should instead set our sights on the much more reasonable goal of peaceful co-existence. Perhaps another King might be a better guide to race relations: as South Central Los Angeles was engulfed in riots, Rodney King famously said: "can't we all get along?" There is no reason black and white Americans cannot get along in their day-to-day lives. Many will surely do much more: they will intermarry, become friends, or serve together as brothers in arms. But it is foolish to believe the whole country will do so.

A NEW RACIAL AGENDA

These goals are well within reach for the Right. The Left's racial frenzy since the beginning of the Great Awokening in the early 2010s has led to mounting racial fatigue in America. It's not that the Left is relenting – in fact, it is as shrill as ever. But a growing number of Americans realize that if everyone is a racist, then no one is. People are getting fed up of both the hysteria and the relentless propaganda about race. This creates a huge opportunity for conservatives. As the economists might say, the demand for uncowed intellectuals and politicians on the Right who are capable of defending the norms of civilized conduct in America currently far exceeds the supply.

For all the talk of defunding the police, emptying the prisons, eliminating admission tests, Americans remain stubbornly attached to basic fairness – the rule of law and meritocracy. Affirmative action has been around for more than five decades and it still has not won over the American public (most polls on this question are misleading as they frame the question in such a way as to conceal the injustice of the practice). In November 2020, less than six months after George Floyd's death, Californians, of all people, upheld the state's ban on affirmative action. And they did so by a slightly higher margin than when they first enacted it in 1996, despite a more "diverse" (i.e., less white) electoral coalition.

Conservatives must forcefully oppose and publicly denounce the metastasizing civil rights regime, which bestows special privileges on blacks (as well as on other so-called people of color and women in general) at the expense of whites (primarily, but not exclusively). The eradication of all affirmative action programs, the elimination of disparate impact theory from our laws (section 105 of the 1991 Civil Rights Act must be repealed or overturned), and the defense of free speech against the hate speech censors should be the three immediate policy priorities of the Right. Eventually, freedom of association will have to be restored (although it is hard to envisage how this could happen within the confines of ordinary politics).

Ultimately, the Right has no choice but to oppose those who would destroy our country in the name of racial justice. This will take moral, intellectual, and political courage. America is becoming unlivable, and will only continue to get worse, unless we definitively break with the elite consensus on race.

NOTES

1   Ibram X. Kendi, quoted in "'When I See Racial Disparities, I See Racism.'
    Discussing Race, Gender and Mobility," *New York Times*, March 27, 2018,
    https://www.nytimes.com/interactive/2018/03/27/upshot/reader-ques-
    tions-about-race-gender-and-mobility.html

2   See, for example, Eduardo Bonilla-Silva, *Racism without Racists: Col-
    or-Blind Racism and the Persistence of Racial Inequality in America*, 5th ed.
    (Lanham, MD: Rowman & Littlefield, 2018).

3   Frederick Douglass, "What Shall Be Done with the Freed Slaves?" in *The
    Life and Writings of Frederick Douglass,* vol 3, *The Civil War*, ed. Philip S.
    Foner (New York: International Publishers, 1952), 189–90.

4   Glenn Loury, quoted in "A Contentious Conversation on Systemic Racism
    in America," *Current Affairs*, November 17, 2021, https://www.curren-
    taffairs.
    org/2021/11/a-contentious-conversation-on-systemic-racism-in-america.

5   Martin Luther King, Jr., "I Have a Dream," in *I Have a Dream: Writings and
    Speeches That Changed the World*, ed. James M. Washington (New York:
    Harper Collins, 1992), 105.

LEAN OUT

Why Women Can't Have it All

Helen Andrews

THE LIE THAT WOMEN can have it all has adherents today because it's not obvious why it should be a lie. Have a career and a family; why not? There are enough hours in the day.

The challenge of refuting the lie that women can have it all – that is, that they can balance career and family equally – rests in the fact that the trade-offs that make it impossible are hidden. If only employers would do more to accommodate working women, people say. If only alternatives could be found to fulfill duties at home that mothers used to do themselves, like childcare and housework. But the more you start thinking about those accommodations and thinking not just about what it means for any one woman to have it all, but for society to be restructured around women having it all, the more impossible those trade-offs become.

Obviously, there are women in America today who are trying to have it all; many appear to be succeeding, at least insofar as they have both children and demanding careers. But look more closely at those households, and almost invariably you'll see that behind every woman who is balancing work and family, there is an army of low-paid labor: immigrant cleaning ladies, nannies who are paid cash under the table, DoorDash delivery men who ferry the meals that mom never had time to cook. It's no coincidence that the vast increase in female workforce participation has coincided with the reappearance of something that the more egalitarian America of the early twentieth century did not have, a servant class.

There is a paradox in American life: although America today is more prosperous than it was seventy years ago, it is no longer possible for an ordinary worker to support a middle-class family on a single income. The story of how that happened is bound up with a lie that has become gospel, the lie that women can have it all.

Establishment conservatism has championed this lie, believing it's possible to be the party of both stay-at-home moms and girl bosses equally. Again, superficially this seems like it ought to be possible. Live and let live, it's a free country. But this bargain is unsustainable in practice. We only have to look at the last thirty years to understand why.

The official position of the Republican Party today is that the government's job is to make it possible for everyone to make the right choice for their family. That's the moderate position. The center right think tank the American Enterprise Institute actually published a paper in 2018 arguing that more women need to enter the work force, because "labor force attachment, especially for women ... is vital for economic growth."[1]

In 2019, Tucker Carlson said on TV that when women make more money than men, as they do in the parts of the country devastated by the decline of manufacturing, you inevitably get bad social effects like low marriage rates, out-of-wedlock births, and higher rates of drug and alcohol abuse.[2] For this factually correct observation he was pilloried. Activists accused him of "arguing there's a moral responsibility to pay women less than men."[3] Advertisers dropped his show over the controversy.

The idea that female success in the workplace might have any downsides is absolutely taboo, on both the Right and the Left. You cannot mention it. You have to stick to the platitude that it's every woman's right to decide for herself whether she wants to put family or career first.

This rhetoric of maximizing choice requires politicians to

talk as if some women will choose to be moms and some will choose to be girl bosses; and it's really fifty-fifty which one you end up being; both are equally valid; who's to say one is better?

But that is false, and it is false according to women's own preferences. The number of women who say they do not want to have children is very low, in the single digits, around 5 percent. And that is just the number who tell surveys that they predict they will be happy not having any kids when their childbearing years are over. The number of women who actually reach old age and feel satisfied with a life of being just a girl boss with no children to keep them company is even lower.

Squaring away family happiness is and ought to be a higher priority than maximizing women's career success. It is also a more urgent priority. A woman cannot simply wake up at the age of thirty-five and decide she wants to have a family. Everyone says that the sexual revolution was brought about by the advent of the contraceptive pill, which supposedly ushered in an amazing age of new human experience thanks to science. But it actually changed less than we think. We have gotten quite good at not having children when we do not want to have them, but the science that gave us the pill has not made us very much better at making children arrive when we do want them.

Look at the Supreme Court, a perfect example. The first woman on the court, Sandra Day O'Connor, had three kids; Ruth Bader Ginsburg had two kids; and both of them had their kids quite young. Both of these women followed the life course of having kids young and then pursuing their career ambitions afterward. Apparently it worked. They wound up on the Court.

Then look at the two women appointed to the court next. Sonia Sotomayor had a brief marriage to a high school boyfriend when she was young. It was annulled shortly after she graduated from law school. Elena Kagan never married. There was some speculation during her confirmation that she might be a lesbian, but her friends confirmed to reporters that she's straight. She just never managed to put it together to have a family.

This generation gap between the female Supreme Court justices born in the 1930s and those born in the 1950s illustrates the paradox of having it all. If you put family first, you can end up doing both. If you set out trying to do both, you are quite likely to end up with just the career. And worst of all, though very commonly, you probably will not end up with a wonderful, stimulating, intellectually demanding career like that of a Supreme Court justice to console you in your childlessness. You are going to have a laptop job doing corporate busywork.

Even among boomers (Sotomayor's and Kagan's generation), childlessness is still relatively rare. That's not the case for millennials. Millennials are on track to be the most childless generation in American history. Projections have it that 25 percent of millennials will be childless – one in four. By comparison, for baby boomers it's closer to one in nine. Millennials are also the least married modern generation.[4] If you want to look at how married a generation is, you look at age 21 to 36. In 1965, 17 percent of that age block had never been married. In 2017, it was 57 percent, and that trend shows no sign of decreasing. In fact, 2014 was the year that the balance shifted and the majority of adults over 16 had never been married before that 36-year cutoff.

Establishment conservatism's conventional wisdom that we should maximize everybody's choices rests on the assumption of informed choice. This means that women in their 20s know what they want, know what they will want when they are older, and have a good sense of what is possible when it comes to deciding their future life course. But this is completely false.

Many young women today lack knowledge of basic facts of biology. Sergey Brin, the cofounder of Google, selected as his second wife a woman named Nicole Shanahan, who, as you might expect, is beautiful, smart, and accomplished. Now that she's a wealthy woman, Nicole Shanahan has chosen to make one of her philanthropic causes female fertility research – or, as she calls it, reproductive longevity.

She told interviewers that when she started to think seriously about motherhood in her early thirties, it was "eye-opening to me that there are biological factors that would impede that dream."[5] She had assumed she could simply freeze her eggs and then come back to them when she needed them. She didn't understand that IVF does not work like magic, that it was possible to, as she did, go through several rounds and end up with nothing. Eventually, she and Sergey were able to have a child; but imagine a woman that brilliant and accomplished lacking this basic knowledge.

Even female doctors don't understand some of these basic facts and constraints. There was an astonishing letter published in the *New York Times* in September of last year in response to an article that it ran about childlessness among female doctors. Writing from Ann Arbor, Michigan, this doctor put it as follows:

> As a reproductive endocrinologist, I have seen countless 40-something-year-old female physicians seeking fertility treatment, only to be genuinely shocked that their peak egg number and quality – that is, their peak fertility – has long since passed.
>
> Often the only reliable treatment in the setting of substantial reproductive aging is using donor eggs from a much younger woman, which is infrequently a desired solution.
>
> Despite decades of medical education, most physicians and other medical professionals have never had sufficient training in basic human reproduction. As you might imagine, the problem is worse among nonmedical professionals.
>
> Family planning, to the limited extent it is taught in our schools, focuses entirely on the prevention of undesired pregnancy. Ironically, no attention is given to the limits of human fertility and the question of how to conceive when

a pregnancy is desired. There is no reliable time in any American's life – including our physicians' – when they are taught even the basic reality and limitations of how to become pregnant.[6]

How in the world did it get so bad, that even our doctors do not understand fundamental biological necessity? One reason is the deliberate suppression of the truth about these matters by feminists. In 2002, the American Society for Reproductive Medicine bought some ad space in movie theaters and on buses in Washington, DC. These PSAs were entirely innocuous, saying things like, "Advancing age decreases your ability to have children." NOW, the Natural Organization of Women, organized a campaign and had those PSAs pulled because "they sent a negative message to women who might want to delay or skip childbearing in favor of career pursuits."

Normally it would be the responsibility of older people to inform younger generations that feminists are lying to them, that family is important, and that it does not just happen automatically. So why haven't elder generations been fulfilling their responsibility to impart that wisdom to younger people, especially to younger women?

In part because of the social taboo, but also because in many contexts it is illegal to do so. If you have ever held a management position, you know that it is illegal to ask a woman in a job interview if she is pregnant or planning to become pregnant. If you are mentoring a female employee at your company and you tell her that your personal advice is that she should have kids before she gets too old, even if that means putting a pause on her career, that remark can get you into legal trouble. If that woman is ever passed over for a promotion, she could turn around and sue the company for sexual discrimination and use your remark as evidence.

In 1981, a female English professor was denied tenure at Boston University. She sued BU for sexual discrimination, claiming the university denied her tenure on the basis of sex. One item of evidence she cited was a speech by university president John Silber at a think tank event in Washington, where he connected the rise in working mothers to a decline in children's well-being. John Silber was known to be somewhat combative, but this particular speech was inoffensive, making the case that "Lack of parental supervision associated with both parents working explains in part that children watch 24 hours of television a week." It was a conventional speech with ordinary, socially conservative observations about women.

During the trial, the professor's lawyer asked Silber on the stand, "So, some of those career women that you denigrated are in universities, including your own. I suppose that's one way to get them back in the kitchens, to get them out of the university. Is that so?" The female English professor won her case, with the university being ordered to give her tenure. In other words, expressing the opinion that motherhood is more important than a career, especially when children are young, is enough to expose your institution to legal liability.

Imagine the following scenario: A boss has a sincerely held opinion that motherhood is important, and he does not want his business to be complicit in taking a mother away from her children, especially when the children are young. This boss wants to operate his business by the rule of thumb that a lot of business owners had before the sexual revolution, which means he does not want to hire a woman who has kids under the age of five (with whatever exception is needed for widows or special circumstances). You might think that the boss should be free to do that, just as a woman should be free, if she has children under five, to disagree and go out and find an employer who is happy to have her. But no. Such a policy has been illegal since 1971.

The Supreme Court case *Phillips v. Martin Marietta Corporation* (1971) established this standard. The case involved a company that had a policy of not employing women with preschool-aged children. The Court found it was a violation of the Civil Rights Act because the company did not also have a policy against employing fathers with preschool-aged children. The idea that mothers and fathers of young children have different responsibilities was dismissed by the Court as an outdated stereotype.

We live in a regime where agreeing that women can have it all is legally mandatory. You cannot express dissent from it or operate your private business according to a different set of opinions.

Has the Republican Party done anything to reverse these legal insanities? No. On the contrary, Donald Trump, in many ways a buster of such orthodoxies, put his daughter Ivanka in charge of a push for paid parental leave, which is a misguided policy that does a lot for girl bosses but gives stay-at-home moms nothing. The idea of rolling back the antidiscrimination jurisprudence described above is a complete nonstarter.

And here we have the reason why the Republican Party's have-it-all fallacy was bound to fail. Once you lead women down the primrose path of thinking they can have a career just like a man and also the family that they want, then millions of women are going to try and do that. And it does not matter for most of them that they eventually fail because, once they all try to do it, they become a constituency. This means that when the math inevitably doesn't quite add up, as we see when we look at today's middle class, they will have enough political heft that they can get the government to step in and make up the difference, subsidizing the lifestyle that is not working for them. That is what is behind the calls from people like Elizabeth Warren for universal child care – getting the government to subsidize a lifestyle that is unsustainable on its own.

Thankfully, we dodged a bullet and did not get Ivanka's paid parental leave plan. But we have to get lucky every time, and the advocates of plans like parental leave only have to get lucky once. Once an entitlement like this one is enacted, it will be very difficult to reverse.

Some conservatives put their hopes in tweaks to the tax code like the child credits enacted under Viktor Orban in Hungary or those proposed here in the United States by Republican politicians such as Senators Mitt Romney and Marco Rubio. These kinds of policies might help boost birth rates a little on the margins, but they are wildly out of proportion to the magnitude of the crisis we are facing. They are too small to make much of a difference in the decline of the family, even if they are tempting to politicians because they can easily be endorsed by liberals who do not share our values on family and feminism.

The knockdown argument of the people who say women can have it all is that, quite simply, it's my family and you don't have the right to tell me how to run my family. And there's some validity to that. Thankfully, right now my policy wish list for providing for the American family doesn't involve telling anybody how to run their family.

There are three things we could do right now that would put a big dent in the multiplying lies that have come from feminists for the last forty years about women and careers. First, stop subsidizing college so much. One of the main reasons why marriage rates are so out of whack right now is that so many more women than men are going to college. Of people aged twenty-two to twenty-nine – the age when we ideally want people to marry – there are more than a million and a half more women with college degrees than there are men with college degrees.[7] That is to say, there are four women with college degrees in that demographic for every three men. That is going to lead to a lot of women with college degrees who do not end up getting married. We need to reform the student loan system and stop making it a government policy objective that as many people as possible should go to college.

Second, the Right can do more to promote male-dominated industries. Reviving American manufacturing and cracking down on China's unfair trade practices isn't just an economic and national security issue; it's a gender issue. Several of our economic policies for the last few years have led to a lot of growth in so-called pink-collar industries dominated by women, and to the collapse of blue-collar industries dominated by men. The Right has been operating under the assumption that that is fine, but we have in the last five years crossed over a once unimaginable threshold: there are now more female employees in the economy than men. There are more women working than there are men working. This is not something that was foreseen in 1975 or even in 1999. Frankly, there are a lot of reasons to think that replacing factory workers with home health aides is not a good idea for our economy, but gender relations is one of them.

And the third and final one is: do not subsidize childcare. A lot of people, from Elizabeth Warren on down, think it should be the next big push for helping working moms. It is true that many working moms are struggling, spending almost as much on childcare as they are bringing home from jobs. That might actually be good information the economy is trying to tell you – namely, that it is not worth it for you to pay somebody else fifteen dollars an hour to raise your children so you can go out and earn fifteen dollars an hour. Maybe the division of labor that every other civilization in history settled on is actually pretty smart. However this may be, any government childcare entitlement program would put a thumb on the scale in support of the two-earner family model as opposed to the one-earner family model. It would be massively unfair.

The illusion that women can have it all exists in the minds of millions of Americans today only because elite culture is fully dedicated to promoting it, the law punishes dissent from it, and the federal government subsidizes it. Lies cannot endure. They will eventually fail. The lie that women can have it all will do so of its own accord, if we will only stop supporting it with the massive economic and legal power of the federal government.

NOTES

1	Aparna Mathur and Isabel V. Sawhill, "The AEI-Brookings Working Group Report on Paid Family and Medical Leave: Charting a Path Forward," AEI Brookings, September 2018, https://www.aei.org/wp-content/uploads/2018/09/The-AEI-Brookings-Working-Group-Report-on-Paid-Family-and-Medical-Leave.pdf.

2	Paul Bois, "Tucker Carlson Says Women Earning More Than Men Has Some Bad Effects, Gets Hit With More Boycott Calls," *Daily Wire*, January 3, 2019, https://www.dailywire.com/news/tucker-carlson-says-women-earning-more-men-has-paul-bois.

3	Judd Legum, Twitter, January 7, 2019, 12:45 p.m., https://twitter.com/JuddLegum/status/1082332319908806656?s=20&t=14dpD34YrN4fiviZuJM5Rw.

4	Wendy Wang and Kim Parker, "Record Share of Americans Have Never Married," Pew Research Center, September 2014, https://www.pewresearch.org/social-trends/2014/09/24/record-share-of-americans-have-never-married/.

5	Bonnie Rochman, "Don't Count on Having Kids if You Freeze Your Eggs," *MIT Technology Review*, August 14, 2019, https://www.technologyreview.com/2019/08/14/133377/mothers-journey-egg-freezing-parenthood/.

6	Natalie C. Stentz, "Infertility Among Women in Medicine," *New York Times*, September 23, 2021, https://www.nytimes.com/2021/09/23/opinion/letters/covid-booster-shots.html.

7	Wendy Wang and Kim Parker, "Chapter 4: Never-Married Young Adults on the Marriage Market," Pew Research Center, September 24, 2014, https://www.pewresearch.org/social-trends/2014/09/24/chapter-4-never-married-young-adults-on-the-marriage-market/.

CONSERVATIVES AND OUR QUEER CONSTITUTION

Scott Yenor

For the last fifty years, the Republican Party has professed the family to be, as its election-year platforms state, "the foundation of the social order" (The Platform of 1980), "society's central core of energy" (2000), and "the foundation for a free society" (2016). Much ink has been spilled. Billions of dollars have been spent. Organizations have been formed. Yet conservative opposition to the sexual revolution has amounted to very little. In fact, things seem only to get worse: birth rates have declined; more children are born outside wedlock; divorce has increased; and more people live together outside marriage.[1] The conservative movement's broad trajectory on family is one of loss after loss: feminism, followed by the gay revolution, followed by same-sex marriage, and followed soon (perhaps) by trans rights. The reversal of *Roe v. Wade* may point to a partial victory, depending on what states do and whether a culture of life becomes a culture of motherhood; few seem willing to stick their necks out for such an outcome.

Many conservatives made sincere, intelligent efforts to oppose gay rights. Those who were associated with Jerry Falwell's Moral Majority in the 1970s understood that relaxing proscriptions against homosexual conduct would lead to sexualizing childhood. Anita Bryan's "Save our Children" campaign in Florida recognized that emancipating same-sex attraction would tend to corrupt children.[2] Yet much of conservatism's mainstream was embarrassed by such prophetic admonitions. After the hard-fought victories of the 1970s and 1980s, conservatives eventually settled on maintaining "fiscally conservative, socially liberal" gestures and attitudes. Indeed, partly to avoid confrontation, the conservative family policy agenda became mostly *economic* in nature by the 1990s. Child tax credits, for example, were passed in the 1990s. The so-called marriage penalty has been mostly repealed.

Genuine conservatives – Old Right and New Right – sense that the future of the country depends on reversing family decline, but family decline at this point seems (dare we say?) inevitable and fated, sown into the American regime and indeed the modern situation.

As it pertains to marriage, the rolling revolution begun in the 1960s is about liberating sexual desire from procreation, marriage, and parenthood.[3] Sometimes this means embracing contraception so sex is detached from procreation (hindering nature). Or it can mean encouraging women to shun childbearing and child-rearing and to prioritize careers (compromising nature) Sometimes it means celebrating cohabitation and single parenthood (a realization of autonomy). The accumulation of these practices, always done in the name of autonomy or conquering nature, has everywhere led to the decline of family life. This rolling sexual revolution cultivates a new sexual ethic supporting what may be called the Queer Constitution (in contrast to our former Straight Constitution), which has become central to Americanism and its ruling class.[4]

Securing individual autonomy and overcoming nature are at home in celebrations of LGBTQ+ Pride as well. The move from gay rights to public recognition of gay identities is always justified in terms of securing and then affirming personal autonomy. Every Supreme Court decision expanding same-sex freedom in this sphere is done in the name of personal autonomy.[5] Much the same is also true of the LGBTQ+ relation to nature. No LGBTQ+ advocates ever recognize that their practices bring psychological and physical harms, including dreaded diseases. These elements of nature are always attributed to social stigma or "minority stress" syndrome. The natural harms are attributed to homophobia and are used to justify great changes in social arrangements.[6] Monogamous, man-woman marriage, for instance, was rearranged to prevent same-sexers from experiencing the insult of not having their relations affirmed and other social costs. Nature is not thereby conquered, but its role in human life is reduced to following one's sexual desires by those who embrace sexual liberation.

THE QUEER CONSTITUTION

Every country has a sexual constitution: a set of laws and opinion, which use shame and honor to shape and guide sexuality.[7] The old marital constitution was, shall we say, the Straight Constitution, which honored enduring, monogamous, man-woman, and hence procreative marriage. It also stigmatized alternatives. This Straight Constitution upheld a vision of marriage that, among other things, limited divorce and proscribed fornication, contraception, sodomy, and adultery, promoted a family wage (under some circumstances), and imagined marriage for the purposes of procreation and educating offspring. We lived under the Straight Constitution until roughly the 1970s.

That constitution no longer exists, or perhaps just barely. We currently live under the Queer Constitution, which claims to, and in fact does, reject the Straight Constitution. The Queer Constitution was developed by winning legal battles in the service of broader cultural recognition of what once were called alternative lifestyles. It moved from gay rights in the 1970s, to proclaiming "Gay Pride" a virtue in the 1990s, to a legal recognition of the constitutional right to sodomy in the early 2000s, to making the Boy Scouts and the US military accept homosexuals, to constitutionalizing same-sex marriage in the 2010s, to protecting gender identity under the civil rights laws in the 2020s, to practically banning intellectual and legal opposition to the Queer Constitution on speech platforms.[8]

Some conservatives fought these changes. Nonetheless, nearly all acquiesced to them serially – fighting against new extensions while accepting their previous defeats. Rarely have conservatives acted as if the future of practices encouraged under the Straight Constitution – with its manner of directing passions and ordering loves – depended on reversing efforts to queer our sexual constitution.

At the Queer Constitution's core are two ideas. First, that all sexual behaviors, if consensual, are equal and dignified. Second, that society's binary, heteronormative gender identity is an iron cage, hampering individual expression and happiness. The Queer Constitution honors all manner of sex. Laws restricting contraception, sodomy, and fornication are, by its lights, unconstitutional. These changes in law are but the first part of an effort to normalize and then celebrate premarital sex, recreational sex, men who have sex with men, childhood immodesty, masturbation, lesbianism, and all conceptions of transgenderism.

The live-and-let-live attitude, hoped for by conservatives and promised by revolutionaries, cannot in principle hold. Indeed, the move from legal tolerance to public celebration is perfectly logical. Human beings are social and political animals. Many parts of their lives take place in private, but society nevertheless recognizes and applauds public manifestations of private acts. Under the Straight Constitution, no one watches a husband and wife having sex, but the public celebrates their weddings and their births, and the public recognizes their common property. Weddings themselves are a recognition of the importance of the marriage for the couple and for society as such.

Advocates of the Queer Constitution wanted and needed such public affirmation for their private acts. From the private protection or tolerance of "gay rights," advocates moved on to taking pride in "coming out of the closet." Failure to show a similar pride is a public insult, punishable through social opprobrium, as violations of hate speech codes, or worse. Advocates sought and won legal recognition for same-sex marriage, visitation rights for same-sex partners, and the right to adopt children, but they did not stop at such a legal infrastructure.[9] That is because the Queer Constitution demands public celebration of queerness. School curricula *must* be queered, the better to educate children before "homophobia" sets in. Men dressed as sexualized women *must* read children's books to children in public libraries, lest they grow up to think transgenderism is abnormal.[10] "Love makes the family" – rather than a mother and a father – *must* become the morality of every generation. Christian bakers *must* be made to bake the wedding cake for gay couples, lest failure to bake the cake insult the gay couple.

As to the next frontiers: strictures against adult sex with children are being "problematized" and are now eroding. Calls to lower the age of consent and to embrace pedophilia chic are beginning, including among politicians.[11] Incest taboos are already being subjected to critical questions.[12] "Live and let live" turns into "comply or else." Many pro-family activists pretend dishes of the Queer Constitution can be accepted à la carte without ordering the whole Queer menu.

Beyond the law and public morality, the Queer Constitution rules in the scientific professions, our major corporations, our education system, the Boy Scouts, the American military, and countless other commanding heights in our culture and within our families. Even churches openly support it. What had been considered bad under the Straight Constitution must now be considered good under the Queer Constitution, and vice versa. Many conservatives refused to see the Queer Constitution as the Left's imperial project, one aimed at subverting and dishonoring the Straight Constitution. Now this imperial project has gone international. Conservatives can no longer indulge in libertarian fantasies. Peaceful coexistence between a queer and a straight constitution is not sustainable.

THE COSTS AND THE PATH

The laws and mores of the Straight Constitution fade wherever the Queer Constitution is embraced – just as the advocates of the Queer Constitution expected. The gay rights branch of the Queer Constitution is not responsible for all its effects (surely feminism, which also advocates for the end of all sexual taboos, bears a responsibility as well). Yet the Queer Constitution has coincided with the amazing rise in nonmonogamous relationships, a public acceptance of alternative lifestyles even among conservative Americans, cohabitation, the sexualization of childhood, and the consumption of pornography. It has also coincided with the decline of marriage rates, marriage stability, the priority of marriage, the character necessary to sustain marriage, and birth rates. The social costs of the Queer Constitution are broad and deep.

	Rate in 1972	Rate in 1996	Rate in 2018
Number of marriages per thousand people[13]	10.9	8.8	6.5
% of children born outside marriage[14]	12.4%	32.4%	39.6%
% of Americans saying sex before marriage is always or almost always wrong.[15]	46.5%	32.5%	24%
Total fertility rate[16]	2.01	1.98	1.73

At its deepest level, the Queer Constitution elevates sexual pleasure and sexual self-expression as the goods of adults that have a dominant hold on the human heart, instead of procreation, familial duties, and parental responsibility.[17] One's sexual identity becomes who one is. Expressing sex in whatever way becomes a crucial right. All eros becomes sexual eros. Dealing with the consequences of sex – including, most crucially, children – becomes someone else's problem or not a problem at all, since there are fewer kids. In contrast, under the Straight Constitution, sex is something one does, not who one is. Life under this constitution encourages individuals to make sex serve something higher, like the duties of parenthood or finding its place within a marital regime. When people are taught that sex is who they are, they are less likely to see beyond sex to higher duties. The duties associated with marriage and parenthood necessarily wither as the Straight Constitution shapes fewer and fewer lives.

Moreover, the victory of the Queer Constitution promotes more and more queerness. Honoring queer sexuality has done much to shape a new queer and nonmarital culture. More than ever before, Americans identify as either lesbian, gay, bisexual, transgender, or as possessing other sexual characters. Though the number of such persons relative to the population as a whole had remained steady at under 4 percent for decades, these numbers approach 20 percent among females under twenty-five years of age.[18] Young girls are especially sexualized and vulnerable to those who force the Queer Constitution, since girls are uniquely subject to social pressures and media. As our culture points them toward the Queer Constitution, they are much more likely to follow it. This new constitution of sexuality affects the thoughts, words, and deeds of all to some extent.[19]

This social contagion has profound effects on individual happiness and social health. Indeed, sexual constitutions do not create human desires, but they play a large part in shaping them. Like a command-and-control economy, our reengineered ways work poorly, damaging men and women. Suicide rates and rates of drug abuse have spiked.[20] People are more and more medi-cated. Health crises proliferate, depending on the lifestyle. Life expectancy sinks. A sense of personal mission, centered on fam-ily life, fades, and with it fades human ambition and purpose. Children mutilate themselves, at parental, medical, or teacher suggestion. Damage to transgender children is irreversible. Soci-ety as a whole is less happy, less trusting, less confident.

MODELS FOR A STRAIGHT FUTURE?

Where the Queer Constitution sees nonprocreative sex as supe-rior (or at least equal) to procreative marital sex, a new Straight Constitution would hold that there can be no equality between man-woman procreative sex within marriage and other kinds of sex. Society must honor man-woman, marital procreative sex over other expressions of sexual mingling if it wants to survive and thrive over the long haul. Only then will birthrates start to recover. Only then will a superior sense of joint creation inform parental responsibility. Only then will a genuine love that tran-scends the point of individual interest become the glue for mar-ried couples. Only then can lives be reinvigorated with purposes, informed by nature and justifying sacrifices. But this appears to be far removed from where things stand.

Old family-advocacy conservatives have, in recent years, gen-erally been relegated to seeking carve outs for decent family life within the laws and mores provided by the Queer Constitution. A few exemptions here, a little tolerance for families there. Those advocates pray that nature will be strong enough to withstand the imprudent whispers of the Queer Constitution and that many or enough citizens will still be drawn to "natural" marriage (as family advocates, hopefully, call it), as it responds to deep human needs. Perhaps, they hope, the Queer Constitution is a temporary madness that will solve itself if queers do not reproduce them-selves. But it is not. Old family advocates have been standing athwart the Queer Constitution and shouting "Nature" for decades. Things only get worse. Nature is not enough to withstand the imperial Queer Constitution. It cannot be contained with compromising half-measures and carve outs. Advocates are seeking converts.

A rejuvenated conservatism would recognize, as did leftist activists a generation ago, that easygoing coexistence between a decent straight constitution and the Queer Constitution is not possible. As a result, the family must be self-consciously repoliticized. Given the centrality of politics, as the New Right appreciates, the Queer Constitution must be rejected root and branch and replaced with a new straight constitution, duly changed for our circumstances, supporting man-woman marriage, enduring marriage, procreative sex, and parental responsibility. From the perspective of the New Right, the Old Right may have hoped to achieve the goal of a decent family life, but the Old Right did not will the means to achieve it.

The Old Right is correct in seeing that nature provides materials from which decent family life might arise, but the manner of guiding nature is crucial. The queer revolutionaries long ago recognized that sexual passions and priorities could be bent away from enduring marriage – and they built a queering ethic to accomplish it. The New Right must work with the building blocks of nature, but it must also show that our Queer Constitution is a source of misery and social decline, and that a new Straight Constitution is more humane, fosters happiness, and creates an enduring social fabric with lasting man-woman marriage at its heart.

What are these natural building blocks? Differences between men and women are natural. It is a natural fact that only man-woman sex can produce children. Sexual impulses are natural in the sense that they are spontaneous; and they are mostly, absent a countervailing cultural tendency, toward man-woman relations. Men and women in the main have crucially different psychologies, fitting them for life together and raising kids and reflecting something like checks and balances. Childhood is naturally a state of helplessness for human beings. The family, like the sex integrated into it, is based in nature but it is always mediated by laws. A decent sexual constitution would take all these facts into account, while pointing to better, sturdier relations to make them serve human happiness, personal excellence, and the social good.

What would a decent sexual constitution look like in our context? It is difficult to say, but answers to this question center on the relation between stigma and legal proscriptions. In the past, many civilizations pursued the harshest option, painful to mention, involving putting laws with real teeth, like Mosaic or Islamic laws, on the table, as the legal machinery necessary to maintain a real stigma against those who oppose a straighter constitution. Those religious traditions, in their own words, banned sodomy, women who lie with women, people who desire to sexualize or to have sex with or to dance sexually with children, and others, others who should, in a decent society, to differing degrees, face real social stigma grounded in tough legal sanctions. Such scary depths, smacking of tyrannical control, can hardly be uttered today. Many of the world's societies – in Africa, the Middle East, Eastern Europe, and Asia – have been on this path, or are about-facing toward it. Many of those nations are consciously choosing to continue down this path based on their experiences of the West over the last few decades. This option is hardly congenial to Western public opinion today and is thus not desirable or possible.

Those who hope for a pro-marriage straight constitution may see the American Founders as precursors. In the beginning, America's sexual constitution pointed men to fatherhood and women to motherhood, and it pointed sex toward fruitful marriage. For instance, adultery was outlawed, as were fornication, incest, rape, polygamy, and other sexual and marital practices. Laws commonly discriminated between men and women, suggesting different roles for them.[21] The proddings of culture were thought to benefit both sexes. Men owned the family property in their own name, controlled the family finances officially, and were the voting representatives for the family. The ideal, such as it was, of public man–private woman reigned in law and culture. The Founders' sexual constitution was supposed to link natural desires to a republican, Christian society that allowed for natural growth and responsible parenthood. The sexes would be separate for some of their daily lives, but they came together for common private purposes. Men would have suitable outlets in commerce and politics, while women would raise children, mind the home, and build community.

Making man-woman procreative sexual desire normative meant, on the Founder's sexual constitution, stigmatizing some sexual desire. Laws against sodomy were on the books in all thirteen states at American independence. It was viewed as "an offense of so dark a nature, the very mention of which is a disgrace to human nature, a crime not fit to be named."[22] Nevertheless, the Founders' sexual constitution never had as hard of an edge in practice as it had in law. Few malefactors were really punished. When punishments came, they were much gentler than the law could have allowed. Clearly, however, the time of even the Founders' somewhat tepid resolution is over.[23]

Today, public authorities must at least stop getting behind the institutions of Gay Pride. The light must be shed on the institutions of Pride. Serious journalists and politicians must poke through the endless propaganda on issues relating to the Queer Constitution. Deep investigations into what the gay lifestyle actually does to people should be matters of public interest, just as efforts to normalize sex among children and to mainstream gender reassignment are beginning to draw attention from journalists. Journalists must dare to speak the name and seek the consequences of the love so central to Pride. Twenty-eight percent of men who have sex with men have had over one thousand lifetime partners, according to one study.[24] Fidelity is hardly a norm among men who have sex with men. Lesbian relations break up at rates several times that seen in the rest of the population. People should know about these pathologies.

Proscriptions against sex with children and the sexualization of children must be maintained, while our public schools should be subject to scrutiny and skepticism for what they promote and what they leave undone. Sex education programs, all funding the leading edges of our Queer Constitution, should be subject to withering congressional oversight and ultimately be discontinued, since they cause infinitely more harm than good. States should reject sex education funding, knowing that its leading edges always support the Queer Constitution. In the states new obscenity laws for a more obscene world should be adopted. Pornography companies and websites should be investigated for their myriad public ills like sex trafficking, addictions, and ruined lives. The justice of anti-discrimination must be revisited.

The Old Right could not conserve a decent society, though many knew the stakes. Eventually conservatives compromised, hoping for the best, which resulted in the step-by-step adoption of the Queer Constitution. Perhaps they could do no different, given the class arrangements of our new managerial elite. Becoming elite meant acquiescing in the Sexual Revolution. Resisting the Revolution meant irrelevance. But this bargain is up: conservatives are now outside the ruling classes and inconsequential. For society, embracing the Queer Constitution combines the costs of having weak, adult-focused marriage customs with all the costs associated directly with this constitution. The result has been individual misery, social decline, and a barren future. The perversities will keep mounting, as advocates for the Queer Constitution are clearly coming for the children, a fact they themselves now openly admit.

All civilizational founders recognized the importance of promoting a straight constitution and stigmatizing its alternatives. The New Right must follow the deep wisdom of such founders where it leads. Only a return to an uncompromising straight constitution can reverse our decline.

NOTES

1   Patrick T. Brown, ed., 2022 *Family Almanac: 83 Charts on the Health and Well-Being of America's Families* (Washington, DC: Ethics and Public Policy Center, 2022), https://eppc.org/wp-content/uploads/2022/06/2022-EPPC-Family-Almanac.pdf.

2   See Seth Dowland, *Family Values and the Rise of the Christian Right* (Philadelphia: University of Pennsylvania Press, 2015), 59–71.

3   For a discussion of the rolling revolution, see Scott Yenor, *The Recovery of Family Life: Exposing the Limits of Modern Ideologies* (Waco, TX: Baylor University Press, 2020).

4   Darel E. Paul, *From Tolerance to Equality: How Elites Brought America to Same-Sex Marriage* (Waco, TX: Baylor University Press, 2018).

5   Katherine Shaw Spaht, "The Current Crisis in Marriage Laws, Its Origin, and its Impact," in *The Meaning of Marriage: Family, State, Market, And Morals*, ed. Robert P. George and Jean Bethke Elshtain (Dallas, TX: Spence Publishing, 2006). See also *Lawrence et al. v. Texas*, 539 US 558 (2003), https://www.supremecourt.gov/opinions/boundvolumes/539bv.pdf; *Obergefell et al. v. Hodges, Director, Ohio Department of Health*, 576 US 644 (2015), https://www.supremecourt.gov/opinions/preliminaryprint/576US2PP.pdf.

6   Yenor, *Family Life*, 177–82.

7   George Gilder coined the term "sexual constitution" in *Sexual Suicide* (New York: Quadrangle / The New York Times Book Co., 1973).

8   For such a history see Robert R. Reilly, *Making Gay Okay: How Rationalizing Homosexual Behavior is Changing Everything* (San Francisco: Ignatius Press, 2014), 3–14, and 143ff. For a celebratory look at the same story, see Mark Brandon, *States of Union: Family and Change in the American Constitutional Order* (Lawrence: University Press of Kansas, 2013), 211ff.

9   Paul, *From Tolerance to Equality*.

10 See Christopher F. Rufo, "The Real Story Behind Drag Queen Story Hour," *City Journal*, Autumn 2022, https://www.city-journal.org/the-real-story-behind-drag-queen-story-hour.

11 See, for instance, Margo Kaplan, "Taking Pedophilia Seriously," *Washington and Lee Law Review* 72, no. 1 (2015): 75–170; "Inbred Obscurity: Improving Incest Laws in the Shadow of the 'Sexual Family,'" *Harvard Law Review* 119, no. 8 (2006): 2464–85, http://www.jstor.org/stable/4093513.

12 Tatjana Hörnle, "Consensual Adult Incest: A Sex Offense?," *New Criminal Law Review* 17, no. 1 (2014): 76–102, https://doi.org/10.1525/nclr.2014.17.1.76.

13 See Esteban Ortiz-Ospina and Max Roser, "Marriages and Divorces," Our World in Data, Global Change Data Lab, 2020, https://ourworldindata.org/marriages-and-divorces#marriages-are-becoming-less-common.

14 See Michelle J. K. Osterman, Brady E. Hamilton, Joyce A. Martin, Anne K. Driscoll, and Claudia P. Valenzuela, US Department of Health and Human Services, Centers for Disease Control and Prevention, National Center for Health Statistics, Division of Vital Statistics, B*irths: Final Data for 2020; National Vital Statistics Report*s, vol. 70, no. 17, February 7, 2022, tables 9 and 10, https://www.cdc.gov/nchs/data/nvsr/nvsr70/nvsr70-17.pdf.

15 "Sex Before Marriage," GSS Data Explorer, NORC at the University of Chicago, accessed November 8, 2022, https://gssdataexplorer.norc.org/variables/631/vshow.

16 "U.S. Fertility Rate 1950–2022," Macrotrends, accessed November 8, 2022, https://www.macrotrends.net/countries/USA/united-states/fertility-rate.

17 The Left celebrates such developments, in history after history. See, for instance, Steven Mintz and Susan Kellogg, *Domestic Revolutions: A Social History of American Family Life* (New York: Free Press, 1988); Nancy F. Cott, *Public Vows: A History of Marriage and the Nation* (Cambridge, MA: Harvard University Press, 2000); and Hendrik Hartog, *Man & Wife in America: A History* (Cambridge, MA: Harvard University Press, 2000). For a complete treatment, see Yenor, *Recovery of Family Life*, 39–41.

18 Compare Edward O. Laumann, et. al., *The Social Organization of Sexuality: Sexual Practices in the United States* (Chicago: University of Chicago Press, 1994), 294–306 with Jeffrey M. Jones, "LGBT Identification Rises to 5.6% in Latest U.S. Estimate," Gallup, February 24, 2021, https://news.gallup.com/poll/329708/lgbt-identification-rises-latest-estimate.aspx.

19 For the generational shifts among Christians and between non-Christians and Christians, see David J. Ayers, *After the Revolution: Sex and the Single Evangelical* (Bellingham, WA: Lexham Press, 2022).

20 Amy Case and Angus Deaton, *Deaths of Despair and the Future of Capitalism* (Princeton, NJ: Princeton University Press, 2020).

21 Thomas G. West, *The Political Theory of the American Founding: Natural Rights, Public Policy, and the Moral Conditions of Freedom* (Cambridge: Cambridge University Press, 2017), chaps. 9–11; Scott Yenor, "The True Origin of Society: The Founders on the Family," Heritage Foundation, October 16, 2013, https://www.heritage.org/political-process/report/the-true-origin-society-the-founders-the-family.

22 Blackstone, *Commentaries*, vol. 4.

23 West, *Political Theory of the American Founding*, 242–43.

24 Alan P. Bell and Martin S. Weinberg, *Homosexualities: A Study of Diversity Among Men and Women* (New York: Simon and Shuster, 1978), 314.

CONSERVATIVISM IN PROTESTANT AMERICA
What Went Wrong?

Joshua Mitchell & Aaron Renn

CONSERVATISM OF THE last generation is a movement without any appreciable Protestant voice. And yet all America's political movements, from the Founding to this very day, are the outworking of Protestantism, deformed or otherwise. The First Great Awakening, the American Revolution, the Second Great Awakening, the Civil War, the social gospel movement, Progressivism, Prohibition, the civil rights movement, perhaps "the 1960s," and certainly contemporary identity politics – all are unthinkable without the Protestant self-understandings that animated them.

From its outset in the 1950s, the modern conservative movement has been allayed against this Protestant ascendency that, notwithstanding wave after wave of immigration, has remained intact. The Ellis Island era immigration in the latter half of the nineteenth century did not alter the fact that the country remained majority Protestant. The Immigration Act of 1924, which effectively closed the borders, and the travails of the Great Depression and the Second World War, acculturated the hodge-podge mix of non-Anglo peoples who had arrived less than a century earlier into a nation that took for granted that White

Anglo-Saxon Protestants (WASPs) would lead the nation. There was contestation, of course, but the exceptions confirmed the rule rather than refuted it.

Sociologically, modern American conservatism is something peculiar: it is a conservatism of religious outsiders. The leaders who developed America's postwar conservative movement were disproportionately Catholics, Jews, and Eastern Europeans. Writers as different as Kevin Phillips[1] and Samuel Francis[2] have commented on how unrepresentative of the American demographic mainstream were the twenty-five conservative luminaries who appeared on the dust jacket of the first edition of George Nash's canonical history of conservatism, *The Conservative Intellectual Movement in America Since 1945*.[3] Michael Lind also described conservatism as a Catholic-Jewish project, and broke with it in part over their letting evangelical Protestants in the door.[4]

It is notable that few of the WASP upper class were drawn to what we today call conservatism. Prewar conservatism, if such a term can be used, had featured important WASP figures like Henry Cabot Lodge and Robert Taft. The untimely death of Taft in 1953 represented the de facto end of the WASP lineage in American conservatism, and arguably the end of the prewar conservative tradition. There were Protestant presidents after this de facto ending – Eisenhower, Johnson, Nixon, Carter, Reagan, Clinton, Bush, Obama, and Trump – but almost none of them came from the old WASP lineage, and they did not in any way seek to buttress it. While postwar conservatism, invented by William Buckley, Russell Kirk, and Irving Kristol, was almost exclusively a movement of socioreligious outsiders expressing minority perspectives, it was, nevertheless, able to attract a large Protestant voting bloc in the aftermath of *Roe v. Wade* in 1973. The group it attracted, however, was lower status evangelical Christians, not WASPs and mainline Protestants.

The Christian wing of the conservative leadership class has, from the beginning, been Catholic. Today, it has been elevated to a sort of normative status within elite conservative circles. Few

Protestants hold key leadership positions in major conservative institutions. Of those, almost all are quietly Episcopalian. From a leadership perspective, Evangelicals, who comprise the largest and most important Republican voting bloc, are largely frozen out of movement conservatism. This has not been entirely without warrant; evangelicals, as we will point out later, have been ill-equipped to assume leadership roles.

Conservatism wanted an America without Protestantism, whether by killing it or letting it die. But what conservatives got wrong, and why their movement failed, was that they thought, and continue to think, that there can be an America without Protestantism and a conservative movement without Protestants. They have the latter, but they do not understand that the former is impossible.

PROTESTANT CONFUSION AND CONSERVATIVE IMPOTENCE IN THE POST-PROGRESSIVE AGE

During the twentieth century, conservatives lost the war against Protestant progressives. Today, across the country, mainline Protestant churches are defending identity politics and its catechism. Protestants who should be opposing identity politics for the heresy that it is have succumbed to that heresy. "Is not the inner truth of the Gospel," they wonder, "that our mortal task is to identify and revere *innocent victims* as the Christ-like among us? Is not George Floyd *Christ for us*? Does the Gospel not declare that man, or rather some men, are *irredeemable*; and that to remove the sins of the world, a *scapegoat* is needed?"

These three correlative notions – the innocent victim, irredeemable stain, and the scapegoat – are, of course, present in Protestantism and Catholicism alike; but it is in Protestantism that these notions achieve their starkest articulation. In both Protestantism and Catholicism, Christ, the one sufficient scapegoat, the innocent lamb of God, takes away the sins of the world.[5] But in Catholicism, original sin is less acute of a problem than it is in Protestantism; and the church is the viceregent of Christ on earth, whose sacrament of confession dissipates the explosive force of sin to which Protestants are exposed, and for which the scapegoat and innocent victim are so immediately necessary, and always so firmly in view.

In Protestantism, irredeemable stain, the need for a divine scapegoat, and the innocent victim provide the conceptual framework within which the mystery of suffering and the inscrutability of God's redemptive economy are worked through. And it is in its Protestant form that Christianity has configured American culture. Should we then be surprised that something like identity politics should emerge as Protestants begin to lose their way in the twentieth century – as WASP culture implodes, the mainline churches suffer decline, and evangelicals withdraw from American public life?

Fixing firmly on the divine scapegoat who takes away the sins of the world, Protestantism was once able, more or less, to direct its practitioners away from the disposition, natural to man, to scapegoat others. In proportion as Protestantism has faltered, an identity politics deformation of the once-prominent Protestant formulation has replaced it. Ill-disposed toward Protestant understandings of man's sin and God's redemptive self-scapegoating (what Nietzsche contemptuously called "the ghastly paradox of God on the Cross"[6]), conservatives have made no room for Protestantism within their movement and, as a consequence, have little understanding or capacity to push back against identity politics, which appropriates Protestant formulations for its own prideful purposes. The mainline churches, it is true, are now complicit in identity politics; and Evangelicals seem content to steer clear of cultural battles they long ago lost. These currently give no encouragement to conservatives looking for intellectually theologically serious partners. Conservatives have, however, reached the wrong conclusion from these facts. A weakened Protestantism gave rise to identity politics; only a stronger one will dispose of it.

The consequences of this ill-fated decision have been predictable. Unable to grasp the deformed Protestant roots of identity politics, conservative outsiders to Protestantism today fall back on the tired explanations they have put forth since the 1950s. Identity politics, they say, is a further development of Cultural Marxism or of Progressivism. It is not. Identity politics is not Marxism: Marxism attends to class oppression, while identity politics gives you a pass on your class privilege, as long as you signal your solidarity with so-called innocent victims. Nor is it Progressivism, because Progressivism was based on expert competence, while the core idea of identity politics is not competence, but innocence and transgression.

That our elite colleges and universities have altered their mission over the last decade or so, from producing competent citizens, who were to join the ranks of the expert class that Progressivism required, to producing "woke" subjects, whose only lens for discernment focuses on innocent victimhood, confirms that the Progressive age is now behind us. It remains fashionable on the Left to continue to self-identify as progressive but, as with pronouns, saying you are *this* rather than *that*, does not make it so. The twentieth-century Protestant Progressive project has been supplanted by the twenty-first century Protestant heresy that is identity politics.

Protestantism has not prepared itself for real political leadership. When elite Protestantism rejected postwar conservatism, the faction of Protestantism that did join the movement were largely evangelicals, a middle-class, socially subaltern group that has made peace with its status. In 1994, historian Mark Noll famously wrote in *The Scandal of the Evangelical Mind*, that the scandal is that evangelicals did not have a mind.[7] That is to say, evangelicals have been actively and stubbornly anti-intellectual. Rather than developing the life of the mind, evangelicals have been more focused on saving souls and doing ministry, leaving political theology to Roman Catholics. When chatting with Richard John Neuhaus, Chuck Colson is said to have quipped about Roman Catholics and Evangelicals, "You supply the ideas; we supply the votes."

This has left evangelical Protestantism not only unable to lead the charge against identity politics, but vulnerable to it themselves. Because of its reliance on Protestant themes and symbols, evangelicalism easily and speedily absorbed identity politics, and large tracts of the evangelical world have now embraced it. Wheaton College, Calvin College, and a host of other once-serious Protestant training grounds have become seedbeds for identity politics. Protestants can hardly push back against identity politics if their training grounds have been appropriated. Woke Protestants are not alone in producing this movement, of course. The creators of Critical Race Theory may not themselves be Protestant, but they have utilized historic Protestant themes and symbols to penetrate the culture in the way that, say, foreign Marxists symbols – notably, the symbolism of class – could not. Identity politics today is not a church doctrine, it is a theologico-political doctrine, with conversion rates seen only in previous periods of American religious awakening.

One hears that Roman Catholicism in on the rise in America. But its converts are dwarfed by an ever-growing number of adherents to the identity politics heresy within Protestantism. The American "melting pot," long an object of derision on the Left, is consolidating in front of us; it takes the form of the Establishment Church of the New Elect. The post-Progressive Left has created it. Americans today seem less interested in solving problems than in siding with perceived victims. This same dynamic will constitute the core of future elections. A post-Progressive consensus has developed, gathering those who may *think* they are atheists, Protestants of all stripes, Catholics, Jews, and Muslims. They have, in fact, been assimilated into the Protestant heresy of identity politics.

THE OLD ROOTS OF WORLD-PURIFYING AND WORLD-DESTROYING FAITHS

Though seemingly distant from today, the French Revolution was the central political event of the modern world. Although it sought to overthrow Christianity, it turned out to be itself an incomplete religion.[8] As Alexis de Tocqueville observed, this meant that the French Revolution did not destroy Christianity but replaced it with fragments of Christianity. "Liberty, equality, fraternity" were a dreamy hope of a postlapsarian order, complete with a new calendar, and without the social stratification that sinful human societies always produce. The deeper, theological meaning of the French Revolution amounted to the repudiation of God the Father, and the elevation of a new communion of the saints, those committed to "liberty, equality, fraternity, or death." We can extend Tocqueville's analysis. Marxists, no less contemptuous of Christianity than the French Revolutionaries, also promulgated an incomplete religion. Understood religiously, Marxist theology gives us man, who was cast out of the Edenic splendor of primitive communism, and who stands on the threshold of ending his long labor amid the thorns of creation for his daily bread, thanks to the productive fruit of that bitter tree, cruel capitalism.

From this sort of account of the French Revolution and of Marxism, we can conclude that when Christianity falters, one or another incomplete religion will step in to fill the vacuum of the soul. You do not get secularism after Christianity falters; you get distorted, fragmentary, remnants of Christianity, which, like secularism, purport to have transcended Christianity, yet whose revolutionary fervor disrupts rather than contributes to the tranquility defenders of secularism suppose emerges once Christianity no longer reigns in the souls of citizens.

The conservative movement in America has focused a great deal of attention on these two incomplete religions; indeed, from its beginning to the present day, they have been its target. This is not surprising in light of the fact that it is a movement of socio-religious outsiders whose frame of reference is continental Europe, where the first and second incomplete religions emerged. One of its divisions offers a stringent defense of "tradition" against the equalizing tendencies of the French Revolution and of Progressivism, that American movement also dedicated to the destruction of mediating institutions; the second, counterbalancing division, hostile to Marx's vision and thoroughly modern, hallowed Smith and Hayek and the "free markets" it thought an important support for liberty.

Today, America faces a far greater challenge – namely, identity politics, the third incomplete religion to emerge, after the French Revolution, and after Marxism. This new enemy has captivated one portion of America by its promise of a spiritually purified world. The penetration of identity politics into our institutions and into our minds has been extraordinarily rapid, while Marxism has never really taken hold in America, for the reason we gave earlier: Marxism's fundamental category was *class*, which Americans are never going to accept, while the fundamental category of identity politics is *guilt*, by which residually Christian Americans are haunted.

In a canonical book often cited by conservatives, Eric Voegelin famously wrote that "Marxism immanentizes the eschaton." Marxism offered modern man, who had religious longings even if his religious tastes had soured, a redemptive narrative of history, as did Christianity. Identity politics, the third incomplete religion now upon us, does something different: it *immanentizes the scapegoat*, a Christian heresy, while at the same time affirming that a scapegoat is necessary to take away the sins of the world – an article of Christian faith. How shall we understand this? Man, tainted by sin, can only be saved by Christ, "the [sacrificial] lamb who takes away the sins of the world" (John 1:29). Moral cleanliness and purity are unachievable by mortal effort alone. *Everything* this side of heaven is impure. Because uncleanliness cannot cleanse itself, only Christ, the divine irruption who is "without blemish or spot" (1 Peter 1:19), can atone for man's uncleanliness, and save him from the eternal fires of hell to which his uncleanliness condemned him.

Identity politics offers a variant of this formulation, unthinkable without Christianity, but a defection from it. Man's stain is still the consuming issue. But moral cleanliness and purity are *not* purchased through Christ; instead they are purchased by scapegoating another person or group said to be responsible for the sins of the world. "Not *all* of mankind is unclean," declare our identity politics priests, "just the white race." All the others gathered under the categories of people of color, nonheteronormative, etc., are, in fact, clean. The one must pay; the other is to receive just compensation. The unclean must be purged from our midst. If *you* happen to be white, you must convince yourself and everyone else that not you, *but rather those other white people*, are filthy and irredeemably stained. *They* must pay, eternally, so that *your* white ledger balance carries no debt. That is why you put BLM signs on your front lawn. That is the way social death passes you over. In the New Awakening that is identity politics, cathartic rage is directed toward whiteness and all that it has supposedly wrought in human history.

In the First Great Awakening, God's grace and forgiveness heal man, cover over his filth, and cancel the debt owed to God that man could not pay. A divine gift alone cleanses the world and pays off man's debt, so that tomorrow might be lived with a clean ledger. The relationship of debt and payment is, so to speak, *vertical*. The audacious wager of the New American Awakening is that the gift of Christ's blood sacrifice is meaningless – indeed, an *embarrassment* no one in polite company need talk about. There are *no* gifts for which we should be thankful, *no* payment made on our behalf, *no* mercy that we must extend to others because it has been divinely extended to us. Hope, faith, and charity are foolishness. "Equity" is the order of the day, a never-ending reminder to the irredeemables that their tomorrow will *never* be lived with a clean ledger. Equity is the never-ending reminder that the relationship of debt and payment is, so to speak, *horizontal*. In the New American Awakening, justice involves the calculation of what one group *permanently* owes another, not the thankfulness man should show God every minute of every day that he has life and breath, which is beyond price.

WHAT IS TO BE DONE?

Identity politics is a Protestant problem, which Protestants must themselves address, by recovering for their churches, and disseminating in their churches, the theological insight that identity politics does not go *too far*, but rather does not go *far enough*.

Identity politics will be defeated only by the *more* profound theological insight that a scapegoat does indeed take away the sins of the world, but that there will be no end to trouble if that scapegoat is mortal rather than divine. As we indicated above, in the *vertical* relationship of innocence and transgression proffered by Christianity, Christ alone is the innocent victim, and all mankind is guilty. That insight is the only antidote to identity politics that can cure its practitioners of the disease from which they suffer. Not by rejecting the three corelative notions of identity politics – irredeemable stain, the scapegoat, the innocent victim – will it be overcome, but by returning them to the confines of Protestant churches, where they belong.

Responding to the challenge of identity politics requires that evangelicals free themselves from the allure of its flaccid teaching, rediscover their own distinct theological answers to the problem of sin in the world, and aggressively confront identity politics on the field of theology for what it is: a heresy.

They must also reconnect with remaining faithful Protestant elites in the mainlines and elsewhere, and develop their own capable elites who can assert themselves as leaders within conservatism, and within society at large. Parishioners in the Church of identity politics who are currently captivated by the idea of irredeemable stain will only find what they are really looking for – a deep account of irredeemable stain – in Reformed theology, however enfeebled it is at the moment. Absent this development, conservatives will continue to throw stones at identity politics but have no real armaments against it, and American politics will be dominated by the misguided effort to work out the salvation of society and its citizens. America, in a word, will succumb under the destructive weight of an incomplete religion that promises much but can deliver only despair.

Aside from the necessary theological work, there are intermediate political positions that must be staked out. These, however, must be understood as supplements to the necessary theological work, not substitutes for them.

The cabal that is the alliance of elite whites and elite blacks must be exposed to the light of day. There is indeed a race war in America. Identity politics promulgates it. It is between the *right* kind of white man and the *wrong* kind of white man; the *right* kind of black American and the *wrong* kind of black American. The identity-politics, "right kind" alliance seeks to humiliate the wrong kind of white man, which is to say anyone with the temerity to challenge identity politics; and it silences black Americans who refuse to abide by the upper-middle-class white, racist narrative that they are but innocent victims. This cabal requires of black elites that in exchange for their standing as untouchable, they must allow the black wound to be leveraged for the purpose of advancing feminism, gay and lesbian rights, and now transgender rights – movements that a vast swath of black Americans do not support. If you are black and are in the running for the Supreme Court, then your answer to the question, "what is a woman," must be, "I cannot say."[9] This cabal requires of white Americans that they denounce the *essentially racist* character of America, and call out the wrong kind of white man. Do that, and then you can rule America – but only if, as President Joe Biden did, you come before the court of the Black Congressional Caucus and receive its blessing. Fail to do that – refuse to do that – and you are cast into outer darkness, among the deplorables. A vast swath of Americans, neither white nor black, or white and black who are disgusted with being characterized by anything other than their common citizenship in this great but agonized country, have had enough. They await a public leader who can give voice to their revulsion.

Finally, competence matters. The whole of human history confirms that nations thrive internally, and ascend in the competition of nation against nation, only when they put the competence of their citizens first, and their attributes second or not at all. This universal law of history can be suspended only if we are at the end of history or, in a rare historical interlude, one nation is so privileged that it need not, for a time, compete with other nations. America from 1989 to 2016 had such a privilege. Antiwar activists of the identity politics Left should note that the ascension of this movement was made possible because America prevailed over every nation that emerged or consolidated after World War II. That historical moment is now behind us. The competition between nations has resumed. The sooner a yet unknown public leader can convince a nation wallowing in the shameful self-indulgence that all we need to do now, at the end of history, is call out transgressors and coddled innocent victims, that history *has resumed*, the sooner we will get on with the business of rebuilding the competence of our citizens. It goes without saying that this task can only be accomplished with the kindred insight that it is through the churches, not through politics, that the mystery of sin and redemption are revealed – not fully, but enough so that we carry on in a broken world, unbroken by it.

NOTES

1   See Kevin Phillips, *Post-Conservative America* (New York: Random House, 1982), 41.
2   See Samuel Francis, *Beautiful Losers: Essays on the Failure of American Conservatism* (Columbia: University of Missouri Press, 1994), 227.
3   See George Nash, *The Conservative Intellectual Movement in America Since 1945* (New York: Basic Books, 1976).

4   See Michael Lind, "Why Intellectual Conservatism Died," *Dissent*, Winter
    1995. This social dimension of the conservative movement helps illumi-
    nate the uproar that accompanied the publication of William F. Buckley's
    God and Man at Yale. It was not simply that the WASP elites who ran Yale
    and the other major American institutions at that time did not like the
    book's content (although they did not); it was also that the Irish Catholic
    upstart Buckley, whom they had invited into the inner sanctum of one of
    their key citadels – Yale was founded as a college for Protestant ministers –
    had the temerity to respond with such ingratitude.
5   See John 1:29; 1 Cor. 5:7.
6   See Friedrich Nietzsche, *Genealogy of Morals*, trans. Walter Kaufman (New
    York: Random House, 1967), First Essay, §8, 35.
7   See Mark Noll, *The Scandal of the Evangelical Mind*, (Grand Rapids, MI:
    Eerdmans Press, 2022).
8   See Alexis de Tocqueville, *The Old Regime and the French Revolution*, ed.,
    Francois Furet and Francoise Melonio (Chicago: University of Chicago
    Press, 1998), bk. 1, chap. 3, 101.
9   See "Sen. Blackburn asks Supreme Court nominee to define 'woman,'"
    USA Today, YouTube video, 1:07, https://www.youtube.com/watch?v=B-
    WtGzJxiONU. See also Senator Josh Hawley, "Far Left Berkeley Law Pro-
    fessor Melts Down When Sen. Hawley Asks Her if Men Can Get Pregnant,"
    YouTube video, https://www.youtube.com/watch?v=uU7nzwbJ-Hk.

EDUCATION

How to Destroy and Reconquer

Arthur Milikh & Scott Yenor

PERHAPS NOWHERE HAVE the Right's failures been more consequential than in American education. In America's public
schools, children are often taught to despise themselves and their
country. Our history is distorted. Our constitutional traditions
trashed. Through our textbooks, our literature and heritage are
ignored or rendered ugly; through "comprehensive sex education," students are encouraged to transition genders, and are
manipulated and exploited; through "anti-racism" doctrines,
now renamed "culturally responsive pedagogy," students are
taught whites are inherently evil and racist. No country can
countenance, much less subsidize, schools that destroy a decent
social fabric.

This moral corruption is only part of the story. American
schools were once competent at the basics. Foreigners came to
America to study, and to copy our infrastructure, from high
schools to flagship state universities. Our system generated the
talent required to sustain our scientific infrastructure, so critical
to our prosperity and international competitiveness. That era
may well be over. Today, about 55 percent of all students taking
the Graduate Records Exam for graduate school in math, computer science, and engineering are foreign nationals.[1] Astound-
ingly, America ranks fifth among the Organization for Economic

Cooperation and Development in total education expenditures, but only twenty-fifth in math proficiency among early stage high schoolers and lower in other areas.[2] American taxpayers are foolishly funding a system that produces unseriousness and inability.

As stated in *Nation at Risk*, a report commissioned at the onset of the Reagan administration: "If an unfriendly foreign power had attempted to impose on America the mediocre educational performance that exists today, we might well have viewed it as an act of war."[3] The situation is even worse today. The Left controls the real levers of power in education – the teacher preparation programs, the curriculum business, the accreditation programs, the state departments of education, the US Department of Education, the teacher's unions, and the professional organizations. The Left also controls the moral high ground and thus the teaching narrative.

The Right's defensive crouch is present in everything it does: While the Left writes and implements curriculum and educates the educators, the Right seeks educational choice. While the Left burrows into administrative roles and teacher colleges, the Right demands testing and accountability. While the Right is concerned about declines in literacy, numeracy, and citizenship, the Left sees these declines as part of closing the racial achievement gap. While the Left obtains vast funding for woke education, the Right begs for "opt-outs" from sex education programs and seeks to ban pornographic books from school libraries.

In its current state, this Right can only fritter around the edges of the Left's institutional conquest. It more or less tacitly accepts the Left's moral goals of sexual and racial radicalism. The growing anger on the Right at the incompetence, expense, and moral corruption in our schools is not matched with a plan to take away the Left's institutions or to provide an alternative vision of education. The Right's solutions are so based in narrow policy-wonkery and so lacking in spiritedness that even if all its policy fixes were instantly implemented not much would change. This is what political defeat looks like. The New Right must endorse government and private actions to harm, humiliate, and destroy our education establishment and rebuild a competitive, patriotic, moral educational model suitable for a great country.

WHAT WENT WRONG

In many cases, the Right's policies were pursued on the assumption that the education establishment, controlled by the Left, welcomed accountability and would react rationally to incentives for better outcomes. Conservative education reformers of the last generation (like Jeb Bush and Lamar Alexander) sought to make teachers' pay dependent on students achieving higher test scores, and they hoped that such incentives would lead to higher standards.

The truth is, partly out of corruption, partly because of ideology, the leftist-controlled educational system simply absorbed the standards and testing movements without the promised improvements and reforms.[4] Merit-based pay for teachers soon became detached from student achievement, allowing most teachers to be deemed worthy of merit-based raises.[8] Moreover, testing proved inequitable across racial lines, so the system deemed testing racist. Accordingly, teachers' unions turned against tests, as did many parents.[6] To avoid public embarrassment, data are ignored, hidden, or manipulated.[7] Meanwhile, the embrace of higher standards has coincided with historic declines in achievement scores for math and reading since 2015.[8] The whole accountability movement, a centerpiece of conservative reform for a time, died a quiet death.[9] Meanwhile, the Left is more united than ever in pushing sexual license and antiracist-based education, all the while (successfully) demanding more money.

Rather than counterattack, conservatives have focused on creating exit strategies. First, they made homeschooling legal in all states. Many more students are homeschooled today than were ten, twenty, or thirty years ago.[10] The quality of homeschooling has also improved. But recourse to homeschooling cannot be counted on to change the country's trajectory, since most people will not homeschool. Second, conservatives invest great hope in educational choice. Earlier generations embraced charter schools, magnet schools, and targeted means-tested school choice programs. Now education savings accounts (ESAs) is the new goal. ESAs take the money that the state would have spent on a child and give it to parents directly. In West Virginia and Arizona, which have adopted ESAs for everyone, parents can now spend the money on private schools or on tutors or for homeschooling.

Both the rise in homeschooling and the achievement of more educational choice are welcomed expressions of public dissatisfaction. Given the situation, walking away from the public system is a reasonable. Parents should be lauded for saving their children from America's failing and corrupting public schools. Today's educational system attacks charter schools,[11] ESAs, and homeschooling as if they are mortal threats to their monopoly. They may drain the public system of students and money and honor.

In the end, however, both homeschooling and educational choice are insufficient strategies of reconquest for four reasons. First, schools are more thoroughly conquered by leftist ideology than was previously imagined: many charter schools have been conquered by the Left, including KIPP, a charter school giant, which recently retired its motto "work hard, be nice" because the demand for working hard was viewed as demeaning to black students.[12] Notable exceptions, of course, exist, but many schools are staffed with teachers certified by the Left, use curriculum produced by the Left, and are run by administrators credentialed by the Left.

Second, Americans remain committed to a public system. Only a trickle of students have taken advantage of ESAs for everyone in West Virginia (about 1–2 percent of West Virginian students used their Hope Scholarships in 2022) and Arizona (about 12,000 of Arizona's million or so students used universal school choice in the first year).[13] Perhaps, someday, 25 percent of students in red states will use ESAs for alternatives to public schooling.[14] That would be terrific progress. But it may not be the game changer the establishment Right advertises unless it is accompanied by corresponding changes in the traditional public schools.

Third, educational choice programs assume that education is essentially private, protected from the rest of society. Thus, they assume that parents, school administrators, or teachers can operate in defiance of the reigning national moral orthodoxies. School choice, combined with alternative teacher certifications, or no certification programs, with loose state accreditation, independence from school boards or state agencies will, on this reading, allow schools to operate outside the system. And *to a certain extent*, this hope may be realized.

One can see the insufficiency of the education choice movement and the importance of reigning orthodoxies most easily in higher education. Americans have educational choice in higher education. Student loans or out-of-pocket expenses follow students to their chosen higher educational institutions. Institutions can maintain their own distinctiveness – some are Catholic, others Protestant, others public. They can organize their curricula in different, creative ways, if they choose. Yet universities reflect a stultifying monotony, with the same kinds of general education requirements, the same majors, the same cookie-cutter policies in nearly every university. Nearly every university is saddled with faculty and administrators that directly or indirectly agitate against or denounce the country. The same Diversity, Equity, and Inclusion (DEI) policies are everywhere. Similarly, even without ESAs many private Catholic K–12 schools and other private schools have adopted leftist ideology over the last generation.[15] Choice does not guarantee diversity because education is inherently political – so the battle must be fought on that basis.

Finally, school choice is a strategy for avoiding a showdown over what American education should be.[16] At its best, this strategy reflects the liberal hope that mutual tolerance and forbearance have their place in a pluralistic country. At its worst, school choice advocates forget an inescapable truth: education is inherently political in the sense that a vision of education is always guiding a political community. For instance, either the country is good or at least worth saving as our own – or it is not. Either the body and soul are connected and biological reality exists – or there is no necessary connection and gender identity is fluid. Either educational excellence should be recognized as an individual achievement – or bemoaned as a sign of white supremacy.

Dwelling on school choice masks deeper weaknesses in the Right's position. Unspoken moral confusions plague the Right's effort to wage a counterrevolution. While the Left pushes sexual liberation, the Right is not clear about its own teaching. The Right opposes pornography in the libraries, but what does it want to do about sex education? While the Left is clear on race, the Right is confused. The Right opposes equality of results and Jim Crow, but what is it for? Nor is the Right able to stomach the group disparities that would arise when standards are enforced. For now, it cannot seem to clearly defend civic nationalism. At the core, it may be moral confusion, shame, or wanting it both ways, that prevents the Right from joining the real fight on the level of politics. The Left wins without a shot being fired.

For similar reasons, efforts to reform higher education have proved even more futile than they have in K–12 school programs. Conservatives first sought to engage university trustees. They promoted free speech policies. They tried to ban racial preferences. They tried to attack tenure, mostly in opinion but sometimes in policy. They have, more recently, poured millions of dollars into funding centers on campuses, hoping to keep the flame of liberal, patriotic education alive. All, broadly speaking, to no avail. America's universities and colleges ratchet ceaselessly to the Left.

Fifty years of futility should teach conservatives many lessons. As in K–12, nothing can be done to repair our ruined education system without offering an alternative vision of education. And nothing can be done without using perfectly legitimate powers that the Right has shied away from using. When the leftist educational system controls all the institutions, only external force can impose discipline. Just as the Progressives marched through the education institutions while casting aspersions on the old education system, so the Right's policies must be confrontational and destructive with the aim of recovering and rebuilding on a more solid foundation.

THE PATH FORWARD: FEDERAL AND STATE ACTIONS

Conservatives must pursue a dual track. On one hand, they must use state powers to raise the costs for the Left and to strip its funding at the state and national levels. On the other hand, they must identify people and build institutions to win back public schools. The same applies to colleges and universities.

A ROADMAP FOR A NEW EDUCATIONAL VISION: K–12 AND HIGHER EDUCATION

States must first declare independence from the national government's inducements in matters of education and from the educational establishment in general. The federal government, often with the help of large private foundations, has adopted a pay-for-play system: if states want money, for instance, for disabled children, they must teach transformative social and emotional learning. This cycle is replicated over and over.

Of course, it would be best to dismantle the Department of Education, but this will not happen, even if conservatives talk about it for another generation. Conservatives might settle for the half-measure of allowing states to opt out of federal strings while still taking federal money, as has been recently proposed.[17] States can also act preemptively to keep the system out of their jurisdictions by refusing federal funds for fear of the strings that are attached to them. This declaration of independence takes many forms: a rejection of federal funds for K–12 schools; a rejection of implied national standards; and banning establishment forms of therapeutic education like transformative social and emotional learning or trauma-induced practices, along with private causes of action to enforce them.

Other steps must be taken. One is to eliminate state teacher certification standards, so that schools can hire anyone they deem adequate to be a teacher; often, new teachers are needed to lead a new system of education. Following this, state legislatures should defund existing state schools of education that simply serve to prepare teachers for our current corrupt system. States have ceded accreditation to corrupt private actors. Instead, legislatures should take back degree-granting authority and establish standards themselves or simply eliminate accreditation in K–12. Either way, accreditation should reflect the reality that education is inherently political and that the people's representatives must weigh in on its future shape. Teachers who disagree can find employment in places more suited to their tastes.

Trusting our education establishment is often the same as trusting leftists who have openly declared war on the country. State legislators should mandate their own curriculum for K–12 and higher education. For K–12, legislatures could simply mandate that public schools use a particular curriculum like E. D. Hirsch's knowledge-based curriculum or the one currently being written by Hillsdale College. In higher education, the Texas university system practices a miniversion of this in its general education, where it mandates courses in American history and American government.

Teacher jobs must be made less comfortable so as to decrease the benefits of being associated with our corrupt public system. Different pay scales should be adopted so that teachers are not overpaid compared to people working similar jobs in the private sector. Mandatory collective bargaining between teachers unions and school boards or collective bargaining altogether should be brought to an end. No sovereign immunity for teachers and other public employees should be given, so that when they peddle pornography to students, they are subject to the same criminal and civil penalties as any normal citizens committing such crimes would be, and are treated as pedophiles or pedophilia-enablers.

But in breaking the current system, there must be a clear alternative vision. No one under the age of sixty has known an American public school system based unapologetically on the ideas of competitive merit, physical fitness, a decent patriotism, deep historical wisdom about America's heritage, and respect for the moral foundations of the American republic. We should be preparing a genuine American elite for leadership of our country and its states. Some of that elite must know classics of American heritage and governance. Others must be pushed in mathematics and the sciences. All should be prepared to physical excellence and health from an early age. We should be trying to get people earlier into jobs to which they are suited.[18] High schools should encourage the trades and prepare students for them. Many elements of America's pre-1950s education system could be revived by red state legislatures, which are, after all, sovereign over their education systems.

Take two examples. First, physical fitness. Students could start building obstacle courses at an early age, learning to how to construct a wall and how to adapt the wall for climbing. Students should work on competing through these courses, being timed against their best time and against one another. Wrestling should be mandated in middle schools. Students could learn to build and shoot guns as part of a normal course of action in schools and learn how to grow crops and prepare them for meals. Every male student could learn to skin an animal and every female to milk a cow. This is what a training in citizenship looks like – fitness, independence of mind, skills in living, all undistorted by sophistry. There is no reason that education systems must confine students to institutions for book-learning all day, for nine months per year.

Second, physical fitness, mathematical skills, and excellence in the trades can be combined. Building obstacle courses is a beginning in practical math. Excellence in mathematics must once again be a national and individual ambition. Gifted and talented programs and academic tracking are stigmatized as inequitable. Instead, we must adopt a policy designed to create a leading corps of STEM experts, unapologetically, whether results are "inequitable" or not. If we are willing to identify state champions in high school sports, we should be more willing to identify state champions in physics, algebra, and inventions. State, national, and global competition should bring benefits and honors to America's high school students.[19] De-emphasizing competition has been a chief reason that American boys continue to be outperformed by American girls at nearly every level of education.

Educational visionaries should think about how to integrate competitiveness, physical fitness, a decent patriotism, and deeper historical wisdom about America's heritage into every facet of education. We should study modern countries like Israel and adapt their methods. New wine must get into those old wineskins, or new wineskins must be made for this new wine.

UNIVERSITIES: CRUSHING AND REBUILDING

Much the same confrontational attitude must inform the New Right when it comes to higher education. An attitudinal shift is needed: our universities and colleges are assets of the Left; they are defrauding taxpayers and undermining our country while hiding behind the authority of science. Our colleges and universities function as government-sponsored monopolies, with the national government funding the vast majority of university budgets through student loans, grants, and research support.

Many disciplines in higher education simply cannot be reformed and must be eliminated by state legislatures overseeing public universities. First, DEI offices must be identified, defunded, and disbanded. The personnel associated with DEI offices should be fired. Second, any university major with "studies" associated with its name is guilty unless proven innocent and should be defunded. This includes Women's and Gender Studies; African and African Diaspora Studies; Latin American Studies; Latino

Media Arts and Studies; Lesbian, Gay, Bisexual, Transgender, and Queer/ Sexualities Studies; and Critical Disability Studies (all of which are available at the University of Texas, Austin, for example).

Third, intellectual corruption has been sown into professional standards for many disciplines, such that few scholars have a living memory of genuine intellectual pursuits. Disciplines like sociology and social work must be jettisoned from public universities. State legislatures should do what it takes for such programs to lose accreditation.

Fourth, enforcement mechanisms should be added to bans on racial preferences. Such torts could allow third parties to challenge policies, make discriminating bureaucrats personally responsible for their practices, and force universities into large damages if they fail to comply.[20]

A declaration of independence at the university level will prove much more difficult given the current structure of university funding. Today, federal student loans flow only to accredited universities and colleges. The Left then controls the accreditation standards, in order to ensure its ever-deepening grip on how universities are run. The national government controls the access to funds. Both sides of this equation must change, but it is not completely in the hands of state governments to change them. Experiments in alternative accreditation should be tried, as should seed money for student loan–free public universities.

States control much more than they think, first in the necessity of attendance at colleges and universities; and second, in the nature of the education. When it comes to attendance, states should work with professional groups to encourage college workarounds for entry to various professions. Apprenticeships and other forms of alternative certification can be used for entry into many blue-collar and white-collar professions. Prohibitions on using IQ tests in hiring processes could be lifted, allowing employers yet another way to identify candidates with potential. Universities should never have a monopoly on the future of an

American worker. There should always be a way to be certified and hired that does not involve having the proper college major.

Moreover, state universities should be broken up. No matter how much we wish it were not so, general education at modern universities is most often poisonous. Red states could break up universities between "hard sciences" and "pretend sciences," funding only the hard sciences with public monies, while allowing the others to compete or wither away on the vine. The relatively healthy and competitive science portions of schools could be detached and made independent from the corrupt humanities and social science portion. Business schools could be detached from the corrupt humanities schools, too. Without general education, the Florida university system, for instance, could establish a University of Florida (STEM in Gainesville); a Florida State University (business in Tallahassee); and a University of Central Florida (sociology and humanities in Orlando). Each could have its own tuition, administration, and curriculum. None would fund the others. The Florida regents could even privatize its university of sociology and humanities. If it dies, it dies.

At the federal level, reforms can be achieved when public opinion reaches a boiling point. Elected officials must prepare public opinion. Conservatives have settled for the appearance of reform for a generation. Conservatives must have an active national agenda, since colleges and universities are dependent on federal funds for their existence. Congress can end all student loan programs, and should not guarantee any private loans for higher education. Congress should end research funding for universities that promote DEI or undermine free speech or practice racial preferences. Congress should tax university endowments instead of pretending that universities are anything but big businesses that harm the common good while defrauding the taxpayer and creating a pseudo-intellectual revolutionary class that agitates against the country.

The newly emerging flagship universities, which will be elevated because of these reforms, should make it their goal to hire up the faculty from the universities pushed into failure. Governors must attract talented but disgruntled scientists from all over the country to boost their own science departments, perhaps even doubling their salaries as an incentive, and paying to transfer their laboratories. Picking up the pieces from the old order will be a generational opportunity.

The slow draining of the legitimacy of the education systems is not enough. It is true that new universities are popping up; that the number of universities working outside the system is growing; and that charter schools and classical Christian schools are growing exponentially in K–12. All their numbers, however, are quite small. These efforts will come to naught unless they are matched with an equally determined effort to destroy and dishonor the current K–12 and higher education systems. Destruction followed by reconquest is necessary and proper.

NOTES

1   Enyu Zhou, "Graduate Enrollment and Degrees: 2011-2021," Council of Graduate Schools, November 2022, https://cgsnet.org/wp-content/uploads/2022/11/CGS_GED21_Report_v1-1.pdf.
2   See Arthur Herman, "America's STEM Crisis Threatens Our National Security," *American Affairs* 3, no. 1 (Spring 2019), https://americanaffairs journal.org/2019/02/americas-stem-crisis-threatens-our-national-security/. See also the OECD test results for 2018 found in the PISA report, https://www.oecd.org/pisa/PISA%202018%20Insights%20and%20Interpretations%20FINAL%20PDF.pdf. Spending reports are found in the OECD library at https://www.oecd-ilibrary.org/sites/5e4ecc25-en/index.html?itemId=/content/component/5e4ecc25-en.
3   The National Commission on Excellence in Education, "A Nation at Risk: The Imperative for Educational Reform," April 1983, https://edreform.com/wp-content/uploads/2013/02/A_Nation_At_Risk_1983.pdf.
4   Cf. Frederick M. Hess, "How the Common Core Went Wrong," *National Affairs* 21 (Fall 2014), https://www.nationalaffairs.com/publications/detail/how-the-common-core-went-wrong.
5   In Colorado, for instance, 94 percent of teachers were found to be "effective" or "very effective." See Erica Meltzer, "No Longer Every Teacher, Every Year: Union-Backed Bill Would Change Colorado Teacher Evaluation Law," *Chalkbeat*, March 6, 2019, https://co.chalkbeat.org/2019/3/6/2110

6988/no-longer-every-teacher-every-year-union-backed-bill-would-change-colorado-teacher-evaluation-law.

6   See Finn and Hess, "The End of School Reform?"

7   See Luke Rosiak, *Race to the Bottom: Uncovering the Secret Forces Destroying American Public Education* (New York: Broadside, 2022), 31–45, 119–24.

8   "NAEP Long-Term Trend Assessment Results: Reading and Mathematics," The Nation's Report Card, https://www.nationsreportcard.gov/ltt/?age=9.

9   Chester E. Finn, Jr. and Frederick M. Hess, "The End of School Reform?" *National Affairs* 52 (Summer 2022), https://www.nationalaffairs.com/publications/detail/the-end-of-school-reform.

10 Indeed, according to the National Home Education Research Institute, about 6 percent of American students are homeschooled in 2022, up from 3 percent in 2019 and around 1.5 percent in 2000. See "Homeschooling: The Research," National Home Education Research Institute, September 15, 2022, https://www.nheri.org/research-facts-on-homeschooling/.

11 See Thomas Sowell, *Charter Schools and Their Enemies* (New York: Basic Books, 2020).

12 See "Retiring 'Work Hard, Be Nice' as KIPP's National Slogan," KIPP Public Schools, July 1, 2020, https://www.kipp.org/retiring-work-hard-be-nice/.

13 Both these numbers come from interviews with school choice advocates in West Virginia and Arizona.

14 Perhaps this is an underestimate: According to a 2022 survey, 38 percent of parents say they would not send their kids to public schools if other options were easily available. See Colyn Ritter, "EdChoice Public Opinion Tracker: Top Takeaways July 2022," EdChoice, August 4, 2022, https://www.edchoice.org/engage/edchoice-public-opinion-tracker-top-takeaways-july-2022/.

15 There are, however, exceptions, as Catholic schools depend on the views of their particular diocese. Nevertheless, the broad trend is true.

16 Libertarians embrace school choice for precisely this reason. See Neal P. McCluskey, *The Fractured Schoolhouse: Reexamining Education for a Free, Equal, and Harmonious Society* (Lanham, MD: Roman & Littlefield, 2022).

17 Jude Schwalbach, "A PLUS Spells Relief for States During the Coronavirus," Backgrounder 3519, Heritage Foundation, August 26, 2020, https://www.heritage.org/sites/default/files/2020-08/BG3519.pdf.

18 We should also be preparing young men and women for different destinies, including a more fundamental teaching to all our citizens about nutrition, the benefits of having children earlier, and the different social roles that men and women play in family life.

19 For thoughts on how American math education could improve, see Percy Deift, Svetlana Jitomirskaya, and Sergiu Klainerman, "As US Schools Prioritize Diversity Over Merit, China is Becoming the World's STEM

Leader," *Quillette*, August 19, 2021, https://quillette.com/2021/08/19/
as-us-schools-prioritize-diversity-over-merit-china-is-becoming-the-
worlds-stem-leader/.

20 See Louis K. Bonham, "Enforcing the Coming Affirmative Action Bans: A
Modest Proposal," *Minding the Campus*, October 27, 2022, https://www.
mindingthecampus.org/2022/10/27/enforcing-the-coming-affirmative-
action-bans-a-modest-proposal/.

HOW CONSERVATIVE ECONOMICS GAVE BIRTH TO A MONSTER

David P. Goldman

Apple Computer, entrepreneur Peter Thiel observed, spent the first ten years of its existence selling products invented by the US government.[1] The most successful (in terms of stock market capitalization) and emblematic enterprise of the Reagan boom years got its start as the marketing arm, as it were, of the Defense Advanced Research Projects Agency, which funded, among many other things, the research and development (R&D) that led to the graphical user interface and the mouse, Apple's first signature product.

It wasn't only Apple. The invention of complementary metal oxide semiconductor chip (CMOS) manufacturing, which made possible cheap mass production of powerful integrated circuits, powered the digitalization of everything from look-down radar in American fighters to wristwatches. The semiconductor laser made possible optical networks, including cable television as well as the internet. Cheap chips and high-capacity networks made possible Apple, Microsoft, Google, Cisco, and the other technology giants that have driven the rise in American equity indices for the past thirty years.

The Reagan tax cut encouraged corporate managers to start

their own enterprises and motivated investors to back them. But the Reagan Revolution entailed more than a supply-side field of dreams where, if you cut taxes, they will come. The 1981 Kemp-Roth tax cut gave entrepreneurs a powerful incentive to take risks, but the entrepreneurs did not find the technology under a cabbage leaf. Rather, to win the Cold War, the United States invented the digital age, with revolutionary advances in physical science and manufacturing techniques ranging from plasma displays to chip manufacturing, materials science, and lasers. The personal computer, flat displays, optical networks, cheap and powerful chips – the elements of the new industries that arose during the 1980s – required entrepreneurs to commercialize them. But the entrepreneurs needed the great national effort that brought forth these technologies.

Regrettably, the conservative movement learned only one trick from the Reagan era – cutting taxes to promote growth – and did nothing else for the ensuing forty years. As Talleyrand said of the Bourbons, the American Right has learned nothing and forgotten nothing. It watched with approval as the disruptive entrepreneurs of the 1980s gave way to digital monopolies supporting a toxic liberal utopianism. And it viewed with favor the abandonment of manufacturing by American corporations, who decided to shift to capital-light software businesses while relinquishing low-margin manufacturing businesses to Asia. America's share of world manufacturing fell to 18 percent today from 29 percent in the early 1980s, manufacturing employment fell to twelve million 2022 from eighteen million in 1989, and America's chronic trade deficit has left us with a net foreign asset position of negative $30 trillion.

The goal of Reagan's presidency was national revival, in which America's sense of purpose guided the different policies he brought to bear. The economic revival was a geostrategic policy, just as the Strategic Defense Initiative and other transformations of military technology were an economic policy. And Reagan's economic and national security policies both drove a cultural agenda: the revival of America's self-confidence and belief in its unique mission. Driving this was a great public-private partnership: the federal development budget – funding for prototypes and testing of new technology – spent about 1 percent of GDP, compared to about 0.3 percent today.

HAMILTONIAN ECONOMICS REINVENTED

Supply-side economics was an answer to the stagflation of the 1970s. The supply-siders argued that economies could enjoy high growth and low inflation through incentives to increase the supply of goods and services. That contravened the conventional wisdom, which prescribed austerity as a cure for inflation. In economic theory, supply-side economics began with Robert Mundell's insight that government debt issued to fund the temporary loss in revenue from a pro-growth tax cut constituted an increase in wealth. In effect, Mundell recreated Alexander Hamilton's 1790 Report on the Public Credit. Tax cuts may increase future household income, but markets can't capitalize future household income family by family. But they can capitalize expected tax revenues from expected income growth. Mundell's approach inspired the 1981 Kemp-Roth tax cut, which reduced the top US marginal tax rate on personal income to 40 percent from 70 percent. The government deficit jumped temporarily, but the impact of the tax cut, in tandem with the tight monetary policy of Paul Volcker's Federal Reserve, led to growth.

Mundell's approach contrasted sharply with the prevailing wisdom on the Right, which supported tax cuts to "starve the beast" and force a reduction in government spending. Politically, it allowed Republicans to promote tax cuts without demanding cuts in popular government spending programs. *Wall Street Journal* opinion writer Jude Wanniski promulgated the "two Santa Claus theory" – if Democrats played Santa with spending, Republicans could play Santa with tax cuts. Although mainstream Republicans like George H. W. Bush derided this as "voo-doo economics," it worked, both as a political platform and as an economic policy.

Like Hamilton, Mundell showed that government had an active role in helping the market to turn long-term expectations into investment, in this case by issuing debt supported by rising tax revenues. But government had an equally important role in funding basic research at the frontiers of technology, driving the discoveries that gave us the digital age and unleashed a tidal wave of entrepreneurship.

The digital economy that drove economic growth depended on federal support for innovation conducted mainly at corporate laboratories. The federal R&D budget exceeded 2 percent of GDP at the peak of the Apollo program and 1.3 percent of GDP during Reagan's Strategic Defense Initiative. The United States invented every component of the digital age: fast and cheap mass production of computer chips through the CMOS process, LED and plasma displays, the optical network, the Graphic User Inter-face, the computer mouse, and the Internet, among others. With-out exception, every one of these technologies began with a research grant from NASA or the Defense Advanced Research Projects Agency, although researchers frequently discovered things more useful and important than the original grant had envisioned. Private capital commercialized innovations that never would have materialized without federal support.

There was a dimension to Hamilton's thinking, elaborated in his Report on Manufactures, that never entered into Mundell's consideration. That is the role of federal spending in promoting growth. There is a world of difference between government spending to promote "internal improvements," to use Hamilton's term, and handouts for consumption. The content of the federal budget during the Reagan years shifted away from transfer pay-ments to federal investment, and the military budget supported innovations that formed the basis for a dozen new industries.

FEDERAL R&D (ESPECIALLY DEVELOPMENT) SHRINKS AS A SHARE OF GDP

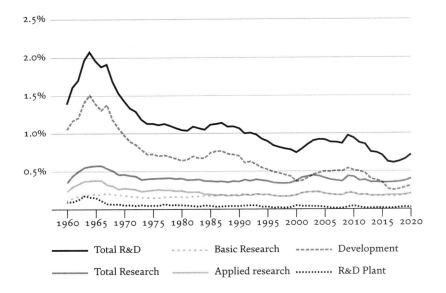

The federal development budget (funding of new technology prototypes) collapsed during the Clinton years, as a complacent America basked in its status as the sole superpower. Many in the US government at the time wanted to believe that competition had once and for all ended. Reagan was, in fact, a big-government conservative when it came to military spending but a small-government conservative in cutting transfer payments, which fell from 50 percent of total expenditure in 1980 to 40 percent in 1990. The biggest increment in transfer payments as a proportion of spending occurred under Nixon, and the second biggest took place under Clinton. Government employment, moreover, shrank to 16.3 percent of the total in 1989 from 17.8 percent in 1979.

As a share of gross domestic product, transfer payments stabilized during Reagan's 1981–89 tenure, while federal investment rose as a share of GDP. This was the overall trajectory that determined the coming decades.

TRANSFER PAYMENTS
AS % OF FEDERAL EXPENDITURES

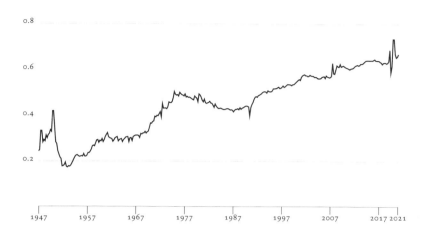

FEDERAL GROSS INVESTMENT VS.
TRANSFER PAYMENTS AS % OF GDP

ENTREPRENEURSHIP ISN'T ENOUGH

The conventional economic model of savings and investment presumes that societies first must save in order to invest – on the model of a neolithic tribe that must save part of its harvest to expand acreage the following year. Yet we know that entrepreneurs do not necessarily need to save to start companies, especially in industries like software in which brainpower is more important than plants and equipment. If they have a credible business plan, they can hire talented workers and pay them with stock options, and conjure capital out of thin air – that is, out of expectations of future income. Entrepreneurship became the watchword of the new Republican economics.

Many, including myself, went headlong into this vision of economics.[2] But we were nightmarishly wrong. Instead of a new era of entrepreneurship, we unleashed two related monsters that ate American business: the establishment of monopolies, and the destruction of our industrial base, which led to vast trade deficits based on consumer pathology.

The internet-enabled network effects turned the startups of the 1980s and 1990s into giant monopolies. Microsoft eliminated Lotus 1-2-3 and WordPerfect; Google became the dominant search engine; and Facebook eliminated or acquired rivals. By 2014, the revenue of the Fortune 500 companies reached 72 percent of GDP – up from 58.5 percent in the 1990s and 35 percent in 1955. In 1994 (the earliest date for which numbers are available) companies with fewer than 250 employees still provided the majority of US jobs. By 2016, large companies had 54 percent of all jobs, versus only 46 percent for smaller companies.

To the supply-siders, this represented the triumph of entrepreneurship and the victory of the creative new economy over the old, uninspired manufacturing economy of the past. In 1991, as the global head of credit strategies at Credit Suisse, I invited my old friend and colleague Art Laffer to give a seminar for the banks' credit analysts. Laffer informed us that there was no rea-

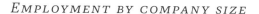

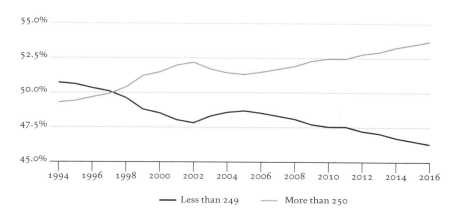

son for the United States ever to manufacture anything ever again: We Americans would do the design and the rest of the world would do the dirty work of actually making things.

Art Laffer only applied his gift for hyperbole to the prevailing conventional wisdom among Republican economists. By the time the Republicans returned to office with George W. Bush, globalization had become Republican dogma. The United States lost 30 percent of total manufacturing employment during the Bush administration – from 17.4 million in November 2000 to only 12.6 million in January 2009. Implored by consultants, driven by quarterly earnings, and unrestrained by laws, American companies shifted employment offshore at an unprecedented rate.

As such, US imports from China doubled or tripled every three years during the George W. Bush years. By 2008, Chinese exports to the United States equaled 9 percent of China's GDP. And by 2006, America's current account deficit rose to 6 percent of the GDP.

Indirectly, that set the stage for the Great Recession of 2008–9. America's current account deficit put trillions of dollars in the hands of foreigners, who wanted to invest them in relatively low-risk assets. Wall Street obliged by creating trillions of dollars of derivatives from home equity loans, subprime mortgages, high-yield debt, and other risky assets. Structured financial products supposedly turned low-quality assets into triple-A rated bonds. When the US housing market sagged, the structured triple-A bonds lost most of their value, leaving major banks around the world technically insolvent. A $700 billion rescue funded by US taxpayers prevented a collapse of the financial system in the aftermath of Lehman Brothers' bankruptcy in September 2008.

Republicans were blindsided by the Great Financial Crash. Tax rates were low, they thought, so how could anything bad happen? A handful of Republican economists, including this writer, warned of an impending implosion. The Republicans paid a steep price at the ballot box in 2008 for their incomprehension.

TRANSFER PAYMENTS
AS % OF FEDERAL EXPENDITURES

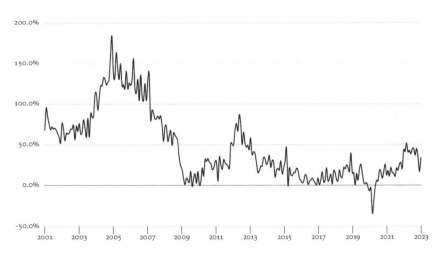

Even worse, the real hourly earnings of US factory workers peaked in 1979 and fell thereafter. The average factory wage in 1947 was one dollar an hour. That has risen to twenty-five dollars today, but prices have risen sixteen-fold, so the real wage is less than two 1947 dollars.

MANUFACTURING HOURLY WAGES IN 1947 DOLLARS

Manufacturing productivity peaked in 2009 and declined afterward.

US MANUFACTURING OUTPUT BY MANHOUR

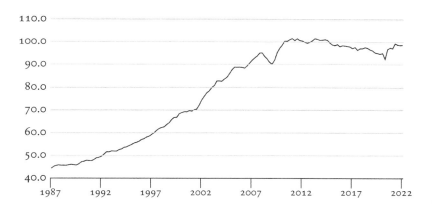

These two data points are related. Productivity increased during the Bush years because America shed a third of its manufacturing jobs. When the great offshoring was over, productivity growth came to an end. After the recession of 2000, investment in manufacturing dropped sharply. Venture capital commitments to hardware production of all sorts virtually disappeared. Software and biotech absorbed the whole of the venture capital budget. Productivity and real wages stagnated.

Tech giants like Google and Microsoft are natural monopolies sustained by network effects, and conventional antitrust enforcement is not a remedy. We use one search engine and post cat pictures on one social media site, not because Google or Facebook use nefarious means to suppress competition but because it is convenient to do so. But the government has given them unfair advantages by commission as well as omission. As Senator Josh Hawley proposes, internet giants should be designated "common carriers," and required to open their platforms to all points of view. Tax dodges such as the parking of intellectual property in offshore low-tax venues like Ireland should be eliminated. Government has an interest in suppressing social media practices that promote pathologies – for example, Instagram's impact on the body image of adolescents. But the worst problem is a sin of omission. The atrophy of government support for technological innovation has left the brightest young Americans writing smartphone apps rather than pushing the envelope of physical sciences. As the manufacturing base has shrunk, so has innovation. The corporate laboratories at the Bell System, General Electric, IBM, and RCA shut down. As American corporations shrank their manufacturing business, they laid off the engineers and scientists who collaborated with production personnel to test and develop new industrial products. With the end of the Cold War, federal funding for experimental research disappeared as well. America's great productivity machine was dismantled.

If the industrialization of the late nineteenth century was founded on railroads, the consumer monopolies of the 1990s and 2000s were founded on the internet and consumer vices. Productivity growth in the information technology sector surged – the cost of memory fell seventy-fold between 2000 and 2020 – but IT productivity had little impact on the rest of the economy. This is remarkable, but not unprecedented. Hero of Alexandria invented both the steam engine and linear programming in the first century AD, but he used them for magic tricks and puppet shows. The Age of Discovery after the conquest of the New World drew on a range of new technologies, but it made little impact on the daily life of Europeans. The entirety of Spain's capture of precious metals went to India and China to pay for luxury cloth and spices, historian Fernand Braudel has calculated. Meanwhile, the African slave trade instituted by the Portuguese and later the British first produced sugar in Brazil and the Caribbean, which was turned into cheap intoxicants for the European market. The use of slave labor to produce these vices probably reduced the West African population by a third.

Spain's passion for Asian luxury goods ultimately bankrupted its empire. Britain financed its trade deficit through the second half of the nineteenth century through India's opium exports to China, while its once-dominant manufacturing industry atrophied. During the nineteenth century, in order to sell cheap cotton cloth to India, the East India Company arranged for Indians to grow opium and for the Chinese to buy it. All the silver mined in Latin America, which two centuries earlier had passed to China to pay for silks, found its way back to Europe to pay for opium.

Today the wealth of the United States derives from the sale of digital bread and circuses, while we depend on China, Japan, South Korea, Germany, and others for industrial imports. As noted, our net foreign asset position is now negative $30 trillion. We are headed down the same slippery slope as imperial Spain and England.

CULTURE COMES FIRST

During the heyday of supply-side economics, Irving Kristol, an early supporter of the movement, admonished his followers to pay more attention to culture. He did so in 1992 at a conference that Jude Wanniski's consulting firm Polyconomics held for its clients and at which I spoke on the same panel. Wanniski stood up and remonstrated, "But Godfather, you told us to concentrate on the economics!" Kristol laughed and agreed. If ever culture led economics, it did so during the Internet Age.

Mainstream Republicans often forget that the world-beating achievements of the American economy ultimately depended on a culture of exploration, discovery, and combativeness. To win the Cold War we transformed technology. This was a bipartisan effort – that is, a cultural expression of what the United States used to be. It was a Democratic president, John F. Kennedy, who pointed to the moon in 1962 and told America that we would go there. And it was another Democratic president, Jimmy Carter, who entrusted the Department of Defense to one of our best physicists, Harold Brown, whose efforts developed most of the technologies that would help Reagan win the Cold War.

Reagan removed the tax "wedge" that separated innovators from investors. The Reagan tax cuts, in combination with Volcker's monetary policy, opened the floodgates for entrepreneurs to exploit the technology that the Cold War had brought forth, to which the Defense Department stood as godfather. But we failed to understand how devasting would be the post–Cold War culture of hedonistic complacency and the abandonment of government and corporate backing for innovation. The Right today defends economic growth almost solely in terms of consumer choice, which is a sophisticated expression for hedonism. But such an economy spends its vital juices and eventually exhausts itself: not only in its shallow innovations, but in the effects of these supposed innovations on consumers.

Growing GDP and rising equity valuations are not the measure of success. In fact, the GDP can be grown in foolish ways that provide a temporary boost but undermine the nation in the long run. We could, for instance, boost GDP by several percentage points in an instant, by legalizing all recreational drugs, and by incorporating what is now an off-the-books activity into the official count of transactions. Much of the conservative establishment would go for this bargain even today, refusing to see how shortsighted and self-destructive this would be.

Today, our manufacturing base is so depleted that our imports from China have risen from $410 billion a year in August 2019, when President Trump imposed tariffs on Chinese goods, to nearly $700 billion a year today. We manufacture less than we did in 2008, according to the Federal Reserve's index of industrial production. We cannot find companies willing to invest in manufacturing, and we cannot find workers willing to take manufacturing jobs. US companies now advertise a million unfilled manufacturing jobs, an unprecedented number. Given the poor compensation for factory work, it isn't surprising that Americans don't want to take them. We are in a vicious cycle where underinvestment has left productivity stagnant, low productivity keeps labor compensation down, and workers eschew manufacturing work, which is harder and less remunerative than the alternatives.

We succeeded in the past not because government played a bigger role in the economy, but because government played a special kind of role: Spurred by the exigency of the Cold War, the American government asked its citizens to do great things, and it helped give them the means to do them. We Americans are a Protestant country with the spirit of an evangelical tent meeting, and we need leaders who can use the bully pulpit of the presidency to inspire us to great accomplishments. Perhaps the challenge of a rising China will elicit from us the determination and energy we need to lift ourselves out of our present malaise. But that will require us to summon all our resources and undertake an effort for national renewal as great as any we have attempted in the past.

WHAT'S REQUIRED OF US NOW

First, the Right must recognize the real causes of growth that took place during the 1990s and 2000s: federal investment in R&D in the previous generation. Today, this means that we should fund federal R&D at similar levels – that is, an additional

1 percent of GDP, or roughly $2 trillion over ten years to revive the system of public-private partnerships that allowed the federal government to subsidize basic research while leaving the risk of commercialization to private entrepreneurs.

Second, we need a radical revision of tax and regulatory policy to favor capital-intensive manufacturing, in place of our present tax code that allows Big Tech to keep intellectual property offshore in low-tax venues. Industry should be able to write off the entire cost of capital investment in the year that it is made. Otherwise inflation reduces the value of depreciation allowances over time, raising the after-tax cost of investment. Immediate depreciation, moreover, encourages manufacturers to buy the latest stuff rather than hold onto obsolete equipment.

Third, we need selective subsidies for mission-critical industries, including semiconductors, advanced materials, quantum computing, quantum communications, high-speed broadband, and other technologies that have a radiating effect on all of industry. Before its breakup under antitrust action in 1982, the Bell System constituted a monopoly that kept the cost of telephony high, but it funded Bell Labs, which invented the transistor, among other building blocks of the digital age, and earned three Nobel Prizes. Rather than let China's Huawei Technologies take world leadership in broadband infrastructure, the United States should have subsidized the buildout of 5G broadband, the carrier technology for a host of Fourth Industrial Revolution applications.

Fourth, we need to shift our educational priorities toward engineering and hard science, and state-of-the-art vocational training for industrial skills on the model of the European apprenticeship system. This can be done at the level of the states as well, but the federal government should lead. A few community colleges provide advanced industrial training for skilled workers. This is something to build on. A public-private partnership that brought curriculum and teachers from industry to teach students earning degree credits could train the skilled workers America needs to restore manufacturing leadership.

Fifth, we need to shift defense priorities away from legacy systems and toward innovation, including space-based missile defense, directed-energy weapons, cyber war, and drone swarms. The requirements of national defense force us to push the envelope of physics and make fundamental innovations. A defense driver for technology has always been the prerequisite for major advances in technology. The Second World War gave us nuclear power, space flight, the first working computers, and jet aircraft. The Cold War gave us fast and inexpensive chips, optical networks, and the internet. We cannot envision what technologies our national defense requirements might generate, but we know that without fundamental innovation, we cannot reverse our national decline.

Above all, we need inspired presidential leadership of the kinds that John F. Kennedy offered with the Apollo program and that Ronald Reagan provided with the Strategic Defense Initiative, a national challenge that inspires our young people to achieve national greatness.

NOTES

1   Peter Thiel, "The Tech Curse," National Conservatism Conference, Miami, Florida, September 13, 2022, YouTube video, 37:39, https://www.youtube.com/watch?v=balGGAd6ZrI.
2   "David P. Goldman, "Savings, Capital Gains and Risk-Taking: Toward and Entrepreneurial Theory of Growth," *Journal of Applied Corporate Finance 7*, no. 1 (Spring 1994): 103–12.

WINNING THE ECONOMIC WAR

How to Defeat Woke Capital

Matthew Peterson

AMERICANS ARE DIVIDED about what men and women, the family, citizenship, and nation-states are and ought to be, as well as when human life begins and when it ought to end. In other words, Americans are now divided over the building blocks and the purpose of their country's civilization. Since nearly every major institution in America – whether commercial, cultural, political, or educational – is now in the grip of a totalizing, ethical system of woke thought and ways of life, it ought to be no surprise that the views of roughly half the population of America are increasingly suppressed, delegitimized, and harmed by most major corporations and media outlets.

Currently, nearly every major corporation in America, along with "woke capital" or the financial complex that supports these corporations, bows to this ideology publicly, accelerating change for the worse. Anyone paying attention now realizes that half of America faces a dire threat from within: Big Corporate increasingly works directly with the administrative state to deplatform, debank, and unperson dissenting political and cultural organizations, citizens, and political movements.

The American Right has already lost this battle and must now wholly rethink its approach if it is to win the war. There are no easy solutions, but there is a clear strategy to pursue, which is in contradiction to the views the Right has espoused for the last generation. The first step is to boldly and publicly acknowledge that our economy is a political and cultural warzone, and to act accordingly. There are two paths forward that must ultimately converge if we are to stop woke capital and all it now controls. The first is legal and political; the other is a new commercial-cultural movement.

HOW WE GOT HERE

In a very different America, the Right set out to *conserve* American institutions and an American way of life through partisan political action and advocacy. The Right hoped to fight the "culture war" within explicitly political spaces, via explicitly political means, while holding that businesses and the economy were explicitly "neutral" spaces, subject to discipline from shareholders and market demand. This flawed, narrow understanding has long since been falsified by events.

This way of thinking became so dominant that the true history of ideas on economic issues has been lost or forgotten. But neutrality was manifestly not the approach of the Founders or in the early Republic, nor even that of the birth and reign of the Republican Party from 1860 to 1932. Although there is not sufficient space here to fully elaborate the point, Noah Webster, who was typical of the founding era, was greatly concerned about the relationship between "the morals of the people" and "the influence of money on men's sense of justice and moral obligation."[1] Commerce was seen as subservient to the good of the citizenry. Moreover, as Charles Kesler has pointed out, Lincoln's Republican Party "inherited their support for protective tariffs from their predecessors in the Whig Party, who stood for Henry Clay's 'American system' of protection and internal improvements, and who had in turn inherited their protectionism from the Federalist Party and its leading economic thinker, Alexander Hamilton" – to say nothing of Theodore Roosevelt's policy of "Americanization" and "trust-busting."[2] The idea that commerce was morally, politically, or culturally neutral, and should accordingly be left alone, was not mainstream.

The rise of the notions of the morally neutral expert and systems of law and policy throughout the twentieth century infected the thinking of the American Right. Abstract libertarian economics and a sloppy, overgeneralized application of laissez-faire rhetoric began to intertwine with the Right in its opposition to the rise of the administrative state and communism. After World War II it was much easier to speak of neutrality – both because of the intellectual culture of the age and because of the urge to directly support the rapid rise of American global trade (and the wealth that came along with it) against the backdrop of the Cold War. After all, there were no commissars here – and our economy was growing, surpassing all others.

By the time the Cold War ended, as Republicans began to face down the "social justice" movement and the "political correctness" police, they no longer had a cohesive understanding or language of justice applied to commercial life with which they could respond. They often relied instead on the claim that politics should be kept separate from business, and that globalization was financially good for everyone – a message supported by their corporate sponsors. This was never an adequate counter to both the negative effects of globalization and the long unfolding takeover of corporate culture by the Left.

As woke activists correctly point out, in our present context neutrality itself is a political position. There are at least two reasons for the inadequacy of "going back" to neutrality as a goal. The first is practical: our civil rights regime, our laws, our institutions, and our culture have long since baked in the necessity of allegiance to elite-sponsored wokeness and identity politics. Although the initial Civil Rights Act was sold to Americans as a way to ensure we judge individuals by the content of their merits, it quickly metastasized into a system based on the opposite notion: by law, all workplaces must now take racial and many other identities into account and hire, fire, and promote people accordingly. The system is not neutral. Moreover, it is partly run by an ideological federal administrative state and its corollaries in the individual states themselves. And thus far, no one has been able to roll back this regime of laws and customs, which fights under the seemingly inspiring banner of social justice.

The second, deeper reason that a return to neutrality is impossible is that it was always a smokescreen. All civilizations possess an informal social credit system of some kind and an idea of human virtue that its members use to "signal" to others that they are not merely successful, but good. Any human community requires a shared vision of the good life, and broad but real agreement on what that life entails. This agreement is precisely what has broken down in America. The markets, our financial institutions, and our corporations were never "neutral" – it was just that in the past there was broader agreement on fundamental principles and purposes. It was far easier in the past to claim that whatever was good for General Motors was good for America, but the claim that whatever is good for Google is good for America is now absurd to millions of Americans.[3]

What the last decade has revealed is that relying on shareholders and market demand – that is, clinging to the "Go Woke, Go Broke" mantra – is not an actionable strategy. It is a strategy of denouncing while wishfully waiting around. But, fundamentally, it will fail for two reasons.

First, the corporations in question are so large that they can weather many storms over time. The increasingly publicly woke Walt Disney Company, facing anger on the part of right-leaning consumers for increasingly woke content and public stances, has seen its stock fall 40 percent in 2022. But even if we assume that this drop was entirely owing to an informal boycott, at the time this essay was written its market cap is still $172 billion. Disney may not be too big to fail, but it is large enough to remain a global entertainment colossus for years to come.[4] Many large corporations are now akin to gigantic cargo ships that have been overrun by pirates who have a long way to go before they plunder all the loot now available to them.

Second, corporations have already determined that the Left is a far greater and more powerful obstacle if they refuse to go along than is the Right. And, as of now, they are correct. For instance, Jack Dorsey, the former CEO of Twitter, does not seem to be a woke radical; rather, he was constantly contending with forces far more powerful than anything the American Right could muster.[5] As the corporations merge with the administrative state and/or America's intel state (as is the case with Twitter), this is increasingly true. Twitter not only opened itself up to direct federal influence. The company also hired numerous members of the intelligence community. It is now public knowledge that Facebook and other companies have developed similar arrangements.[6]

Neutrality is simply no longer possible. Any free market is free to the extent that force or law not only protect but shape its contours. Business, innovation, and investment cannot be separated from political realities such as a nation's borders or questions about what furthers or obstructs a healthy culture or political life. Moreover, all products and services are sold around an attractive vision of a desirable way of life. Without understanding the truths about commerce – namely, that it is embedded within politics and culture – truths that have been conveniently ignored by the American Right in favor of cartoonish libertarian rhetoric, we cannot reverse the overwhelming tide of woke corporate control.

REVERSING THE STATUS QUO: POLITICS AND LAW

The first line of attack is to use the weapons already available to us. As those engaged in current legal battles have pointed out, whether it be free speech, antitrust, or common carrier laws and regulations, there are plenty of avenues already available to protect consumers and attack the corporations now wielding their power against employees, customers, and competition to further a political agenda.[7] What we lack is the *will* to deploy them. If we jettison the blinders of the past and instead engage in the full-scale economic war that corporations are already waging against us, we will unleash the talent and creativity of politicians, policy-makers, and lawyers at a much greater scale with much greater effectiveness than we've seen thus far. The Left successfully carried out such a program over the past decades.

Until recently, the Right has not tried very hard. The reality is that for too long think tanks and others on the Right have been effectively bought off by funding from Big Tech and other sectors. But these were not Third World bribes, where a clear quid pro quo is attained. The corporations acted cynically, while the think tankers believed the dogmas. The mind of the Right has been distorted by such influence. The pre-WWII Republican Party believed that wisely crafted antitrust legislation was *good* for commerce, as monopolies by their nature stifle innovation. But today, the legal and established corruption of the system swings in one direction. When it comes to antitrust measures, for instance, it is well known that federal lawyers often go to work for the same large corporations they are supposed to be investigating and prosecuting after they leave public service. Yet the examples of a growing group of state attorneys general in states like Texas, Florida, Missouri, and elsewhere make clear that many victories are possible using the framework of existing law – and such actions as filing suits against Google for antitrust violations or the Biden administration for colluding with Big Tech are popular with voters and many donors alike.[8]

But applying existing law in stronger ways to meet the moment is not enough. When corporations grow to such a scale that they disregard the national good in favor of their own and have a significant negative effect on American citizens, the contours of the free market must change accordingly. If American companies like Google, for instance, are working on advanced Artificial Intelligence – one of the most potent burgeoning technologies in existences – with China but not the United States, merely maintaining the status quo is suicidal. When new technologies radically alter society and the marketplace alike, threatening national security and the fundamental rights of the citizenry, laws and regulations must often adjust accordingly.

It is absurd to call this socialism. Never in recorded history did any serious civilization allow corporations to dictate what is and is not good for the nation. That is what statesmen do, not self-interested CEOs. The Constitution itself was designed to rectify the unjust and failing financial practices of the early American states, which the Federalists vehemently decried in moral terms.[9] If the Right can abandon the failed intellectual framework of the past few decades and join the fight, there are plenty of areas in which new or radically reformed laws and regulations can reshape the commercial landscape for the better. This includes obvious measures such as pushing anti-ESG legislation and forbidding banks from discriminating against their customers, but much more creative legislative approaches are within reach with the right motivation and focus.[10]

One other obvious principle of action for red states is to stop giving billions of taxpayer dollars to corporations that hate them. At one level, this means pulling out huge amounts of money now in the hands of BlackRock and other large investment vehicles that have weaponized the trillions of dollars they control. West Virginia State Treasurer Riley Moore and others have begun leading the way forward, but such measures and more must become the new norm across the nation.[11]

The same principle should apply to all large red state contracts with notable woke businesses that oppose and attack the interests of the residents of those states. The correct response to the large group of corporations that involved themselves in the dispute over Georgia election law in 2021, for instance, would have been to threaten them en masse with real financial disincentives in applicable red states.[12] It is notable that although in the past Hollywood has threatened to pull productions from Georgia, this never came to pass since too many productions wanted to utilize the state's questionable film tax credit.[13] This is the sort of leverage that must now be weaponized. If Salesforce continues to involve itself in Texas politics and attack Republicans, for instance, offering to pay its employees to transfer out of the state, any and all benefits or breaks they receive by operating in Texas at the state and local level should be considered fair game.[14] This is not only a matter of simple justice: continuing to fund one's enemies reveals a lack of seriousness, if not suicidal ideation. Although no single action of this sort will likely dissuade some of the large corporations in question, this line of attack is vital. It not only raises awareness of the problem but actively creates a new ecosystem to foster and reward *alternative* businesses and financial institutions, which can then start to capture real market share away from the worst offenders.

On the same principle, all special arrangements and giveaways that state and local governments have designed in the past for corporations that are now actively opposing the interests of the residents of red states need to be systematically reexamined. What Governor Ron DeSantis did by dissolving Disney's local governing power in Florida is a model for the rest of the nation.[15] The idea that such action violates conservative principles is absurd. Strict libertarians have argued for decades that special cut-outs for businesses distort what should be a level playing field, so getting rid of them should be good. The entire complicated landscape of our so-called free market is already a distorted and corrupt warzone, with states like California and New York ceaselessly rewarding their friends and punishing their enemies. While specific cases may vary, as a general rule maintaining special benefits and relationships with companies actively working to subvert the interest of the people is not principled, but foolish.

In the past, the discipline of boards and shareholders was a more trustworthy lever to limit the political activity of a company. Ownership today, however, is often not your grandfather's capitalism: woke finance owns significant shares of large companies, and does not operate by the long-term and responsible rules of the gray-haired wise men that still exist in the imagination of many conservatives. Many corporate boards have long since been co-opted by activists. A tangled web of NGOs, politicians, and political organizations has succeeded over the years to take over even the industries they despise, such as the energy sector. In California, for instance, all corporations are required to put women and "underrepresented communities" on boards.[16] The real impetus behind the cries for "diversity" on corporate boards is simply to leverage power for political purposes.

Here, too, the Right has simply not tried very hard to counter this movement. There is no reason in principle that nonprofits, politicians, political organizations on the Right could not act in similar manner to the Left in this arena; there is only lack of will. One goal would be to unite aligned shareholders and run pressure campaigns against wokeness like the Left does for climate change and a host of other issues. Some new organizations are even looking to band together to buy shares in certain companies as a group for the sake of corrective activism. Yet much more is needed and is still possible: to take one example, why does a consumer's union to represent tech platform users and advocate on their behalf not yet exist? Such an organization would file a few high profile lawsuits a year break down ever-changing terms of service, educating consumers about their rights and tech privacy practices; and rank social media platforms, calling attention to their worst actions.

At the center of what needs radical legal and political reform, however, is the woke human resources regime established on the basis of the 1964 Civil Rights Act. There can be no real victory until the Right takes aim at the massive body of rules and regulations emerging from it, which provides the commissars their command centers in every major business in America. Without freedom of association, we do not have a free country. While the experiment may have begun with noble aspirations, it has become a tyrannical tool of radical ideology. We must no longer require that race and other identities be taken into account in the workplace. Dismantling this complex is such a monumental task that many despair at the attempt. But there is no longer any way around fighting the weaponization of race and sexual "identities" in the workplace if there is to be any hope of saving the American economy.

At the very least, the concept of disparate impact – which practically means that any inequality is the result of oppression and must be rectified accordingly – needs to be publicly dismantled by revisiting and revising the 1964 Civil Rights Act and all the subsequent legislation that has been built upon it. The Right can rest assured that despite the success of its enemies, millions of regular Americans and business leaders still value excellence and despise the working environment they now find themselves in. What's required to help them is a brave new political movement that takes direct aim at this body of law.

Any such movement needs to start with an accurate description of the problem that completely rejects the rhetorical straitjacket the Left has put its opponents in for decades. The framework we must adopt has nothing to do with racism or sexuality, but with the question whether we still value competence and innovation or not. The Right must argue not merely that woke HR is inefficient but that it is fundamentally unjust and morally wrong. The Right must clearly articulate the difference between the competence (or merit) regime versus the group quota regime. There are two competing notions of justice in play: the traditional American understanding looks to merit or what equal citizens owe each other; "equity" means categorizing human beings into an ever-changing array of identities and treating all group differences as the result of injustice or oppression. As this notion of justice is imposed on the workforce, our commercial world will collapse owing to the toxic atmosphere this creates in the workplace, the removal of all standards of excellence, and the replacement of the purpose of business with radical political ends. The most successful businessman in the world, Elon Musk, recently declared: "Unless it is stopped, the woke mind virus will destroy civilization and humanity will never reach Mars."[17] If Republicans can't say the same and explain why, they should not expect to defeat woke capital.

COMPETITIVE VISION

The geographic, digital, and financial movement of millions of people and billions of dollars out from under the control of woke states, woke digital technology, and woke corporations and capital has already begun. But if the Right is to succeed, it will need to actively foster, grow, and channel it. Many on the Right do not see it and even doubt such a movement exists; many more do not think it likely or possible. Yet it has begun.

Along with his public denunciation of ESG, Elon Musk's purchase and reform of Twitter could be described as an act of statesmanship for the twenty-first century. His public speech and actions rely on presuppositions about a preferable way of life that is diametrically opposed to woke capital. Others, like Peter Thiel, one of the most thoughtful American entrepreneurs and investors, have called ESG and all that surrounds it a "hate factory" equivalent to the Chinese Communist Party.[18] Vivek Ramaswamy, a successful entrepreneur and the author of *Woke Capital*, recently announced the creation of Strive Asset Management, "to restore the voices of everyday citizens in the American economy by leading companies to focus on excellence over politics." He rightly says established competitors such as BlackRock and Vanguard are part of an "ideological cartel." These figures reveal signs of life and hope. They are models for the dithering Right and its unnatural conceptual separation of politics from commerce, culture, and technology.

What these leaders currently lack is a robust connection to red state America and a full articulation of what the broad-based, popular movement the American Right must now help foster is substantially about. But we will not defeat a positive with a negative. Wokeness, ESG, and "social justice" were created as positive movements by a concerted effort on the part of many kinds of organizations and talented people. Any positive movement pointing in another direction will fail to launch unless it includes the same key stakeholders. Nonprofits and intellectuals must lay out definitions and guidelines and promote and advocate for them; businesses must adapt and be able to innovate and advertise based on them; and, at the center of it all, the media must showcase this attractive vision to the public.

Woke capital operates by means of its capture of billions of dollars from the very people it opposes. A key reason for its success is the lack of nonwoke options currently on offer for millions of Americans. The Right needs to foster a new class of investors and founders who refuse to break to its demands. True, many people tied to the current system cannot completely break out of it. But they can assist new efforts outside it that can. True, change is nearly impossible in the short term within our large corporations. But the real way to take on woke capital is to draw actual blood. And that means competition.

The same forces driving geographic migration from blue to red states apply with even more force to the one-party controlled workplace, marketplace, and, especially, digital technology platforms. When the divide in understanding about fundamental things is so deep, people are pushed by necessity and pulled by desire to get out from under woke control. Any way you count the numbers, millions of Americans – who, as a group, would constitute one of the largest GDPs in the world – want to stop supporting companies and cultural institutions that hate them. Half the nation, in other words, wants alternatives. If we can put together the historic levels of talent now available to meet increasingly ravenous demand, this is the single biggest business opportunity in our lifetime. It is also needed to save America.

This requires family offices, financial institutions, and investment banks coming together to facilitate all of the above – our own smaller but sharper versions of McKinsey, Goldman, and Bain, seeking to find opportunity in reshoring supply chains and American jobs, fighting to fend off woke H R and promote excellence, and helping build an ecosystem that restores health to American life. It requires decentralizing rather than centralizing woke control of financial transactions, and giving us search results we are actually interested in based on our values when we search for books and movies and products and services.

This would mean, say, a crack team of business leaders purchasing a small clothing company in good position with products capable of replacing woke Patagonia's clothing, with capital from aligned and experienced investors, for the express purpose of growing that business into a competitor that directly appeals to red state America and beyond.

This would mean media outlets and communities in tech that drew consumers and investors together to highlight and support new ventures like multiple ongoing efforts on the part of young, energetic, accomplished entrepreneurs to create dating apps that reject hook-up culture and explicitly seek to lead people into meaningful, long-term relationships and marriage.

In sum, this would require a very different form of ESG focused on what we know threatens our civilization most right now in the West – namely, the disintegration of the family and standards of excellence, beauty, and healthy human behavior. Businesses that were part of this movement would recognize that the destruction of family life, and the sexual mutilation of children, woke education, and so on, is forming millions of increasingly dysfunctional people in the workforce – and would therefore promote civilizational and cultural health as part of this countermovement. This is not fantasy. This is the reality of what is now required to win.

NOTES

1   Noah Webster, *A Collection of Essays and Fugitiv Writings: On Moral, Historical, Political and Literary Subjects* (Boston: I. Thomas and E. T. Andrews, 1790), 97, 114.

2   Charles R. Kesler, "The Republican Trump," *Claremont Review of Books*, Winter 2016/17, https://claremontreviewofbooks.com/the-republican-trump/.

3   Robert W. Patterson, "'What's Good for America …'," *National Review*, July 1, 2013, https://www.nationalreview.com/2013/07/whats-good-america-robert-w-patterson/.

4   Rick Munarriz, "3 Things Disney Got Right in 2022 Despite the Stock Falling 40%," Motley Fool, December 12, 2022, https://www.fool.com/investing/2022/12/12/3-things-disney-got-right-in-2022-despite-the-stoc/.

5   See "Exhibit H," Elon Musk Text Exhibits (Twitter v. Musk), accessed December 14, 2022, https://www.documentcloud.org/documents/23112929-elon-musk-text-exhibits-twitter-v-musk.

6   Name Redacted (@NameRedacted247), "@elonmusk, Your new company @Twitter has many ex FBI/CIA agents in high ranks. Should probably do a little housecleaning," Twitter, December 6, 2022, 9:31 p.m., https://twitter.com/NameRedacted247/status/1600316966182715393; America First Legal (@America1stLegal), "BREAKING: Following the #Twitter Files, AFL has obtained new documents uncovering a secret Twitter portal U.S. Govt officials used to censor dissenting COVID-19 views and violate the First Amendment," Twitter, December 6, 2022, 4:49 p.m., https://twitter.com/America1stLegal/status/1600246196102389760?s=20&t=XFXvq3ro5jn3C1Iom1RrdA; Felix Livshitz, "Facebook and US Gov't Have United Against Americans with 'Wrong' Views," Free Thought Project, October 7, 2022, https://thefreethoughtproject.com/free-speech/facebook-and-us-govt-have-united-against-americans-with-wrong-views; Alan Macleod, "Meet the Ex-CIA Agents Deciding Facebook's Content Policy," MintPress News, July 12, 2022, https://www.mintpressnews.com/meet-ex-cia-agents-deciding-facebook-content-policy/281307/.

7   Harmeet K. Dhillon, "Congressional Testimony of Harmeet K. Dhillon on September 27, 2018," House Judiciary Committee, Subcommittee on the Constitution and Civil Justice, September 27, 2018, https://docs.house.gov/meetings/JU/JU10/20180927/108458/HHRG-115-JU10-Wstate-DhillonH-20180927.pdf.

8   Eric Schmitt, "Attorney General Schmitt Files Suit against Google for Alleged Anticompetitive Actions in Relation to App Store," Eric Schmitt: Missouri Attorney General, July 8, 2021, https://ago.mo.gov/home/news/2021/07/08/attorney-general-schmitt-files-suit-against-google-for-

alleged-anticompetitive-actions-in-relation-to-app-store; Nihal Krishan, "Missouri and Louisiana Attorneys General Accuse Biden of Colluding with Big Tech," *Washington Examiner*, May 5, 2022, https://www.washing-tonexaminer.com/policy/missouri-and-louisiana-attorneys-general-accuse-biden-of-colluding-with-big-tech; Ken Paxton, "Alaska, Florida, Montana, Nevada and Puerto Rico Join Texas-Led Bipartisan Antitrust Lawsuit Against Google," Ken Paxton: Attorney General of Texas, March 16, 2021, https://www.texasattorneygeneral.gov/news/releases/ag-paxton-alaska-florida-montana-nevada-and-puerto-rico-join-texas-led-bipartisan-antitrust-lawsuit.

9   Matthew J. Peterson, "The American Founding Was Not Libertarian Liber-alism," *American Mind*, June 14, 2019, https://americanmind.org/features/why-the-new-right-rises/the-american-founding-was-not-libertarian-liberalism/. See also Noah Webster, *A Collection of Essays and Fugitiv Writ-ings*, 97, 114.

10   Richard Vanderford, "Florida's DeSantis Takes Aim at 'Woke Capital,'" *Wall Street Journal*, July 28, 2022, https://www.wsj.com/articles/floridas-desantis-takes-aim-at-woke-capital-11659043495?mod=latest_headlines.

11   Riley Moore (@RileyMoore), "Today I announced my office will no longer use BlackRock, Inc. investment fund for banking transactions," Twitter, January 17, 2022, 4:53 p.m., https://twitter.com/rileymoorewv/status/1483195751345930243; Lydia Moynihan, "Republican Treasurers With-draw $1B from BlackRock over ESG Investments," *New York Post*, October 10, 2022, https://nypost.com/2022/10/10/republican-treasurers-withdraw-1b-from-blackrock-over-esg-investments/; Danielle Moran and Saijel Kishan, "Florida Will Pull $2 Billion of Assets From BlackRock Over ESG," *Bloomberg*, December 1, 2022, https://www.bloomberg.com/news/articles/2022-12-01/florida-will-pull-2-billion-of-assets-from-blackrock-over-esg.

12   Rachel Treisman, "'Based On A Lie' – Georgia Voting Law Faces Wave Of Corporate Backlash," *NPR*, April 1, 2021, https://www.npr.org/2021/04/01/983450176/based-on-a-lie-georgia-voting-law-faces-wave-of-corporate-backlash.

13   Ross Williams, "What's Wrong with This Picture? State Auditors Give Georgia's Movie Tax Credit Mixed Reviews," *GPB News*, November 1, 2022, https://www.gpb.org/news/2022/11/01/whats-wrong-picture-state-auditors-give-georgias-movie-tax-credit-mixed-reviews; Chris Lindahl, "Strong Tax Incentives May Be Enough for Hollywood to Stay in States Restricting Abortion Access," IndieWire, June 24, 2022, https://www.indiewire.com/2022/06/georgia-film-tax-credits-abortion-1234736475/.

14   Associated Press, "Salesforce to help workers leave states over abortion laws," *AP News*, September 11, 2021, https://apnews.com/article/

technology-business-texas-greg-abbott-marc-benioff-98094859a
011193d3c83d6a4ff1e7a8a.

15 Michael Kranish, "How DeSantis Used Disney's Missteps to Wage War on
Corporate America," *Washington Post*, October 19, 2022, https://www.
washingtonpost.com/politics/2022/10/19/desantis-disney-corporate-
america-war/.

16 Shirley N. Weber, "Diversity on Boards," Shirley N. Weber, Ph.D.: California Secretary of State, accessed December 14, 2022, https://www.sos.ca.
gov/business-programs/diversity-boards.

17 Rita Li, "Elon Musk Calls Out TikTok Over 'Civilization' Risk," *Epoch
Times*, June 19, 2022, https://www.theepochtimes.com/elon-musk-calls-
out-tiktok-over-civilization-risk_4543023.html.

18 Harry Wilmerding, "'Hate Factory': Peter Thiel Blasts Woke Investing
Craze Sweeping Corporate America," *Daily Caller*, April 8, 2022, https://
dailycaller.com/2022/04/08/peter-thiel-esg-warren-buffett-bitcoin-
conference/.

DIGITAL RULE, BIG TECH, AND A DIGITAL RIGHTS AMENDMENT

James Poulos

I<small>F WE DO NOT</small> reassert the right kind of control over our technology, our technology will increasingly control us. This presents a problem for the Right. Over generations, conservatives have come to feel that they are blocked from limiting technological advancement. Even those who worry that technology is exerting an unhealthy control over our lives are usually uncertain how to respond.

The reasons for this hesitancy are twofold. First, many conservatives, particularly those of the establishment stripe, are committed to free markets. They say the following sort of thing: "We willingly gave the tech companies our data and so we must allow them, within the law, to do what they wish with it; to do otherwise would be 'socialism.'" And that's that. As I argue below, this way of thinking has prevented "establishment" conservatives from even admitting tech presents a problem, let alone dealing with it.

Second, among those who do recognize that digital technology poses a danger, their solutions, such as antitrust action, are inadequate because they fail to recognize the most challenging obstacle to reform: the belief that no matter how great technology's harms, America's very existence hinges on our military domination of the planet. And this domination, in turn, depends on a priestly class of elite experts and spies with restricted and secret access to the world's most powerful technology, or so it seems to conservatives. According to this view, the citizenry *should not have access* to the cutting-edge tools and information that run the world because they are not to be trusted. They will leak them to other countries. Better to trust the experts, say politicians on both sides of the aisle.

The roots of this point of view are understandable. It arises from the successful aversion of serious crises, including the Cold War. Understandable or not, however, it leaves us believing that we must accept slavery and destruction at the hands of our machines in order to avert slavery and destruction at the hands of foreign powers. But in fact this is a bargain we do not have to make. We can have both. We can use our superior technology to defeat our foreign enemies but without sacrificing liberty at home. If we do not do this, unelected technocrats will continue to use advanced technologies as weapons to end our constitutionally guaranteed form of government and our way of life. The America we knew and loved will be replaced – indeed, it is now being replaced – with a new and alien cyborg form of government, one that fuses social credit and social justice into an automated system, where the woke religion is ingrained and enforced by machines that act like people, and by people who act like machines.

HOW WE GOT HERE: BUCKLEY'S DREAM, EISENHOWER'S NIGHTMARE

The mistaken belief that we are hostage to technology can be traced to contemporary conservatism's founding documents: William F. Buckley's 1955 mission statement for *National Review*, which lays out as its first and third "credenda" two convictions in uneasy alliance with each other. He first claims that "It is the job of centralized government (in peacetime) to protect its citizens' lives, liberty and property"; "all other activities of government," he says, "tend to diminish freedom and hamper progress." This required fighting utopian social engineers. Buckley goes on: "We consider 'coexistence' with communism neither desirable nor possible, nor honorable; we find ourselves irrevocably at war with communism and shall oppose any substitute for victory." For Buckley, and the movement he forged, centralized government's primary role was to comprehensively fight and unconditionally win the struggle for world domination. What Buckley failed to fully appreciate was that the fight against communism could easily lead to a large, unaccountable, controlling government, the very thing that threatened liberty at home.

Even before the launch of *National Review*, there was reason to worry: the Manhattan Project had created a massive and secret state within a state, covertly employing over one hundred thousand people across military installations nationwide. This was what "global dominance" was really starting to look like: an explosive and unaccountable expansion of government, designed to wield the state's unmatched resources and power to harness and create the most up-to-date and lethal technology in the world. This expansion of the technological shadow state was deemed (perhaps correctly) necessary to win control over America's existential enemies. After World War II, conservatives and liberals alike believed they had no choice but to accept, and even to promote, this vast unelected government in order to replace communism as the world's ruling ideology. At this point, there was no getting rid of big government. And big government could no longer be blamed on the social engineers.

President Dwight Eisenhower understood better than Buckley that big government was necessary to defeat communism. He wrote in his farewell address that "we can no longer risk emergency improvisation of national defense," being obliged instead "to create a permanent armaments industry of vast proportions" with 3.5 million workers "directly engaged in the defense establishment." But, at the same time, Eisenhower recognized the attendant dangers. He exposed to the American people the real identity of their menacing form of government and way of life: not socialists larding Washington with red tape and regulations, but "a scientific-technological elite" whose groundbreaking tools for world domination – or annihilation – were "largely responsible for the sweeping changes in our industrial-military posture."[1] Constrained by the "imperative need" of this new regime, he foresaw just one escape from elite control: "only an alert and knowledgeable citizenry can compel the proper meshing of the huge industrial and military machinery of defense with our peaceful methods and goals, so that security and liberty may prosper together." Rather than stressing up-to-date know-how, Eisenhower intimated that a change in spirit alone could restrain the power of America's new globalized military-technological state. Americans "must avoid the impulse to live only for today, plundering for our own ease and convenience the precious resources" absent which future generations would lose "their political and spiritual heritage." Unfortunately, Eisenhower's warning was not heeded.

Rather than increasing their spiritual alertness and knowledge about the inability of innovation alone to provide security, freedom, riches, and vitality, Americans largely grew spiritually dependent on their scientific-technological elite, expecting an ever-stronger stream of more powerful weapons, more engrossing entertainment, and more comfortable living. The old mentality that quintessentially American rights and responsibilities extended into the realm of technology as much as any other was replaced by a tacit new understanding that advancing technology was a kind of welfare benefit underwritten and distributed by the state's super-brains. Now our elites insist that Americans cannot be trusted to use and apply basic digital technologies in a sufficiently socially just manner. Citizens unhappy about this should take a step outside their comfort zone and learn the basics about using digital hardware and software independently of the state-sponsored Big Tech complex. But today they must also organize politically into a clear constituency that demands our innate and constitutional rights must extend into digital life. The loss of these rights online augurs their destruction offline. While they are implicit in the First and Second Amendments, now is the time to make them explicit in state and, if possible, federal law.

THE MILITARY-INDUSTRIAL COMPLEX
GETS A DIGITAL UPDATE

In Eisenhower's day, the cutting edge of technology was atomic fission and space travel. Today, the apex of advanced technologies is digital tech – the computational software and hardware, including programs, protocols, platforms, algorithms, and the devices they link together – that powers and directs our use of ever more machines and that intermediates ever more of our human communications and interactions. In its digital form, the American technomilitary shadow-state has gained fearsome new powers over the minutiae of citizen lives. The sinister intimacy of these technologies has made a mockery of the distinction, already collapsing in Eisenhower's grim vision, between "private" and "public" sectors.

In private, our economic life is reduced to consumption and entertainment. And now it is clear that the spiritual privations – owing to, among other things, ubiquitous pornography – we suffer in private are mirrored by the totalizing control exerted over us by our public "servants." The public sector is an increasingly autocratic realm where limitless technological advancement is coercively used to impose a radically invasive new form of government control over the American people and across the world. The tools used to control us – tools of digital categorization, processing, and analysis – are only put into our hands as playthings. But when wielded solely by the state and by corporate giants they are weapons that advance the state's interests. We no longer control our technology; rather, it controls us.

Public and private communications alike are routinely surveilled, stored, analyzed, censored, and punished. Financial transactions are logged, monitored, and restricted; fines and account closures are imposed on individuals and groups for reasons reflecting the woke prejudices and interests of the state. Agencies whose officials are not elected or removed by democratic means, sometimes not even by the president, collaborate secretly with "nongovernmental" and media organizations to suppress, disrupt, and interfere with the spread of narratives and information they ideologically or spiritually oppose, publicly casting participants in disfavored movements as threats to national security and democracy. Decisions about military conflict are increasingly made by intelligence agencies technologically and legally shielded from citizen visibility, and shadow conflicts are waged around the clock in cyberspace, targeting systems ranging from weapons to communications to infrastructure, without explanation or approval by elected representatives.

COVID lockdowns have increased government control: domestic and international officials have pushed both separately and together for ever more comprehensive digital systems controlling identification, access to benefits and markets, personal movement, social association, and the law in general – from content moderation to health care, from education to parenting, and well beyond.

And most individuals do not seem terribly concerned. They are simply unwilling or unable to function without constant technological connectivity – to virtual goods, services, and pleasures. No matter how corrosive the pleasure (like pornography); no matter how soul-destroying the amusement (like rote and costly app games); no matter how harmful the habits formed (like fruitlessly "doomscrolling" and swiping through "dating" apps) – mass addiction and the demand for "more" and "faster" are endemic.

Today's subjects of the digital world – who, in a sense, cannot properly be called citizens – are not just willing to accept technological slavery; they more and more demand it, rewarding the regime that supplies it. Indeed, on account of this, many Americans have become enlisted as crusaders in a kind of holy war to ensure that this regime annihilates all resistance around the world. The digital way of life is a totalizing way of life, and its adherents feel that it must be totalized both here and abroad.

Such a cyborg jihad would have seemed far-fetched less than a decade ago. But its reality is hard to deny today. Since 2020, all those paying attention have witnessed how the interlocked public and private institutions making up America's globalized woke regime – from the intelligence agencies to the leading tech and business corporations – makes rule by machinery sacred. From murals of George Floyd in Afghanistan to the latest moral imperative to seethe with hatred against not just Vladimir Putin but the Russian people themselves, America's flag is now the rainbow flag, and the sign of fidelity to her is the BLM fist. Our ruling class has announced its intention to oppose and bedevil any nation-state that contravenes these ideals.

Meanwhile, Americans have a vague unease with the technology to which they have willingly submitted. Although they struggle to articulate explicitly what this phenomenon is, it is not lost on them that somehow their concerns about technology are reflected in woke identities – in particular, the "trans" identity, which is lauded and compelled by the new regime. The "trans" person does not, in fact, transform from one biological sex to another, but surgically changes from a biological identity to one that inseparably mingles, in as radical a way as currently possible, the biological with the technological. This transition from human to cyborg puts its practitioners at the vanguard of "progress," making the physical and spiritual mutilation of our sacred humanity the hallmark of social advancement.

In a world where God is dead, living nature is reduced to raw material, technology promises total control, and only our consciousness makes us special, it is no surprise that the sitting administration is officially committed to "protecting trans kids." The rise of "trans" to the top of the stack of identities sacralized by the regime, even against parental objections, shows that the regime now purports to provide compulsory answers to the ultimate questions about human well-being. In this way, our governing elite is responding to technology's potential to disrupt its sovereignty by establishing the woke religion, one in which humans must merge intimately with technology on terms enforced by the regime. On its present trajectory, this new religion spells unlimited global and domestic conflict between the regime and every people or nation unwilling to assimilate into its new order.

The quest to forcibly reorder the world through the mastery of weapons technology is leading to the replacement of America's liberal ideals with the worship of technology's power. Establishment conservatism, however, paralyzed by a commitment to free markets, denies the threat.

To those who argue that Big Tech firms are too big and "endanger American security," American Enterprise Institute's Klon Kitchen, a card-carrying establishment conservative, warns that "Hamstringing these industries will make the nation less safe" and "embolden authoritarian regimes."[2] "Instead of railing against these companies because of their size, argues Kitchen, we instead should be thankful that our free-market economy has produced an alignment of interests where private-sector actors can generate wealth and jobs while also developing capabilities that will provide for the common defense." But this, as the political economist Mariana Mazzucato, among others, has plainly shown, is an out-and-out lie. The leading tech firms (like Google, Facebook, Twitter, and so on) did not grow organically out of the free market;[3] rather, they have worked hand in glove with the military-intelligence complex almost since the beginning, and they have joined in recent years with NGOs and media organizations to forge even more pervasive social controls. They are outgrowths of the military-intelligence complex and the regulatory state.

From GPS to the touchscreen to 5G, virtually every major digital consumer electronics technology is the product or beneficiary of military or intelligence R&D and the bottomless grants it affords.

With exceptions that can probably be counted on one hand, nearly every leading founder and CEO within the Big Tech complex has embraced both the regime's unlimited digital control and the woke cyborg spirituality that the regime is establishing as America's official religion in order to legitimize and cement its control. Such loyalty to the regime was doubtless earned in part by the Obama administration's crucial rubber stamp on the spree of unchallenged organizational acquisitions that made Big Tech so big: by Biden official Tim Wu's count, Google acquired 214 companies, ninety-one for Amazon, and sixty-seven for Facebook.[4] The Obama-era enlargement of Big Tech was doubtless a response to the regime's quest for continued global dominance amid the return of great-power competition.

REFOCUSING OURSELVES ON REAL GOALS

The question is how to right the ship. Some critics of establishment conservatism from the Right understand that the military-industrial behemoth is never going away and that we would be foolish to try and dismantle it. They think instead that we must, as Eisenhower advised, try to control it. Some on the Right – "integralists" on the Catholic side and "Christian Nationalists" on the Protestant – propose swapping our current secular masters for religious ones. Other conservatives propose not to commandeer the machine but to modify it, using legislation or executive action to restrict the features of certain apps or to increase their accessibility, or to break up or ban companies seen as especially bad for the Right, for children, or for national security.[5]

These would-be solutions, whether rooted in more religious or more political urges, will not bring digital technology to heel in a fruitful way. For that, only the free and soulful technological exchange of socioeconomic energy among the people will suffice. That is, the same patterns and principles that established and enshrined the American way of life need to be reproduced and protected in the realm of our basic digital technologies. Compulsory use of these technologies to celebrate or observe official woke state religion must be prohibited. Surveillance and punishment of individuals and groups in an effort to prevent violations before they happen cannot be allowed. Instead, the government and its Big Tech arm must permit online freedom of speech and association in our commercial and cultural life. Ours must be a mature citizenry that "keeps and bears" fundamentally dangerous tech like smartphones, the internet, high-powered processors, and computational protocols, using these things to strengthen, not undermine, our spiritual health, our physical vitality, and our human identity. If we fail here, we become impotent slaves, no matter how notionally well-ordered. And we cease to be US citizens in the truest sense: America has always been, and must be, a large commercial republic.

The Right – indeed, anyone – should focus their political agenda. To get there, we must first and foremost stop seeing ourselves as hostages to technological development. To restore our life and our country, and to become good masters of the machines that have swamped our world, we must stand up and take responsibility for what our computers do, not leaving the work to a priestly caste of administrative machine worshippers. This means not blindly accepting the latest wow-machine, but learning for ourselves what these machines do and how to make them behave differently. High-powered processors can run streaming video games and live pornography – or they can mine Bitcoin to build independent marketplaces for goods and services that are virtuous as well as valuable. Social media can produce infinite scrolls of gossip and entertainment – or it can rebuild productive political action on the basis of trusted personal credentialing within close communities. Surveillance technology can keep its nose out of citizens' business. Elected representatives can put the brakes on suicide pods and artificial wombs. The woke religion can be disestablished as America's reigning justice algorithm. To be sure, a dogged minority of tech founders in America is hard at work using protocols and platforms to make technology support, not undermine, our national identity. But without a broad-based public constituency to support this work and to take the lead in deciding the direction of innovation and the wisdom of research agendas, entrenched institutional elites will steamroll or even prohibit opposition within and outside of government.

The bottom line is this: Americans' right to keep and bear this computational machinery must no longer be infringed. If this right goes, America goes. The right to compute and to communicate and to associate through computing is implicit already in the First and Second Amendments. That digital technologies, such as smartphones, GPUs, and Bitcoin, are "dual-use" – with potential military applications – is no counterargument. These technologies arose from military research, and restricting our use of them to entertainment, especially when that entertainment is destructive to us and our freedoms, does the opposite of protecting our security or our country's. Americans must be free to acquire and to use computational technology in financial, economic, social, and political ways that reflect and advance their interests, without federal or state surveillance, censorship, tracking, manipulation, or prohibition. The citizenry is well aware that the social justice and social credit system built around them is hostile to their commercial and cultural life. Without legal and political support from their elected officials, they will hesitate to build new digital organizations, institutions, and businesses that use leading tech to strengthen our country and our humanity. And after not too long it will be too late. That is why states and, if possible, federal lawmakers must prioritize and pass digital rights amendments, which are broad enough to protect innovation by the people without picking winners and losers through invasive and arbitrary policies.

For our constitution and our republican form of government to endure, it must be extended into cyberspace, and the executive and judiciary branches must not stand in the way. Lawmakers and policymakers must resist the temptation to create dueling laundry lists of rights to particular online practices. The constitutional crisis created by our regime's response to digital technology can only be resolved by amendments, which respond to regime-level digital threats and avoid further aggrandizing the administrative state.

Formalizing the protection of computational and digital rights will shelter Americans from the terror and paralysis they feel in the face of technology's alienating acceleration toward a future in which they have no purpose and play only a servile role. Such a digital bill of rights will shield citizens from the federal apparatus, including the SEC, the DHS, the IRS, and many other intelligence agencies and affiliate organizations that today deprive Americans not only of free speech but of the free association without which free speech is but a parody.

Moreover, such a digital bill of rights will infuse into our digital infrastructure the vitality that produces things of durable and lasting value, instead of trying to replace and substitute our innate human dynamism with digital automation and simulation. It will knock the false god of the machine down to size and help dismantle the establishment of the cyborg church by the woke administrative state. And it will free Americans from having to rely on the occasional Elon Musk to claw out some modest protection against the Left while increasing our dependence on centralized tech. America has always been a commercial republic, and it is in the commerce of the people where our lifeblood must flow, especially in the digital age. To reassert salutary human control over technology in America, it does not suffice for conservatives to tell the woke regime what to do. Confident Americans must themselves tell our most powerful computational devices and protocols how to strengthen our economy and more importantly our hearts and souls – freely writing programs, commanding protocols, and wielding hardware to build new markets and institutions consistent with their ancient religious faith and their founding political principles.

NOTES

1   Dwight D. Eisenhower, "Farewell Address," transcript of speech delivered at the White House, Washington, DC, January 17, 1961, https://www.presidency.ucsb.edu/documents/farewell-radio-and-television-address-the-american-people.
2   Klon Kitchen, "Invoking 'Big Tech' as an Accusation Can Endanger American Security," *The Hill*, October 15, 2021, https://thehill.com/opinion/technology/576267-invoking-big-tech-as-an-accusation-can-endanger-american-security/.
3   Mariana Mazzucato, *The Entrepreneurial State: Debunking Public vs. Private Sector Myths* (London: Penguin Books, 2018).
4   Tim Wu, "How Google and Amazon Got Away With Not Being Regulated," *Wired*, November 13, 2018, https://www.wired.com/story/book-excerpt-curse-of-bigness/.
5   See the agenda laid out by Conservative Partnership Institute senior director of policy Rachel Bovard in "Here's What Republicans Need to Do to Truly Take on Big Tech," Texas Scorecard, March 15, 2022, https://texasscorecard.com/commentary/bovard-heres-what-republicans-need-to-do-to-truly-take-on-big-tech/.

A CENTURY OF IMPOTENCY

Conservative Failure
and the Administrative State

Theodore Wold

JAMES LANDIS IS widely credited with crafting the theoretical architecture supporting President Roosevelt's radical reconstruction – and expansion – of the federal government. Landis shrewdly both established and legitimized the regulatory state, including Roosevelt's creation of new federal administrative agencies, by offering the regulatory state as the solution to the problem of modern governance: the administrative state "is, in essence, our generation's answer to the inadequacy of the judicial and legislative process."[1] The Landis premise took concrete shape through Roosevelt's expansion of the regulatory state, and in doing so, it brought to fruition Woodrow Wilson's progressive intellectual project: rule by experts, insulated from the popular will.[2]

Landis believed the "the administrative process" for which he advocated would "spring from the *inadequacy* of a simply tripartite form of government to deal with modern problems" because modern problems were simply too large and complex to be entrusted to the system based on the separation of powers instituted by our nation's founders.[3] Landis framed this innovation as *consistent* with separation of powers principles because he believed the separation of powers called both for separation but also *coordination* among the branches, and he saw the administrative state as essential to creating that coordination:

> If the doctrine of separation of power implies division, it also implies balance, and balance calls for equality. The creation of administrative power may be the means for the preservation of that balance, so that paradoxically enough, though it may seem in theoretic violation of the doctrine of the separation of powers, it may in matter of fact be the means for the preservation of the content of that doctrine.[4]

What the tripartite branches could not coordinate among themselves directly, Landis believed administrative agencies could coordinate as a substitute. Landis then aimed to create administrative agencies that *themselves* combined the three aspects of government. Years later, the Administrative Procedure Act codified this three-branches-in-one-agency approach to administrative power, defining not only rulemaking authority for federal agencies (a quasi-legislative power), but also adjudicative authority (a quasi-judicial power).

In reality, Landis's three-branches-in-one-agency theory never comported with the separation of powers principles that the Founders embedded in our Constitution. But even if it *could* have been reconciled with those principles as a theoretical matter, the past one hundred years have demonstrated that the administrative state is the single biggest threat that faces the Constitution and the republic it establishes. What began as a type of separation-of-powers "innovation" beyond the Constitution has persisted as nothing less than tyranny. The vast majority of our governance today is created, maintained, and enforced by unelected bureaucrats who are almost entirely insulated from accountability to any branch of government, let alone the people.

This reality was never on fuller display than during the Trump administration, as I witnessed firsthand. From President Trump's inauguration forward, the recalcitrant federal bureaucracy slow-walked his policies, including policy promises that were central to his victorious 2016 campaign (and that therefore commanded significant support from the American people). The Army Corps of Engineers dragged its feet in finalizing plans for the construction of a border wall. The Department of Education refused to withdraw Obama-era memoranda on Title IV and disparate impact. Bureaucrats at the Department of State ultimately blocked efforts to require "extreme vetting" for foreign nationals entering the United States. The idea that the federal bureaucracy is accountable to the president is a mirage.

And yet, for decades now, conservatives have failed to mount any fundamental challenge to the central Landis claim undergirding the administrative state: the inadequacy of the self-governing tripartite branches. There lies the problem for conservative reforms of the administrative state as they have been proposed for the last forty years. Landis believed the complexity of modern problems demanded the administrative state as a solution, and by and large, even conservatives have agreed.

In fact, when conservatives have dared to oppose the administrative state, they have framed their opposition through an economic lens: the administrative state is a vehicle for regulation and government control of the market. As such, conservatives' tools for combatting it have focused almost exclusively on curtailing the authority of the administrative state to promulgate new regulations and affixing costs to its enactments. In this view, the administrative state as seen through green eyeshades is a problem only because it is profligate and burdens the marketplace, not because "coordination" may now work in conflict with the policy preferences and reanimated desires for political control of a free people. The tyranny of the administrative state is not merely an economic tyranny: it is a tyranny over all purposes of government, a capturing of the people's power over all political questions, not merely pocketbook questions.

Perhaps it has been easy for conservatives to adopt the Landis premise because before FDR's remaking of the federal government, conservatives were already committed to the idea that some modern problems were so complex they could not be resolved through the basic instruments of self-governance and instead required the intervention of experts.

When Landis was previewing his ideas publicly prior to working in the executive branch, President Herbert Hoover signed the Reconstruction Finance Corporation Act, creating a new, government-sponsored financial institution that would fit right in with the "independent agencies" of today. The Reconstruction Finance Corporation was a quasi-public corporation that borrowed its funds over its lifetime almost entirely from the federal government for the purpose of lending directly to banks and other financial institutions. The RFC was composed of professionals hired outside the civil service system, and the federal government appointed its executive officers and board of directors. Even the leading conservative of the time, Senator Robert Taft of Ohio, favored the RFC and would later back New Deal agency programs, including subsidized loans for farmers and homeowners and accelerated public works spending. In retrospect, the RFC was a template for the New Deal federal agencies that FDR later created, including the Tennessee Valley Authority, a quasi-governmental corporation, the Works Progress Administration, the Federal Communications Commission, the Federal Housing Administration, and the Securities and Exchange Commission. More importantly, it was a harbinger of decades of conservative capitulation: In creating the RFC, conservatives like Taft had essentially adopted the Progressive view that modern problems required credentialed experts and technocratic governance. As Taft would posit, laissez-faire individualism was a political-philosophical perspective that required mediation from governmental authorities.

The solution to the administrative state, however, depends on *resisting* the Landis premise and accepting instead that even modern problems can be solved *without* administrative agencies, or that the price of solving those problems is too high if administrative agencies are the only means of doing so.

THE FOUR PAST ATTEMPTS TO RESTRAIN
THE ADMINISTRATIVE STATE

THE ADMINISTRATIVE PROCEDURE ACT OF 1946

The Administrative Procedure Act might be considered the first attempt at restraining the administrative state. Passed in 1946, the APA followed FDR's Second New Deal by about a decade and came at a time of concern in the United States for the rapid rise of the administrative state. Conservatives publicly worried that its growth impaired individual liberties (by allowing federal agencies to impose regulations that burdened individuals' freedom to work and contract, even without explicit authorization from Congress) and the free market (by allowing federal agencies to establish burdensome regulations or effectively pick "winners" and "losers" and interfere with otherwise-free markets). Liberals advocated for the administrative state based on the Landis premise – namely, that unelected experts were needed to create policies and regulations capable of meeting the demands of "modern society."

The APA attempted to assuage concerns about the administrative state's power by grafting onto the administrative state the same types of due process protections that applied to other branches of government. It created formal and informal rulemaking processes to regularize the administrative state's quasi-legislative activities, and it created formal and informal adjudicative process to regularize the administrative state's quasi-judicial activities. It also specified conditions for review of agency action by the judicial branch.

But although the APA was seen at the time as a bipartisan compromise, it was in retrospect a compromise that leaned heavily leftward because it endorsed – and even advanced – the Landis premise. The essential compromise of the APA was biased *in favor of* a large administrative state: the administrative state was a necessary governmental innovation demanded by the complexity of modern society, and the only restraints that Congress could place on its activities were marginal procedural protections intended to mimic the due process protections that applied to the constitutional branches of government. These protections increased public participation in rulemaking by requiring pre-rulemaking notice to and comment from the public, and they increased regularity in agency decision-making by standardizing agency processes. But they did little, if anything, to curtail the reach of federal agency power or to protect the primacy of the constitutional branches of government as set against the unelected and essentially insulated activities of the administrative state.

CHEVRON DEFERENCE

Many prominent conservative jurists, including Justice Antonin Scalia and DC Circuit Judge Kenneth Starr, spent a generation advocating for *Chevron* deference, which was intended to prevent liberal courts from imposing their policy preferences on the executive branch by preserving a deferentially drawn sphere of decision-making in which executive agencies were free to operate. But in protecting this deferential sphere of decision-making power, *Chevron* deference has ultimately proved to be incapable of checking the administrative state's power and growth. *Chevron* deference originated with the 1984 decision *Chevron U.S.A. v. Natural Resources Defense Council*,[5] which created a two-part test for judicial review of the agency's construction of a statute passed by Congress. First, a court must determine "whether Congress has directly spoken to the precise question at issue"; and if it has, and "the intent of Congress is clear, that is the end of the matter," for both the court and the agency "must give effect to the unambiguously expressed intent of Congress."[6] Second, "if the statute is silent or ambiguous with respect to the specific issue, the question for the court is whether the agency's answer is based on a permissible construction of the statute"; if it is, it is entitled to the court's deference.[7]

Chevron itself embraced the Landis premise that difficult policy questions required experts to resolve. It posited that where a statute is ambiguous, Congress might have "consciously desired ... that those with great expertise and charged with responsibility for administering the provision would be in a better position to do so" than Congress.[8] But even if Congress had not so determined, the opinion advocated deference to experts: "Judges are not experts in the field, and are not part of either political branch of the Government," so it should not be for judges to resolve complex policy issues.[9] The *Chevron* Court assured itself that the deference it instituted presented no separation-of-powers problem because "while agencies are not directly accountable to the people, the Chief Executive is, and it is entirely appropriate for this political branch of the Government to make such policy choice."[10] Today, such an argument is untenable, in light of the entrenched nature of the administrative state and the little (or, more often, utter lack) of executive control over its machinations.

Chevron deference is a legal doctrine incompatible with substantial self-governance because it translates statutory ambiguity into complete deference to the *least* accountable arm of modern government – the administrative state.

While conservative jurists today are more skeptical of the doctrine (and, indeed, may even be willing to replace it), the conservative jurists of yesterday embraced it. None other than Justice Scalia himself argued for a relatively expansive definition of *Chevron* deference. In discussing *Chevron*'s "step one," Justice Scalia explained that "congressional intent must be regarded as 'ambiguous' not just when no interpretation is even marginally better than any other, but rather when two or more reasonable, though not necessarily equally valid, interpretations exist."[11] In other words, *Chevron* requires courts to defer to federal agencies even when those agencies adopt clearly *inferior* interpretations of the statutory text passed and signed by the politically accountable branches. It is no wonder, then that the doctrine of *Chevron* deference has done little to check the power and proliferation of the administrative state.

REINS ACT

More recently, conservative legislators in Congress have introduced and advocated for the REINS Act (Regulations from the Executive in Need of Scrutiny Act). Senator Rand Paul (R-KY) first introduced the REINS Act in 2013. The act creates categories of "major" and "nonmajor" rules and requires congressional approval by both houses of Congress before "major" rules can take effect.[12]

The REINS Act, however, begins from the Landis premise as well – namely, that the authority to craft policy properly belongs to experts in the federal agencies. Rather than remove that power from agencies or shift lawmaking authority back to Congress in the first instance, the REINS Act leaves regulatory power with federal agencies in the very same size and scope in which it exists today and merely imposes a requirement of congressional approval on *some* regulatory actions. But even the definition of *which* regulatory actions require such approval is both ambiguous and inadequate. The REINS Act defines a "major rule" to be a rule with "an annual effect on the economy of $100 million or more," or one that causes "major increase in costs or prices for consumers, individual industries, Federal, State, or local government agencies, or geographic regions," or one that has "significant adverse effects on competition, employment, investment, productivity, innovation, or the ability of United States-based enterprises to compete with foreign-based enterprises in domestic and export markets."[13] These definitions are unsatisfactory as a drafting exercise, since they are open to interpretation and admit of ambiguities. Who will determine which rules satisfy these definitions? Who knows?

Worse, these definitions are completely inadequate because they emphasize economic impact alone, as if the administrative state poses only pocketbook harms. Edicts from the Department of Education about the treatment of trans students in the classroom; Department of Commerce regulations about the classification (and therefore, legal availability) of certain firearms and accessories; Department of Defense allowances for same-sex spouse benefits or sex-change surgeries – all of these are culturally transformative regulations that fall short of the economic impacts that trigger greater congressional oversight in the REINS Act.

The REINS Act clearly demonstrates the view of its conservative sponsors and supporters that federal agencies have too much authority to take actions with too great significance; yet rather than remove such authority from those agencies and require *Congress* to exercise it, these legislators are content merely to give themselves an up-or-down vote after the fact – and even then, only for regulations with considerable *economic* impact, not those that answer transformative cultural questions about which ordinary people and their legislators expect to express views and direct policy. Thus, even in the REINS Act, the premise that expertise, after all, lies with the agencies still reigns.

The REINS Act is notable – and rightfully criticized – for another reason, too. It provides that all other rules outside the definitions stated above are "nonmajor" rules, which Congress may *disapprove* under the REINS Act. But surely this is a fact that need not be stated. Of course Congress can negate an action of a regulatory agency if it chooses. The fact that legislators see the REINS Act as a vehicle to state that power is alarming, but it is also illustrative of Congress's impotence in the face of the size and scope of the modern administrative state.

REGULATORY OVERSIGHT AND DEREGULATION

Republicans have long pursued a deregulation strategy as another antidote to the proliferation of the administrative state, although with no more success than any other strategy discussed here. Deregulation and regulatory oversight strategies are executive efforts to exert more control over agency rulemaking, but these strategies fail because the executive lacks fundamental control over the administrative state.

The Reagan administration's regulatory oversight required agencies to prepare cost-benefit analyses for major rules and required that agencies only issue regulations that maximize net benefits (defined as social benefits minus social costs). Similar to the REINS Act, this approach focuses not on the substance of federal regulations but only on their potential costs (and estimating costs depends on accurate forecasting – a dubious proposition). The error of this approach is on display in immigration policy. Federal regulations that grant visas to hundreds of thousands of immigrants might be economically "scored" as beneficial to the country's gross domestic product, but that cost analysis, even if accurate, speaks to only *one* aspect of immigration policy and neglects the transformational effect of immigration on culture, the allocation of labor, the displacement of American workers, and domestic wages. The Reagan administration's regulatory policy focused myopically on the economic impact of regulation, as if regulations could only pose harm by undertaking *economic* decisions without the people's participation through their elected representatives, not social, cultural, or political decisions, despite their obviously transformative nature.

Besides, the Reagan administration's regulatory oversight program can be judged by its fruits. By the final two years of that administration, the pace of new regulations had increased, and that increase continued into the Bush administration. The power of the administrative state to dictate the lives of Americans, divorced from political oversight, did not shrink; it grew.

For its part, the Trump administration attempted a new regulatory strategy targeted more precisely at *de*regulation. The Trump administration pledged to remove two regulations for every one enacted, and even made the promise official by promulgating it in an executive order. The policy sounded good but faced legal and procedural hurdles. For one, *de*regulation requires federal agencies to go through the same notice-and-comment process that applies when affirmatively regulating, so the policy could, at most, require agencies to *initiate* the withdrawal of two regulations for every one proposed. From that point forward, the deregulatory and regulatory efforts had to follow different trajectories, leaving no guarantee that two regulations would *actually* be withdrawn for every one imposed. Nor was there any guarantee that the regulations targeted for withdrawal would be equal in significance to any new regulation being proposed.

Ultimately, the Trump administration's deregulatory initiatives resulted in the enactment of fewer new regulations compared to its predecessor administrations, and the Trump administration did try to remove many regulations as well, but many of these efforts foundered on legal grounds.

Most of the Trump administration's important deregulatory actions, like barring asylum eligibility for certain individuals entering the United States at the southern border or rolling back the Obama administration's Clean Power Plan, were litigated immediately and enjoined. Overall, the Trump administration's track record in litigation was dismal. By one assessment carried out by the Institute for Policy Integrity, the Trump administration succeeded in defending its regulatory actions in court fifty-eight times but was unsuccessful two hundred times. That means a mere 22 percent of the Trump administration's regulatory actions survived judicial review.

The Trump administration's deregulatory efforts come the closest of any conservative strategy to resisting the Landis premise itself: at least under President Trump, the executive branch attempted not merely to layer procedural requirements onto the regulatory process or create greater oversight for economically significant laws, but to actually *reduce regulation directly*. But the Landis premise is so deeply embedded in the modern regulatory state that executive action alone cannot unseat it. Deregulation requires the same procedures as regulation, and it is subject to judicial review, which places it ultimately beyond the executive's sole control. The administrative state results in tyranny because it operates without political oversight. Presidential oversight is an illusion. The president sits atop the bureaucracy but can have precious little effect on its conduct. The president cannot order agencies to act without following the burdensome and time-consuming notice-and-comment procedures; nor can the president rescind past agency action without undertaking the same burdens – to say nothing of the general unresponsiveness of the bureaucracy to pursuing any policy with haste or diligence.

A PROPER DIAGNOSIS

Conservatives have failed to restrain the administrative state because they have accepted the Landis premise – that the administrative state is a necessary governmental innovation required by the complexity of modern society. This intellectual capitulation is what ensures that the balance of power in this country will remain not only in Washington, DC, but specifically with the largely unaccountable administrative state. The federal bureaucracy is the home of the most prestigious jobs in public service, the best salaries and benefits, the greatest esteem, and the most power. Educated and well-qualified individuals who aspire to power and influence want to join the administrative apparatus. These are the experts, after all, and we have entrusted to them the power to rule us.

Never before has the fallacy of expert governance been so exposed as it is today, following the emergence of COVID-19 in the United States. The problem of COVID-19 placed federal public health officials on the national stage, demanding that their expertise direct and save the nation. And they failed. They opposed masking before demanding it universally; they advocated destructive lockdowns that uncannily reflected liberal biases (like shuttering churches on account of public singing while permitting in-person alcohol sales); they ignored the science of child infection in favor of virtual schooling that has disadvantaged (or worse) a generation of children; and they opposed a vaccine as "rushed" when it was President Trump's accomplishment, only to mandate the same vaccine at the expense of one's livelihood once President Trump was no longer in office. *These* are the experts. Their training prepared them for this moment, and when the nation needed them, they proved themselves to be credentialed political hacks.

That is why any conservative response to the administrative state must begin with the counter-Landis premise: that rule by experts and technocrats *is not* the self-evident and necessary solution to the problem of modernity, and that in fact, rule by experts and technocrats is just as likely to *harm* the nation, by impeding individual freedom and restraining economic prosperity. The so-called "expertise" of the administrative state is not expertise at all but simply politics unbridled: it is liberal hegemony divorced from democratic accountability.

The only prescription for the administrative state is *deconstruction*. Dismantling. Eliminating at least some of the nearly two million civilian federal employees (let alone the legions of federal contractors) who comprise the unaccountable and uncontrolled administrative state.

A future Republican president cannot deconstruct even a portion of the federal bureaucracy without significant preplanning that begins well before assuming office. Any Republican presidential candidate must catalog a list of obsolete federal agencies and programs and articulate to the American people the waste and excess required to maintain these frivolous bureaucratic outlets.

At the same time, a future Republican president must be willing to articulate a broader vision for deconstructing significant portions of all federal agencies, including recruiting cabinet officials who are committed to downsizing their agencies.

Realistically, as the experience of the Trump administration shows, a project to deconstruct the administrative state will depend on the participation of Congress in order to be successful. Taking down even a single regulation requires considerable effort and carries little guarantee of success, as shown by the Trump administration's track record in legal challenges to deregulatory efforts. Taking down entire swaths of the federal bureaucracy will face even greater obstacles, including in the form of legal challenges from career federal employees, many of whom are unionized and enjoy special employment protections. Significant policy reforms can proceed only from possession of significant political power. The greatest inroads will be made against the administrative state when the coordinated power of *two* branches can be brought to bear against it.

A tangible deconstruction along these lines will only be possible if conservatives begin by deconstructing the *mindset* of the administrative state. Rule by experts is foreign to our constitutional separation of powers; it is incompatible with democratic accountability and legitimacy; and it has proved itself a failure in our own lifetimes. The political branches and the states must be returned their lawmaking power, and conservatives must relearn to express confidence in that power. Conservatives must accept that some things simply will not be done by a smaller administrative state, *and that is the point*. Policies that can be achieved only through tyranny are too costly. To the extent that they deserve to be pursued, they must be housed in branches or levels of government sufficiently responsive to the people and their elected representatives so that tyranny is averted.

How does this translate into actionable policies for a new Republican administration? With difficulty, of course, but some measures come to mind, particularly where a Republican-led executive branch can work cooperatively with a Republican-led Congress.

First, draft and pass legislation to require a universal sunset for all agency regulations. As it stands, agencies enact regulations frequently but rarely take any down (and, as the experience of the Trump administration shows, taking down regulations is fraught with legal challenges and is not guaranteed to succeed). Yet many good reasons exist for revisiting regulations at some point after their enactment. When regulations are enacted, predictions about their costs, benefits, and effectiveness are speculative at best. Fifteen years on, more can be said about whether a particular regulation has been justified. Mandatory sunsets also require Congress to act if a regulation is to be retained, which restores at least some measure of democratic accountability to a bureaucracy that has been allowed to otherwise run amok.

Second, repeal and reverse large portions of the Pendleton Civil Service Reform Act of 1883 and the Civil Service Reform Act of 1978, with the imposition of term limits for bureaucrats. These acts standardized federal government hiring and required that bureaucrats be primarily hired as nonpolitical positions of expertise. This has had the effect of stultifying the bureaucracy, turning hiring into a quota system and exacerbating the problem of unaccountable bureaucrats remaining in their posts for a lifetime. These reforms could have the advantage of surprise, an advantage already squandered for the Schedule F reforms, which the Trump administration pursued by executive order and the Biden administration immediately rescinded. Much attention has been paid to Schedule F reforms, allowing the Left to mount a public relations counterattack. But finding new ways to control the bureaucracy could allow for the element of surprise once again.

Third, Republicans should ban or restrict public-private partnerships in governance. The idea is a radical one because, at present, both the Left and the Right support these kinds of arrangements. Because government is perpetually behind the private sector in terms of technology, sophistication, innovation, and general capabilities – so the thinking goes – partnering with the private sector to provide government services allows government to compensate for its inadequacies. But this compensation means that government remains able to grow its mandate despite its ineptitude, fanning into an ever-more-expansive oversight of Americans' lives, *and* it does so at the cost of sharing data with private sector businesses that desperately seek to own and profit from it. Consider the Obamacare exchanges, for example, which are run by private entities and host the personal health, financial, employment, and other data of *millions* of Americans – data that private entities are happy to contract with the federal government to control. These kinds of partnerships present increasing threats to the American people (including the threat of a growing and unaccountable federal bureaucracy) even as they decrease in visibility (think "government" websites owned and operated by private entities, with consumers none the wiser). Congress can and should exercise oversight over whether and how the federal government outsources its work to the private sector because private sector innovation and nimbleness allow the administrative state to do things that are beyond its capabilities. Obviously, some nuance is required, because the Department of Defense cannot help but contract with private entities to build military aircraft, and no one would suggest otherwise. Yet the proliferation of public-private partnerships for the purpose of growing government and ceding Americans' data to the private sector is a real problem and one that deserves the attention of any future Republican administration.

These reforms require Congressional cooperation and significant preparation in advance of a Republican presidential administration. But if accomplished, they promise durable change to the administrative state. To be clear: their success depends on the wholesale rejection of the Landis premise and a complete commitment to the urgent necessity of dismantling the administrative state. Upending the belief that only rule by experts can accomplish the aims of modern governance must be the goal of any future Republican administration.

NOTES

1   James M. Landis, *The Administrative Process* (New Haven, CT: Yale University Press, 1938), 46.

2   For a thorough analysis of the deep intellectual roots of the administrative state, see Ronald J. Pestrito, *Woodrow Wilson and the Roots of Modern Liberalism* (Lanham, MD: Rowman and Littlefield Press, 2005); John Marini, *Unmasking the Administrative State: The Crisis of American Politics in the Twenty-First Century* (New York: Encounter Books, 2019).

3   Landis, *Administrative Process*, 1.

4   Landis, *Administrative Process*, 46.

5   *Chevron U. S. A. Inc. v. Natural Resources Defense Council, Inc., et al.*, 467 U.S. 837 (1984), https://tile.loc.gov/storage-services/service/ll/usrep/usrep467/usrep467837/usrep467837.pdf.

6   *Chevron*, 467 U.S., at 842–43.

7   *Chevron*, 467 U.S., at 843.

8   *Chevron*, 467 U.S. at 865.

9   *Chevron*, 467 U.S. at 865.

10 *Chevron*, 467 U.S. at 865.

11 Antonin Scalia, "Judicial Deference to Administrative Interpretations of Law," *Duke Law Journal* 38, no. 3 (June 1989): 511, 520.

12 Regulations from the Executive in Need of Scrutiny Act of 2021, S. 68, 117th Cong. (2021).

13 Regulations from the Executive in Need of Scrutiny Act of 2021.

DECONSTRUCTING
THE DEEP STATE

Robert Delahunty

THE PROBLEM OF the "Deep State" is a central element of the broader problem known as the Republican Security Dilemma,[1] which James Madison lucidly explained in *The Federalist*, no. 37. Liberal democracies, Madison argued, encounter an inescapable tension between having a government that possesses the "requisite stability and energy" to hold foreign and domestic enemies at bay, while also not being so powerful as to endanger "liberty and . . . the republican form." Madisonian concerns about this tension have intensified in recent years, as the reach and power of the "Deep State" have become more obvious, especially during the Trump presidency and its aftermath.[2]

The term "Deep State" is undoubtedly imprecise but, if clarified, may be useful analytically.[3] Although its existence has been questioned,[4] we have it on the authority of former FBI director James Comey that "there is a deep state in this sense. There is a collection of people, CIA, NSA, FBI in the United State military services who care passionately about getting it right, who care passionately about the values we try to talk about."[5] As Comey suggested, the core of the "Deep State" is the eighteen organizations comprising the Intelligence Community,[6] but it extends to the foreign policy establishment[7] and the military high command.[8] Former officials in these agencies should often be included in this network.

The tension Madison diagnosed was easier to resolve throughout most of our country's history, when two large oceans and land borders with weaker powers shielded us from foreign encroachments. But, as the political scientist John Herz argued in the early years of the Atomic Age, nuclear weaponry eroded those traditional defenses.[9] And the first large-scale attack on the continental United States in two centuries, on September 11, 2001, drove the point home. The need for military operations abroad, and for closer surveillance of the American population at home, had, it was felt, become acute.

THE WAR ON TERROR AND HOW WE GOT HERE

Two developments that Madison could not have foreseen have aggravated the danger that the Deep State poses to American liberties: the War on Terror and the Culture of Fear.

Our national security apparatus now exists on a colossal scale. This spring, the Defense Department proposed a FY2023 budget of $813 billion for national defense, of which $773 billion was for the Defense Department itself.[10] The Defense Department employs about 2.91 million service members and civilians at around 4,800 sites in more than 160 countries.[11] The nonmilitary Intel Community budget request for FY23 was $67.1 billion.[12]

The 9/11 attacks triggered one of the largest spending sprees in American history: in the decade following those attacks (which saw wars in Afghanistan and Iraq), military spending more than doubled, representing at its peak about 20 percent of all federal outlays. According to the Costs of War project, as of 2019, "the United States has appropriated and is obligated to spend an estimated $6.4 Trillion through Fiscal Year 2020 in budgetary costs related to and caused by the post-9/11 wars."[13] The War on Terror also stimulated the creation of vast new databases and led to sweeping relaxations of legal controls over monitoring and gathering private communications by American citizens.[14] According to then-director Robert Mueller, in the decade after 9/11 the FBI, which before 9/11 had primarily been a law enforcement agency, was transformed "into a national security organization that fuses traditional law enforcement and intelligence missions."[15] (The FBI's extensive intelligence gathering capacity is now commonly used for warrantless surveillance of American citizens.[16]) The federal government's Terrorism Information and Prevention System (TIPS) recruited as many as one in twenty-four Americans to report on the activities of other citizens, and entailed extensive collusion with corporations like OfficeMax (which reported to law enforcement on "questionable requests" for document copying).[17]

Not only were many of these measures dangerous to liberty; they were overkill. In the aftermath of 9/11, at least 263 government agencies dedicated to counterterrorism were organized or reorganized by 2016. In that period, there were sixty-two documented cases of terrorism and about one hundred apprehensions of terrorists. Thus, the United States created or reorganized more than two entire counterterrorism governmental bodies for every terrorist apprehended or arrested.[18]

THE CULTURE OF FEAR

At the same time, as writers like British sociologist Frank Furedi have argued, Anglo-American societies have been incubating a "culture of fear" – even college campuses, among the safest places in the world, are seen as high-risk environments where "you take your life into your own hands."[19] The readiness of so much of the American (and Western) population to submit to often arbitrary mandates during the Covid lockdowns without considering their collateral costs attests to the growing hegemony of fear in our societies.

The causes of such pervasive but irrational fear are unclear. Furedi suggests that fear arises in societies that suffer from the absence of a moral consensus, causing individuals to value nothing more than bare survival, safety, and health.[20] We live, he argues, in a moral universe of "authority without meaning."[21] The philosopher Lars Svendsen believes that "the fear society is a product of utopian thinking."[22] For the political scientist Corey Robin, some persons desire the widespread experience of fear because they believe that only fear "can turn us from isolated men and women into a united people."[23] For two decades, the United States has been continually on a war footing or in a state of emergency. Fear and the Deep State are reciprocal versions of each other.[24] "Fear entrepreneurs," as Furedi calls them, have been in the ascendant in the government for decades.

A CRITICAL POINT?

With these developments as a backdrop, we seem to be reaching a critical point. There is a growing risk that the combination of the vast and intrusive state security apparatus created during the War on Terror might now be turned against legitimate political opposition within the country, and that manufactured fears of domestic extremism might be used to justify repressive measures. The Biden administration's National Security for Countering Domestic Terrorism, issued in June 2021,[25] is the first such government document to address that topic. It reflects the fact that counterterrorism within the United States is no longer a matter of searching for foreign jihadists or their domestic allies. Since 9/11, jihadist terrorist attacks within the United States have become unusual, and have typically been the work of homegrown individuals.[26] But rather than reducing the domestic security apparatus in light of the receding threat of jihadism, Biden's strategy indicates that the apparatus will be repurposed to focus on domestic "extremism" from the Right. While downplaying the activities of Antifa or Black Lives Matter, the intelligence community affirms that "racially or ethnically motivated violent extremists" and "militia violent extremists" pose the most lethal threats to domestic security.[27] Without denying the reality of such threats,[28] the actual practice of the Justice Department and the FBI under Biden strongly suggests that the focus of "domestic security" investigations will be political conservatives exercising their constitutional rights, such as parents of school children objecting to mask mandates, pro-life activists and licensed gun owners.[29] If the Biden administration were genuinely concerned with countering domestic extremism, why did it drop half the federal charges – including felony charges – against Antifa defendants in Portland, Oregon?[30] Why did it fail to enforce the law against protesters outside the homes of Supreme Court Justices after the leak of the *Dobbs* decision?[31] Why, after purportedly investigating attacks on churches and pro-life clinics by Jane's Revenge and other such extremists for months, has the FBI made no arrests of any suspects?[32] Does this violent onslaught on religious liberty not matter?[33] Is the FBI just incompetent – or is it pursuing a politicized, pro-abortion agenda? For the Biden administration and the intelligence community that services it, violent left-wing domestic extremism seems to be invisible.

Throughout the course of its deeply troubled history, the FBI has all too willingly lent itself to the repression of those it deemed "subversive," including antiwar protesters, civil rights activists, and labor union organizers. Indeed, it was the FBI's sordid dealings with such groups that prompted the investigations in the late 1970s by the (Senate) Church Commission and the (House) Pike Commission and the reforms of the FBI that ensued. The next Congress must ensure that this pattern of conduct, though with a different cast of domestic "subversives" and "extremists," does not occur again.

THE EMERGENCE OF THE DEEP STATE

How did the Deep State emerge? And can anything be done to tame it and reform it – or at least a central component of it, the FBI? The Deep State has been expanding for decades. Its rise was enabled by both Republican and Democratic presidents and members of Congress. President Harry Truman foresaw in 1945 that the FBI was tending in the direction of the Gestapo.[34] The Right (with a tiny handful of exceptions like Senator Rand Paul) must bear a major share of the blame: it has mindlessly saluted it, funded it, protected it, allowed itself to be used by it, and possibly been blackmailed by it.[35] Even after the disclosure of many of its appallingly antidemocratic activities in the past several years, "good" Republicans like Mike Pence,[36] Bill Barr,[37] Asa Hutchinson,[38] and Dan Crenshaw[39] have defended the FBI, occasionally trying to draw a distinction between the agency's leadership and its rank and file. These "good Republicans" have failed to ask themselves why, if the rank and file were so virtuous, only fourteen or so FBI whistleblowers have come forward after years of lawlessness by their agency?[40] (For the sake of comparison, the FBI recently asked Congress for $10.7 billion to support 36,945 positions, including 13,616 special agents, 3,287 intelligence analysts, and 20,042 professional staff.[41])

The Deep State has metastasized because of two twentieth-century world wars, a near half-century of Cold War, and (as discussed above) the War on Terror. It has also battened on fear of domestic disturbances, whether the Red Scare after World War I, the dread of labor unrest, domestic Communism and Soviet infiltration and espionage in the ensuing decades, the Civil Rights movement, the Black Panthers, the American Indian movement and the anti–Vietnam War protests of the 1960s, the dangers of Islamic radicalism in the early 2000s, or, currently, the supposedly "semifascist" threat posed by the millions of (overwhelmingly loyal and law-abiding) supporters of former President

Trump. The Deep State feeds on often delusive fears and insecurities, being obsessed with the idea that America's political institutions are always at grave risk, and that its people are seeded with treason and disloyalty. It manufactures and then exploits pseudo-crises, such as the current hoax about right-wing "extremism."[42] On the pretext of protecting domestic security and the integrity of elections from "disinformation," it colludes with an ideologically aligned Big Tech to censor and suppress political speech.[43]

TRUMP VERSUS THE DEEP STATE

With the fading of the threat of radical Islamic terrorism in the United States and the slow winding down of our wars in the Middle East, the Deep State needed a new adversary. It found it in the person of candidate, then President, Donald Trump. From the outset, Trump appeared to be antagonistic to the agenda and privileges of the Deep State. As Senator Chuck Schumer warned subsequently, he would pay for that.[44]

When historians review the Trump administration, they will see it as the story of a deep, continuing struggle between an elected president and the Deep State. The struggle began even before Trump's inauguration, when "the new notion that the national security bureaucracy might constitute a proper institutional check" on an elected but populist president began to take hold.[45] That phase saw Deep State efforts to sabotage Trump's campaign, spy on Trump Towers (as NSA Director, Admiral Mike Rogers, seems to have warned Trump soon after the election[46]), and set a perjury trap for his intended NSC chief, General Michael Fynn. It carried over into the early days of his presidency, with leaks of his conversations with his counterparts in Australia and Mexico. Most importantly, through the efforts of FBI director James Comey, it led to the appointment of Comey's friend and ally, former FBI director Robert Mueller, as special counsel with the charge of investigating what is now known to be a Clinton campaign–inspired hoax – the "Russian collusion" narrative. It induced Trump's attorney general, Jeff Sessions, to disqualify himself from supervising Mueller's two-year investigation on the specious grounds that he had had a conversation with the Russian ambassador. Mueller's investigation dragged on needlessly for two long years – past the 2018 midterm elections, which resulted in the Republicans' loss of the House – and ended in an abject admission that the collusion charge was spurious.

In a 2020 article titled "The FBI Scandal," the tough-minded journalist Eli Lake summarized the FBI's role in the Russian collusion matter in this way:

> The FBI relied on lurid, sketchy, and sleazy opposition research generated by former British spy Christopher Steele – information so spurious that even liberal news organizations briefed on the so-called Steele dossier before the 2016 election wouldn't touch it with a 10-foot pole. And it used that information in a specious, circular and misleading manner to keep that investigation afloat and active into the first two years of Trump's presidency. Even after the bureau had good reason to doubt its veracity, it didn't share the exculpatory information it had uncovered – not with the public, not with the courts, and not even with the Justice Department lawyers who were supposed to check its work.

The result was a debacle.[47]

More recent disclosures in the trial of Igor Danchenko (Steele's "source") confirm and amplify the "shocking malfeasance" of the FBI in the Russian collusion matter.[48] We have learned, for example, that the FBI withheld from Congress the information that it had offered Steele up to \$1 million to corroborate his dossier – and that he was unable to do so.[49] The FBI's offer underscores that it was aware that the allegations in the dossier were unfounded, even though it later affirmed under oath to the Foreign Intelligence Surveillance Court that they had been verified.

In effect, the FBI was offering a bounty for information leading to proof of Trump's guilt, while lying to the judiciary about the quality of its evidence.

THE DEEP STATE UNDER BIDEN

At a recent "United We Stand Summit" at the White House dedicated to countering "hate-filled violence," President Biden invoked the authority of the intelligence agencies to bolster this claim:

> Our very own intelligence agencies, our own intelligence agencies in the United States of America, have determined that domestic terrorism rooted in white supremacy is the gravest terrorist threat to our homeland today.[50]

Does this "determination" by "our very own intelligence agencies" convince anyone? Apparently so. According to a recent Harvard CAPS-Harris Poll,[51] almost three-fourths of Democrats believe that there are "tens of millions of dangerous MAGA Republicans."

Even granting that white supremacist groups pose a genuine threat to domestic security, it is grotesque to think that "tens of millions of MAGA Republicans" fall into that category. Yet that is precisely the conclusion that Biden, enabled and assisted by "our very own intelligence agencies," invites the American public to draw. This is hardly a cool and realistic analysis of the domestic threats that face the nation. It represents the weaponization of the intelligence community for use against tens of millions of Trump voters who comprise the core of the opposition to Biden's increasingly unpopular and flailing administration. Biden and the Deep State agents assisting him are not defending the nation and its institutions from dangerous threats. They are feeding paranoia, polarizing a divided nation even more deeply, endangering basic constitutional rights, and, in the process, building more powerful and more fearsome bureaucratic empires.

IS TAMING THE DEEP STATE POSSIBLE?

The question whether it is too late to tame the Deep State is fundamentally not an interesting one. The answer is that, regardless of whether or not it is too late, we simply have to try. The stakes for the American people and nation are too high to submit to the Deep State's rule. Here I will focus on the FBI.

REFORMING THE FBI

It is obvious that, as Congress is now constituted, a partisan divide will not permit fundamental reforms of the FBI. The FBI has aligned itself with the Democratic Party,[52] which will not allow any substantive reform measures to pass. So, too, will any Democratic president veto reforms. The only realistic chance of major reform therefore arises from the Republican Party.

The road to reform will be politically rough. Congressional Democrats, their media allies, and the FBI itself will be sure to brand reform proposals as an attempt to "politicize" the FBI. (It is also not unknown for the FBI to use false or derogatory information against politicians: J. Edgar Hoover kept secret, "private" files for that purpose,[53] and leaking disinformation serves the same end.[54]) There will be many "good" Republicans who support those attacks on reforms. Although the public is increasingly suspicious of the FBI's fairness and integrity, the agency retains substantial (if underserved) good will. It will require political courage of a high order to drive major changes through.

Nonetheless, the stakes are surpassingly high, and a corresponding effort is imperative. The current FBI, like the FBI of the 1970s, has manifestly become a threat to civil liberties, lawfully elected government, and the constitutional order. It requires remedies commensurate with the scale and severity of the abuses.

Many of the FBI's recent problems are owing to its *personnel*, particularly those in leadership positions in the Washington, DC office. Other problems are more of a *structural* nature. Congressional action can indirectly bring about some changes in FBI personnel; but for the most part, personnel measures are the pre-rogative of the executive branch, not the legislative. For example, Congress cannot constitutionally mandate the withholding of government salaries from named individuals, thus effectively discharging them.[55]

"Cleaning house" is therefore mainly a project for the next administration, though Congress can lend substantial support to that effort. And although Congress has more power to bring about structural than personnel changes in the FBI, these would seem to offer less immediate and direct relief to the conservative citizens and causes that the FBI is targeting. Personnel is policy, and bad personnel will make bad policy. Thus, without major personnel changes at the top in the Justice Department and the FBI, it is unlikely that those agencies' skewed enforcement pri-orities – such as targeting pro-life activists for arrest while not protecting churches and pro-life clinics[56] – will change until the next administration, even if Congress in the meantime enacts structural reforms in those agencies.

Apart from reforms, Congress can also use its power to block legislative initiatives that would make the current situation even worse. For example, Biden's national strategy indicates that the administration and the intelligence community will seek new statutory authorities to investigate purported threats of domestic extremism and terrorism.[57] Others in the administration and Democrats in Congress have worked overtime to fan such fears.[58] Any such proposals to expand the FBI's investigatory authority should be resisted; and funding to expand monitoring or surveil-lance of American citizens at home on grounds of "domestic security" should be curtailed. The FBI has ample (in fact, over-broad) investigatory authority already.[59] Its recent practice of targeting conservatives indicates that it is clearly unwise to give it either greater authority or more resources.

Instead of providing the FBI with additional funding and personnel for domestic security, Congress should slash those parts of the FBI's budget and reallocate resources to state and local police forces, relying on them to provide safety and security against domestic extremism. Local police have done excellent work in the past in controlling domestic extremism and violence,[60] and placing significant responsibility for such matters in local hands – rather than the FBI's – would reduce the threat the FBI poses to the nation's citizens.

PERSONNEL

Congress has the power to impeach and remove executive officials from office, and it has recently been argued that the next Congress should use that power to remove Attorney General Merrick Garland – to whom the FBI answers.[61] But even if Garland's (or Director Chris Wray's) conduct of office fell within the constitutionally required categories of "Treason, Bribery, or other high Crimes and Misdemeanors" (which seems most unlikely), he could only be convicted and removed after the vote of two-thirds of the senators trying his case. There is zero chance of this. A Republican Congress would spend its time in office much more usefully by exposing FBI misconduct and crafting legislative policies for reform than attempting an impeachment.

This is not to say that Congress should not thin out the existing ranks of the FBI, by mandating reductions in force, offering buyouts, lowering benefits, or engaging in other similar measures with a view to recruiting fresh personnel who have not absorbed the FBI's current culture and ethos. Civil service careerists should be executors of policy, not makers of it – and prolonged incumbency enables careerists (like Andrew McCabe and Peter Strzok) to shape FBI policy to their own ends, not the voters'. Incentives to stay on the job for decades should be sharply reduced. Salaries and benefits should be slashed. (This is true of other federal agencies as well as the FBI.)[62] And Congress should create more positions within the FBI and other agencies for political appointees at the top, rather than having careerists like McCabe supervising other careerists. A major lesson of the "Russian collusion" debacle is that the FBI front office should be filled with persons who, while being faithful to the rule of law, owe their positions to the president, are removable by him at will, and are committed to serving his agenda, not their own.

WHISTLEBLOWER PROTECTIONS

The Deep State not only shrouds its wrongdoing under the mantra of protecting "sources and methods"; it is hostile to whistleblowers in its own ranks. A draft Intelligence Community Inspector General report in 2019 found that intelligence agencies refused to recognize retaliation against whistleblowers in 99 percent of cases.[63] Such self-protectiveness is highly characteristic of the FBI. Senators Chuck Grassley and Dick Durbin have introduced legislation to dismantle the FBI's uniquely self-protective system of dealing with whistleblowers, by conforming the agency's procedures to those of other agencies.[64] A modest first step in reforming the FBI would be for the next Congress to pass this bipartisan legislation. Indeed, Congress should go further by providing for bounties – paid for out of the FBI's budget – to reward FBI whistleblowers who disclose information leading to the exposure of criminal or other serious misconduct by their FBI superiors.

INVESTIGATIVE GUIDELINES

The FBI has no statutory charter; efforts in Congress to enact one in the late 1970s and early 1980s were unsuccessful. Instead of a statute authorizing and regulating its activities – including the investigative techniques it may use – the FBI operates under the broad authority of the attorney general and the Department of Justice. While a statutory charter may be desirable (many thoughtful observers thought so four decades ago), the failure of that proposal suggests that a renewed effort would also fail.

Instead, FBI investigatory activities since 1976 have been regulated by a series of attorney general guidelines, beginning with those issued by President Ford's attorney general Edward Levi. The Levi guidelines were intended to curb illegal and unethical FBI conduct by returning the FBI to its primary mission of crime detection and prevention, and away from monitoring (and inhibiting) disfavored political activities. According to a 2005 special report by the FBI's office of the inspector general, "Attorney General Levi stated that the Guidelines 'proceed from the proposition that Government monitoring of individuals or groups because they hold unpopular or controversial political views is intolerable in our society." The guidelines represented a significant shift in the Department of Justice's approach to domestic terrorism. For the first time, investigations of domestic terrorism were treated as matters for criminal law enforcement, rather than as avenues for intelligence collection."[65]

Over the course of the ensuing decades, several attorneys general issued amended versions of the Levi guidelines.[66] For much of the relevant period, the guidelines retained some form of criminal predicate for the FBI to initiate full domestic security investigations. Thus, the 1989 guidelines provided that a "domestic security investigation may be initiated when the facts or circumstances reasonably indicate that two or more persons are engaged in an enterprise for the purpose of furthering political or social goals . . . through activities that involve force or violence and a violation of the criminal laws of the United States." In that period, the FBI construed the "reasonable indication" standard to require an *imminent* violation of federal criminal law.

The FBI's investigatory authority was greatly expanded after 9/11, first under Attorney General Ashcroft and thereafter under Attorney General Mukasey. The Mukasey guidelines were updated in the FBI's 2011 *Domestic Investigations and Operations Guide*. These documents distinguish three types of FBI authorities: "assessments," which require no allegation or objective facts indicating that the investigation's target may be involved in criminal activity or threaten national security; preliminary investigations, which permit more intrusive techniques but again do not require a reasonable indication of criminal activity or of a national security threat; and "full investigations," which permit agents the use of all lawful investigative methods, and which do require a "reasonable indication" standard. (The required standard is still substantially below the "probable cause" standard needed to obtain a judicial warrant.[67])

Congress should revise and limit these investigatory authorities. In particular it should codify into law a criminal/national security predicate such as existed in 1989, if not a more demanding standard. If the threat of jihadism justified a more permissive standard, the waning of that threat should entail the restoration of a more restrictive one.

Such legislation would likely be supported by civil libertarians on the Left, as well as by conservatives who have grown reasonably apprehensive of the FBI. Earlier this year, the progressive Brennan Center for Justice, in addition to calling for limitations on the FBI's monitoring of social media activities, urged that "opening a full investigation should require articulable facts establishing a reasonable indication that criminal activity is occurring or will occur. Full investigations should be based on reasonable criminal predicates and subjected to regular inspector general audits."

In short, Attorney General Levi's original aim of getting the FBI out of the business of monitoring domestic political activities by US citizens was a worthy one and needs to be reinstated by law.

SEPARATING LAW ENFORCEMENT FROM COUNTERINTELLIGENCE

Taking this line of thinking still further, congressional Republicans should focus their attention on the FBI's *counterintelligence* personnel, programs, and activities, as distinct from the agency's anticrime *law enforcement* functions.[68] While the FBI's traditional law enforcement record is hardly impeccable, some experts argue that the real source of its menace to constitutional freedoms stems from its national security and counterintelligence operations.[69] Proposals have been made in the past to spin off the FBI's law enforcement functions from its counterintelligence functions by creating a separate, freestanding agency tasked only with the latter.[70] Separate agencies for "cops" from "spies" is the norm in most Western democracies.[71] Further, a distinct and smaller counterintelligence agency, if dominated by political appointees subject to presidential removal (rather than by tenure-protected or career personnel) would be more accountable to the president and ultimately to the voters. In 2005, Judge Richard Posner argued that there was "urgent need for a domestic intelligence agency, modeled on the Canadian Security Intelligence Service, that would be separate from the FBI and would have no authority to engage in law enforcement."[72]

Much more recently, intelligence expert Kyle Shideler has argued that the FBI's counterintelligence function is "the most important to break. It is within this division that the FBI spied on the Trump campaign at the behest of the Democratic Party."

Shideler's proposed reform, therefore, is this:

> The FBI's responsibility for counterintelligence should be taken away and vested in the National Counterintelligence Executive (NCIX). Its mandate should not be targeting American citizens (especially elected officials!), but rather policing the intelligence services themselves, rooting out evidence of foreign penetration within their ranks, exploiting and manipulating foreign intelligence services for American national security interests. They do not need law enforcement powers or wide-ranging FISA Court warrants for this job.[73]

ABOLITION?

Proposals not merely to reform but to abolish the FBI have been raised over many years on both the civil libertarian Left[74] and the antistatist Right.[75] The FBI's proclivity to illegal and unethical conduct seems inscribed in its DNA, and its recent shameful attempt to undermine a democratically elected president have taken its wrongdoing to a new level.

The difficulty, however, is that a successor agency, even if populated by an entirely new staff, would likely return to the current agency's patterns and practices if it were to possess the same powers and responsibilities. Madison's "republican security" dilemma is not resolved so easily.

NOTES

1   Daniel H. Deudney, *Bounding Power: Republican Security Theory from the Polis to the Global Village* (Princeton, NJ: Princeton University Press, 2008).

2   Michael J. Glennon's *National Security and Double Government* (New York: Oxford University Press, 2015) is a pioneering work of scholarship in this area. Glennon's distinction between the "Madisonian" State and the "Trumanite" network (or national security apparatus) derives from Walter Bagehot's distinction in *The English Constitution* (London: Chapman and Hall, 1867) between the "dignified" State and the "efficient" State.

3   As understood here, the "Deep State" is a loose and informal network of groups, located principally in the permanent, high-ranking federal bureaucracy in the national and domestic security agencies, but including influential former officials from such positions. It lacks any centralized structure or chain of command but tends to share a broadly similar ethos, outlook, interests, and self-image. It is subsumed by, but narrower than, the "Administrative State." (Thus, as used here, the Securities and Exchange Commission is not part of the Deep State, though some public health agencies might be.) It is, however, broader than the Intelligence Community (though that constitutes its core). The Deep State has robust links to allies in the media, the academy, think tanks, foundations, non-governmental organizations, and members of Congress and their staffs.

4   More recently, the *New York Times*, the *Washington Post*, and other influential voices on the Left have not only acknowledged, but acclaimed, the Deep State. See James Bovard, "The Deep State's Demolition of Democracy," CounterPunch, March 31, 2020, https://www.counterpunch. org/2020/03/31/the-deep-states-demolition-of-democracy/.

5   Daniel Bates, "Ex-FBI Director James Comey Confirms There Is a 'Deep State,'" *Daily Mail*, April 19, 2018, https://www.dailymail.co.uk/news/article-5634373/Ex-FBI-director-James-Comey-confirms-deep-state. html.

6   "Members of the IC," Office of the Director of National Intelligence, accessed November 16, 2022, https://www.dni.gov/index.php/what-we-do/members-of-the-ic.

7   Dean Harold Koh of Yale Law School called on this segment of the Deep

State to resist President Trump in *The Trump Administration and International Law* (New York: Oxford University Press, 2018).

8   Christopher J. Coyne and Abigail R. Hall, *Tyranny Comes Home: The Domestic Fate of U.S. Militarism* (Stanford, CA: Stanford University Press, 2018), 55; Justin Baragona, "Rand Paul: There Are GOP Senators More Loyal to Deep State Than Trump; " Daily Beast, October 21, 2019, https://www.thedailybeast.com/rand-paul-there-are-gop-senators-more-loyal-to-deep-state-than-trump: "'There is an establishment in foreign policy and also in the intelligence community,' [Senator Rand] Paul noted. 'The intelligence community truly is the Deep State.'"

9   John H. Herz, "Rise and Demise of The Territorial State," *World Politics* 9 (July 1957): 473–93, doi:10.2307/2009421.

10 "The Department of Defense Releases the President's Fiscal Year 2023 Defense Budget," U.S. Department of Defense, March 28, 2022, https://www.defense.gov/News/Releases/Release/Article/2980014/the-department-of-defense-releases-the-presidents-fiscal-year-2023-defense-budg/.

11 "About," U.S. Department of Defense, accessed November 16, 2022, https://www.defense.gov/About/.

12 "U.S. Intelligence Community Budget," Office of the Director of National Intelligence, accessed November 16, 2022, https://www.dni.gov/index.php/what-we-do/ic-budget.

13 Neta C. Crawford, "United States Budgetary Costs and Obligations of Post-9/11 through FY2020: $6.4 Trillion," November 13, 2019, Watson Institute, International & Public Affairs, Brown University, https://watson.brown.edu/costsofwar/files/cow/imce/papers/2019/US%20Budgetary%20Costs%20of%20Wars%20November%202019.pdf?rid=84648.

14 Byron Tau, "The Business of Homeland Security Thrives in the Two Decades Since 9/11," *Wall Street Journal*, September 6, 2021, https://www.wsj.com/articles/9-11-triggered-a-homeland-security-industrial-complex-that-endures-11630834202.

15 Robert S. Mueller, III, "Statement Before the House Permanent Select Committee on Intelligence, Washington, DC," FBI, October 6, 2011, https://archives.fbi.gov/archives/news/testimony/the-state-of-intelligence-reform-10-years-after-911. Some would trace the FBI's later misdeeds to the changes Mueller made. See Thomas Baker, "How Robert Mueller Empowered the FBI to Take Out Presidents, Protesters, and Pro-Life Dads," *The Federalist*, October 24, 2022, https://thefederalist.com/2022/10/24/how-robert-mueller-empowered-the-fbi-to-take-out-presidents-protesters-and-pro-life-dads/.

16 The FBI conducted up to 3.4 million warrantless searches in the US in

2021, over half of which were said to be aimed against Russian hacking. See Arjun Singh, "FBI Conducted Millions of Warrantless Searches of Americans' Data in 2021: Report," *National Review*, April 29, 2022, https://www.nationalreview.com/news/fbi-conducted-3-4-million-data-record-searches-in-2021-according-to-report/.

17 Corey Robin, *Fear: The History of a Political Idea* (New York: Oxford University Press, 2004), 219.

18 Coyne and Hall, 182. As of 2007, the Department of Homeland Security's database included potential terrorist targets such as the Old Macdonald's Petting Zoo in Woodville, Alabama, the May Day Parade in Columbia, Tennessee, the Sweetwater Flea Market, the Amish Popcorn Factory and the Apple and Pork festival in Clinton, Illinois. The Department had listed 85,000 targets as of the end of 2004. Frank Furedi, *Invitation to Terror: The Expanding Empire of the Unknown* London: Bloomsbury Academic, 2007), 117. See also Furedi, *Invitation*, 158–60 (reviewing literature).

19 Byron Tau, "The Business of Homeland Security Thrives in the Two Decades since 9/11," *Wall Street Journal*, September 6, 2021, https://www.wsj.com/articles/9-11-triggered-a-homeland-security-industrial-complex-that-endures-11630834202.

20 Frank Furedi, *How Fear Works: Culture of Fear in the Twenty-First Century* (London: Bloomsbury Continuum, 2018), 111–12, 125–26, 141–43.

21 "Fear Psychosis and the Cult of Safety – Why Are People So Afraid?" Academy of Ideas, April 2, 2022, https://academyofideas.com/2022/04/fear-psychosis-and-the-cult-of-safety/; Furedi, *Invitation*, 165–69.

22 Lars Svendsen, *A Philosophy of Fear*, trans. John Irons (London: Reaktion Books, 2008), 128.

23 Robin, *Fear*, 3.

24 Cass R. Sunstein, "Terrorism and Probability Neglect," *Journal of Risk and Uncertainty* 26, no. 2/3 (2003): 121–36.; Furedi, *How Fear Works*, 233–36.

25 FACT SHEET: National Strategy for Countering Domestic Terrorism | The White House.

26 During the thirty-eight year period from 1970 to 2013 – even including 9/11 – the annual risk of death from terrorism in the United States has been one in four million, and the number of people in the United States killed by Islamic terrorists since 9/11 averages about six a year. See John Mueller, *The Stupidity of War: American Foreign Policy and the Case for Complacency* 121–22 (Cambridge: Cambridge University Press, 2021).

27 Paul R. Pillar, "Countering Domestic Terrorism Requires More than a Counterterrorist Strategy," *National Interest*, June 21, 2021, https://nationalinterest.org/blog/paul-pillar/countering-domestic-terrorism-requires-more-counterterrorist-strategy-188292; Gina Ligon and Seamus Hughes, "Biden's Domestic Terrorism Strategy Marks a Change in Course for National Security," *The Hill*, June 19, 2021, https://thehill.com/

opinion/national-security/559243-bidens-domestic-terrorism-strategy-marks-a-change-in-course-for/.

28 See Lisa N. Sacco, Congressional Research Service, *Sifting Domestic Terror-ism from Domestic Violent Extremism and Hate Crime*, updated June 1, 2022, https://crsreports.congress.gov/product/pdf/IN/IN10299. Even on the Left, the FBI's critics believe that "actual crime, violence, and credible threats to national security go unaddressed while FBI agents chase phan-toms of potential future terrorists" (Mike German, *Disrupt, Discredit, And Divide: How The New FBI Damages Democracy* [New York: New Press, 2019], 213). German served for sixteen years as an FBI special agent.

29 Jeremiah Poff, "FBI Opened Multiple Investigations into Protesting Par-ents, GOP Lawmakers Say," *Washington Examiner*, May 12, 2022, https://www.washingtonexaminer.com/restoring-america/fairness-justice/fbi-opened-multiple-investigations-into-protesting-parents-gop-lawmakers-says; Bradford Betz, "Whistleblowers: FBI Targeted Parents via Terrorism Tools Despite Garland's Testimony That It Didn't Happen," Fox News, May 11, 2022, https://www.foxnews.com/politics/fbi-targeted-parents-via-terrorism-tools-despite-garland-testimony.

30 Aruna Viswanatha, "Almost Half of Federal Cases Against Portland Riot-ers Have Been Dismissed," *Wall Street Journal*, April 15, 2021, https://www.wsj.com/articles/almost-half-of-federal-cases-against-portland-rioters-have-been-dismissed-11618501979; "The Biden Administration Drops Dozens of Charges Against Violent Protesters in Portland," Jonathan Turley, May 4, 2021, https://jonathanturley.org/2021/05/04/the-biden-administration-drops-dozens-of-charges-against-violent-protesters-in-portland/.

31 Richard Dahl, "Is It Legal to Protest Outside Supreme Court Justices' Homes?" *FindLaw* (blog), May 12, 2022, https://www.findlaw.com/legal-blogs/courtside/is-it-legal-to-protest-outside-supreme-court-justices-homes/; Aaron Blake, "Yes, Experts Say Protests at SCOTUS Justices' Homes Appear to Be Illegal," *Washington Post*, May 11, 2022, https://www.washingtonpost.com/politics/2022/05/11/protest-justice-home-illegal/.

32 Mary Margaret Olohan, "FBI Won't Provide Updates, Say Whether It Has Arrested Anyone over Attacks on Pro-Life Organizations, Centers, Churches," *Daily Signal*, October 6, 2022, https://www.dailysignal.com/2022/10/06/fbi-wont-provide-updates-say-whether-it-has-arrested-anyone-over-attacks-on-pro-life-organizations-centers-churches/; Elle Purnell, "The FBI Has Announced Indictments of Pro-Life Protesters and Zero Pregnancy Center Firebombers," *The Federalist*, October 19, 2022, https://thefederalist.com/2022/10/19/the-fbi-has-indicted-22-pro-life-protesters-and-zero-pregnancy-center-firebombers/; Laurel Duggan, "'Abuse of Power': Pro-Life Demonstrator Speaks Out after His Indictment on Federal Charges," *Daily Caller*, October 18, 2022, https://www.msn.

com/en-us/news/politics/abuse-of-power-pro-life-demonstrator-speaks-out-after-his-indictment-on-federal-charges/ar-AA137Arr?ocid=msed gdhp&pc=U531&cvid=8b5ef7b1f6b04ce0893c366b9fe7da3a.

33 "Religious Pro-Life Americans Under Attack: A Threat Assessment of Post-*Dobbs* America," Religious Freedom Institute, September 2022, https:// religiousfreedominstitute.org/wp-content/uploads/2022/09/Religious-Pro-Life-Americans-Under-Attack-ONLINE.pdf.

34 Joe Popularis, "Mike Pence's Defense of the FBI is Completely at Odds with Real 'Law and Order,'" The Federalist, August 24, 2022, https:// thefederalist.com/2022/08/24/mike-pences-defense-of-the-fbi-is-completely-at-odds-with-real-law-and-order/.

35 Dale Hurd, "'Get Rid of the Cancer': Why Some Experts Say it's Time to Abolish the FBI," CBN News, October 13, 2022, https://www1.cbn.com/cbnnews/us/2022/october/abolish-the-fbi-some-experts-say-its-time.

36 Brent D. Griffiths, "Pence Whacks Fellow Republicans for Calling to 'Defund the FBI' after Marjorie Taylor Greene Did Exactly That Following the Mar-a-Lago Raid," Yahoo! News, August 17, 2022, https://news.yahoo.com/pence-whacks-fellow-republicans-calling-193203592.html.

37 Mark Judge, "William Barr: Whose Side Are You On?" The Stream, September 3, 2022, https://stream.org/william-barr-whose-side-are-you-on/.

38 Aaron Parsley, "Ark. Gov. Hutchinson Defends FBI, Says Fellow Republicans Should Pull Back on Judging Mar-a-Lago Search," *People*, August 15, 2022, https://www.msn.com/en-us/news/politics/ark-gov-hutchinson-defends-fbi-says-fellow-republicans-should-pull-back-on-judging-mar-a-lago-search/ar-AA10GIko.

39 Merdie Nzanga, "Texas Rep. Dan Crenshaw Calls GOP Demands to Defund FBI 'Completely Wrong,'" *USA Today*, https://news.yahoo.com/texas-rep-dan-crenshaw-calls-174706160.html.

40 Joy Pullman (@JoyPullman), "If the FBI 'rank and file' are so great, why are there so far only 14 FBI whistleblowers, per Sen. Grassley, when there are so many sketchy FBI ops ongoing (MAL raid, Whitmer, PA and MI election meddling, Jan. 6, Spygate, Hunter Biden, terrorist parents, Fortenberry?" Twitter, August 22, 2022, 2:46 p.m., https://twitter.com/JoyPullmann/status/1561801969538371587.

41 Christopher Wray, "Federal Bureau of Investigation Budget Request For Fiscal Year 2023," FBI News, May 25, 2022, https://www.fbi.gov/news/testimony/federal-bureau-of-investigation-budget-request-for-fiscal-year-2023.

42 In letter to Director Wray from July 27, 2022, Congressman Jim Jordan states that FBI whistleblowers have informed him that the FBI is "padding its domestic violent extremist data." "One whistleblower explained that because agents are not finding enough DVE cases, they are encouraged and incentivized to reclassify cases as DVE cases even though there is

minimal, circumstantial evidence to support such reclassification." See Jim Jordan to Christopher A. Wray, Washington, DC, July 27, 2022, https:// archive.org/details/2022-07-27-jdj-to-wray-re-domestic-violent-extremists-32.

43 Robert Delahunty, *Erecting a Wall of Separation Between Tech & State,* Newsweek, Nov. 9, 2022, Erecting a Wall of Separation Between Tech & State, https://www.realclearpolitics.com/2022/11/09/erecting_a_wall_of_separation_between_tech_amp_state_584330.html#! .

44 "'Let me tell you, you take on the intelligence community, they have six ways from Sunday to get back at you. So, even for a practical, supposedly hard-nosed businessman, [Trump] is being really dumb to do this,' Schumer said." Carl Campanile, "Schumer Predicted Intelligence Officials Would 'Get Back at' Trump," *New York Post*, January 11, 2017, https:// nypost.com/2017/01/11/schumer-predicted-intelligence-officials-would-get-back-at-trump/. *Washington Post* columnist Eugene Robinson later echoed Schumer's warning. See Eugene Robinson, "Trump Has Picked a Fight with the FBI. He'll Be Sorry," *Washington Post*, February 1, 2018, https:// www.washingtonpost.com/opinions/messing-with-the-fbi-trump-doesnt-know-history/2018/02/01/53f94f62-0788-11e8-94e8-e8b8600 ade23_story.html.

45 Glennon, *National Security*, 236. In time, the idea flourished, both on the Left (see Eugene Robinson, "God Bless the 'Deep State,'" *Washington Post*, July 19, 2018, https://www.washingtonpost.com/opinions/god-bless-the-deep-state/2018/07/19/de36bd00-8b8a-11e8-85ae-511bc1146b0b_story. html) and on the Neo-Con Right (Bill Kristol [@BillKristol], "Obviously strongly prefer normal democratic and constitutional politics. But if it comes to it, prefer the deep state to the Trump state," Twitter, February 14, 2017, 7:36 a.m., https://twitter.com/billkristol/status/ 831497364661747712).

46 Sundance, "Occam's Razor – Did NSA Admiral Mike Rogers Warn Trump On November 17th, 2016?..." - The Last Refuge, March 3, 2017, https:// theconservativetreehouse.com/blog/2017/03/03/occams-razor-did-nsa-admiral-mike-rogers-warn-trump-on-november-17th-2016/.

47 Eli Lake, "The FBI Scandal," *Commentary*, February 2020, https://www. commentary.org/articles/eli-lake/the-fbi-scandal/ . Lake followed up with a 2021 article that explored the FBI scandal further. https://www. commentary.org/articles/eli-lake/donald-trump-russia-framed-and-guilty/. We have subsequently learned that the FBI withheld from Congress the information that it had offered Steele up to $1 million to corroborate his dossier – and that he was unable to do so. See Natalia Mittelstadt, "Bombshell Revelation of $1M Offer to Steele Shows FBI Misled Congress on Russia Probe: Kash Patel, Just the News, October 11, 2022, https://justthenews.com/accountability/russia-and-ukraine-scandals/

bombshell-revelation-1m-offer-steele-shows-fbi-misled; John Solomon, "John Durham Unmistakably Puts FBI on Trial alongside Its Russian Collusion Informant," Just the News, October 18, 2022, https://justthenews. com/accountability/russia-and-ukraine-scandals/john-durham-unmistakably-puts-fbi-trial-alongside-its.

48 Andrew C. McCarthy, "Utter Proof the FBI Framed Trump and Shielded Hunter Biden," *New York Post*, October 12, 2022, https://nypost.com/ 2022/10/12/utter-proof-the-fbi-framed-trump-and-shielded-hunter/.

49 Mittelstadt, "Bombshell Revelation."

50 Tim Hains, "President Biden: 'White Supremacy Is the Greatest Terrorist Threat to Our Homeland Today,'" September 15, 2022, RealClear Politics, https://www.realclearpolitics.com/video/2022/09/15/watch_live_ president_biden_speaks_against_hate_at_wh_united_we_stand_summit. html. According to agents, Biden has been pressuring the FBI to "cook up" white supremacy cases. "We have more people assigned to investigate White supremacists than we can actually find," one agent said. Leah Barkoukis, "Biden Reportedly Pressuring FBI to 'Cook Up' White Supremacy Cases," *Townhall*, September 16, 2022, https://townhall.com/tipsheet/ leahbarkoukis/2022/09/16/biden-reportedly-pressuring-fbi-to-come-up-with-white-supremacist-cases-n2613187; Ben Weingarten, "The FBI Paid for Russian Disinformation while Punishing a Patriot," *Newsweek*, September 23, 2022, https://www.newsweek.com/fbi-paid-russian-disinformation-while-punishing-patriot-opinion-1745574.

51 *Harvard CAPS Harris Poll*, September 2022, https://harvardharrispoll. com/wp-content/uploads/2022/09/HHP_Sept2022_KeyFindings.pdf.

52 Kyle Shideler, "For the Rule of Law to Reign, the Bureau Must Be Destroyed," *American Greatness*, August 10, 2022, https://amgreatness. com/2022/08/10/for-the-rule-of-law-to-reign-the-bureau-must-be-destroyed/.

53 Some of J. Edgar Hoover's secret files were reviewed by (then) Deputy Attorney General (and later Judge) Laurence H. Silverman, who wrote that Hoover had tasked FBI agents "with reporting privately to him any bits of dirt on figures such as Martin Luther King or their families – information Hoover sometimes used as blackmail to ensure his and the bureau's power." See Betty Medsger, *The Burglary: The Discovery of J. Edgar Hoover's Secret FBI* (New York: Alfred A. Knopf, 2014), 373–34.

54 Mollie Hemingway, "The FBI's Matt Gaetz Operation Sidelined an Effective Republican at a Crucial Time. That Was the Point," The Federalist, September 26, 2022, https://thefederalist.com/2022/09/26/ the-fbis-matt-gaetz-operation-sidelined-an-effective-republican-voice-at-a-crucial-time-that-was-the-point/.

55 US v. Lovett (Sup. Ct. 1946).

56 Olohan, "FBI Won't Provide Updates."

57 Individual Members of Congress have also introduced bills relating to domestic terrorism, e.g., conferring the tools of foreign intelligence gathering on domestic law enforcement. See Charles Doyle, Congressional Research Service, *Domestic Terrorism: Some Considerations*, August 12, 2019, https://crsreports.congress.gov/product/pdf/LSB/LSB10340. Apart from the necessity or wisdom of such proposals, they may well raise constitutional concerns. See Holder v. Humanitarian Law Project (Sup. Ct. 2010) ("We also do not suggest that Congress could extend the same prohibition on material support at issue here to domestic organizations. We simply hold that, in prohibiting the particular forms of support that plaintiffs seek to provide to foreign terrorist groups, §2339B does not violate the freedom of speech.")

58 Joy Pullman, "Democrats Are Framing Americans as Domestic Terrorists So They Can Do to Us What They Did to Trump in Spygate," The Federalist, January 20, 2021, https://thefederalist.com/2021/01/20/democrats-are-framing-americans-as-domestic-terrorists-so-they-can-do-to-us-what-they-did-to-trump-in-spygate/.

59 Michael German and Kaylana Mueller-Hsia, "Focusing the FBI," Brennan Center for Justice, July 28, 2022, https://www.brennancenter.org/our-work/research-reports/focusing-fbi.

60 "Why Local Law Enforcement Is a Cornerstone of Homeland Security", *Corrections* 1, Jul 9, 2018, https://www.corrections1.com/products/online-training/articles/why-local-law-enforcement-is-a-cornerstone-of-homeland-security-g1MKw2lLZviIrSnk/.

61 John Daniel Davidson, "The First Thing Republicans Should Do When They Take Back Congress Is Impeach Merrick Garland" *The Federalist*, October 7, 2022, https://thefederalist.com/2022/10/07/the-first-thing-republicans-should-do-when-they-take-back-congress-is-impeach-merrick-garland/

62 James Sherk, "Deeply Partisan Federal Bureaucrats Selectively Enforce the Laws, Eliminating Equal Justice for All," The Federalist, March 30, 2022, https://thefederalist.com/2022/03/30/deeply-partisan-federal-bureaucrats-selectively-enforce-the-laws-eliminating-equal-justice-for-all/.

63 Bovard, "Deep State's Demolition."

64 "Grassley, Durbin Propose Enhanced FBI Whistleblower Protections," Chuck Grassley United States Senator for Iowa, July 28, 2022, https://www.grassley.senate.gov/news/news-releases/grassley-durbin-propose-enhanced-fbi-whistleblower-protections.

65 Office of the Inspector General, *The Federal Bureau of Investigation's Compliance with the Attorney General's Investigative Guidelines*, September 2005, https://oig.justice.gov/sites/default/files/legacy/special/0509/final.pdf.

66 John T. Elliff, "Attorney General's Guidelines for FBI Investigations,"

Cornell Law Review 69, no. 4 (1984): https://scholarship.law.cornell.edu/clr/vol69/iss4/4/.

67 German and Mueller-Hsia, "Focusing the FBI."

68 The FBI Counterintelligence Division performs three major functions: counterterrorism, counterproliferation and counterespionage. See "What We Investigate/Counterintelligence," FBI, accessed November 16, 2022, https://www.fbi.gov/investigate/counterintelligence; Admin, "FBI Counterintelligence Division Career Information All You Need to Know," Criminal Justice Jobs, January 17, 2022, https://cjusjobs.com/fbi-counterintelligence-division-career/#:~:text=To%20accomplish%20these%20goals%2C%20it%20employs%20over%2036%2C000,Division%2C%20here%20are%20some%20things%20you%20should%20know.

69 Debra Heine, "FBI Whistleblower: The Direction of the Bureau 'Troubles a Vast Majority of the Agents,'" American Greatness, May 11, 2022, https://amgreatness.com/2022/05/11/fbi-whistleblower-the-direction-of-the-bureau-troubles-a-vast-majority-of-the-agents/.

70 "FBI Intelligence Reform Since September 11, 2001: Issues and Options for Congress," Intelligence Resource Program, Federation for American Scientists, April 6, 2004, https://irp.fas.org/crs/RL32336.html.

71 The fusion of law enforcement and intelligence is contrary to the practice of most Western nations. See John R. Schindler, "It's Time to Get the FBI Out of the Spy Business," *Observer*, May 18, 2018, https://observer.com/2018/05/fbi-counterintelligence-activities-should-be-separate/.

72 Richard A. Posner, *Remaking Domestic Intelligence* (Stanford, CA: Hoover Institution Press, 2005), 81–82. Posner wanted to create a new agency, not to restructure the FBI.

73 Shideler, " Rule of Law."

74 Harvey Silvergate, "Reform Isn't Enough; Get Rid of the FBI," *Boston Globe*, December 7, 2021, https://www.bostonglobe.com/2021/12/07/opinion/reform-isnt-enough-get-rid-fbi/.

75 Holman W. Jenkins, Jr., "Abolish the FBI," *Wall Street Journal*, September 21, 2021, https://www.wsj.com/articles/abolish-fbi-durham-indictment-russia-collusion-clinton-sussman-strzok-comey-corruption-11632256384.

REPOSITION, RETRENCH, AND RESTORE
A New, Old Foreign Policy

Michael Anton

WHEN THE COLD WAR came to an unexpected end in the late 1980s, a debate broke out on the Right: what should we do now?

Roughly speaking, one side argued that it was time, if not to withdraw from every foreign commitment and forward deployment, then at least to retrench significantly. The other side insisted that this was America's moment; a world-historical victory of this magnitude should not lightly be squandered. Rather, America's sudden preeminence should be extended for as long as possible and the opportunity to spread "American values" should be eagerly seized.

Intellectually, the first faction was led by Pat Buchanan. Few who know Buchanan's reputation today will be surprised. But at the time, many were shocked that the one-time ardent Cold Warrior had somehow "switched sides." Though, in his view, he had done nothing of the kind. As he saw it, the policy he had supported had fulfilled its stated mission; the logical response, therefore, was to form a new policy. One person who agreed – a fact that shows how much the meaning of terms can change over time – was prominent "neoconservative" (and Ronald Reagan's first ambassador to the United Nations) Jeane Kirkpatrick, whose 1990 *National Interest* article "A Normal Country in a Normal Time" should have been every bit the landmark as her 1979 *Commentary* article "Dictatorships and Double Standards."[1]

On the other side were those we think of today as neoconservatives, in what would come to be the new meaning: maximalist interventionism combined with aggressive "democracy" promotion. Perhaps the two most important protostatements of this view were Francis Fukuyama's "The End of History?" (*National Interest*, 1989) and Charles Krauthammer's "The Unipolar Moment" (*Foreign Affairs*, 1990).[2]

This same debate also wracked the George H. W. Bush administration. It can be hard to remember now, but back then the Republican Party was still home to a lot of patrician foreign policy realists and restrainers, epitomized by Secretary of State James Baker and his deputy (and later, briefly, secretary in his own right) Lawrence Eagleburger. Today those views are at home in the Trump wing of the party, and we think of the Republican establishment – not without reason – as neocon.

But at the time, the neocons were the upstarts. The second wave of neoconservatives, in contrast to the first, was more interested in foreign than domestic policy. They made their name in the 1970s denouncing the Nixon-Kissinger policy of détente (relaxation of tensions) with the Soviet Union, the Carter administration's numerous bunglings, and the security establishment's alleged underestimation of Soviet capabilities. This made them a natural fit for the more confrontational Reagan administration, where many of them found low- and mid-level jobs. The nature of Washington is that, if you were an assistant secretary in the last administration, and you're asked to join the new one, you get to be an undersecretary. Hence the remaining neocons in the Bush administration were promoted from the lower and middle tier to the middle and lower-upper tier. (None of them achieved cabinet rank in either Bush administration, but their ideas nonetheless suffused the second.)

But the country club realists were still around. They favored – though it was not called this at the time – the Buchanan-Kirkpatrick approach. The neocons urged the maximalist strategy. In the final year of the Bush (forty-one) administration, the office of the undersecretary of defense for policy, then the epicenter of neoconservatism in the government, attempted to formalize this approach as "Defense Planning Guidance."[3] Such drafts must be circulated widely within the government before they can be adopted as policy. This one quickly became known derisively as the "Wolfowitz Doctrine," after Undersecretary Paul Wolfowitz. Aghast realists leaked the draft to the *New York Times*, ensuring its quick death.[4] Yet in that strange Washington way in which bureaucratic defeats become strategic victories, the Wolfowitz Doctrine won out and eventually morphed into the Bush Doctrine.

Out of power and ensconced in think tanks, the neocons prospered by roughing up the Clinton administration as Carter redux. Clinton responded by toughening up. He also, like most candidates who on the trail promise restraint, found the presidency's wide latitude in foreign affairs invigorating, especially in contrast to the frustrations of trying to steer a domestic agenda through Congress. And the new president was reacting to a surprising shift among his own party's power brokers, from prolabor to procapital, and anti- to pro-intervention.

In opposition, the Republican Party found it useful to toe the neocon line. Whatever Clinton was doing overseas, they said was not enough – with one exception. The Republican mainstream was still against "nation building," the use of American power to modernize and liberalize other countries (the neocons were all for it). George W. Bush, sounding something like the WASPs in his father's cabinet, ran against nation building and promised a "humble foreign policy."

The last brake on that train was removed in the year or so after 9/11, when "conservative" foreign policy settled into a now-familiar groove: favoring boldness over caution, unafraid to use force, optimistic about what American power can accomplish, seeing the whole world as our sphere of influence, expanding the rubric of "national security" to include almost everything, and convinced that the spread of "Western values" (defined, more or less, as cutting-edge Blue Metro social leftism) is a core US strategic interest.

And we know the result. After initial success in Afghanistan, the Bush (forty-three) administration, egged on by the conservative intelligentsia, set about implementing its maximalist foreign policy. The realists and restrainers who might have opposed this trend had either aged out of policy roles, not been asked to join the administration, found themselves on the losing end of most policy disputes (Colin Powell), or had personally converted to a more interventionist stance. The most notable example of the latter is Dick Cheney, who, as secretary of defense in the first Bush administration, was among the loudest voices defending the decision not to "go on to Baghdad" and remove Saddam at the culmination of the Gulf War, but who, in the second, was a leading advocate for regime change in Iraq.

It's important to remember, however, that at the time of the second Bush administration, while realists were mostly absent from leadership positions, they still dominated portions of the permanent government, notably the Foreign Service and parts of the intelligence community. The State Department, in particular, fought the proposed invasion of Iraq tooth and nail and warned repeatedly against any attempt to democratize the country.

The Bush Doctrine was never officially defined but it came to have two meanings. The first was initially sketched in the president's 2002 West Point commencement speech and definitively explained in the National Security Strategy published that fall.[5] It amounted to an elision of the age-old concepts of preemptive and preventive war. The former means that a nation is not obligated to wait to be attacked by a massing, moving army; if its territory, citizens, or assets are being directly threatened, it can act. The most oft-cited example of preemption is Israel's actions in the Six-Day War when, Egypt, Jordan, and Syria visibly mobilizing to attack, the Israelis struck first. Preemptive war has long been justified, if hesitantly, by theorists of international relations and is even, if equivocally, permitted under international law.

Preventive war, by contrast, means a war begun to prevent a future war, or to prevent a shift in the balance of power that would disadvantage the country that starts the war. The most memorable statement of the logic of preventive war is Thucydides's explanation that the Peloponnesian War arose from "the growth of Athenian power, which putting the Lacedaemonians into fear necessitated the war."[6] International relations theorists have never condoned preventive war and it is unambiguously condemned in international law.

Understandably spooked by 9/11, the Bush administration believed that the obvious response – ousting the Taliban from power in Afghanistan and destroying al-Qaeda – was necessary but insufficient. The roots of the problem went deeper, they argued, with America threatened not just by other hostile regimes but by a transnational movement. The route to safety required going to the root: the deep resentments that give rise to radicalism in the first place.

That was the supposedly hardheaded rationale behind democratization and nation building in Afghanistan and Iraq.[7] Its contours are best laid out in the president's remarks at the American Enterprise Institute dinner in February 2003, a speech to the National Endowment for Democracy later that year, and in his Second Inaugural.[8] The latter, in which Bush pledges that American policy will henceforth be to "end tyranny in our world," is the apotheosis of neoconservative foreign policy.

We know how it worked out – not that we couldn't have known then. Indeed, we should have. Supposed "conservatives" talked themselves into believing that a utopian project with no basis in history or present reality was not only possible to achieve via American power, but that it was fundamental to American interests.

Neither Iraq nor Afghanistan was democratized or meaningfully developed. The wished-for democracy wave known as the "Arab Spring" led to electoral victories by "one man, one vote, once" Islamist parties, and then, where we were fortunate, to the return of military dictatorships we had abandoned but that at least offered stability and nominal friendship. Where we weren't so fortunate, civil wars and failed states followed, or ISIS took over.

While we were busy with this impossible project, our relations with allies deteriorated as we insisted they join us. Those who did futilely spent blood and treasure, alienated their peoples, and fueled, if inadvertently, public anti-Americanism. Those who declined, we sharply lectured – alienating their peoples and governments alike.

China continued its rise, notwithstanding our "pivot to Asia" – which, when finally announced, was too little, too late. Pointless provocation of Russia became de rigueur. Bipartisan elites supported the expansion of NATO and, much more dubiously, of the European Union. Not every trade deal proposed was enacted – sorry, FTAA and TPP – but all enjoyed near-unanimous bipartisan support, which was essential to dragging across the finish line the many that were. Those deals, however much they may (or may not) have boosted our international standing and helped maintain alliances, unquestionably hurt our domestic economy and tore at the social fabric, especially in manufacturing areas where outsourcing and factory closures gave rise to chronic unemployment, substance abuse, and deaths of despair.

The theoretical connection between these strands of policy – preemptive-preventive "war on terror," democratizing the Third World, and further blending together the First World – should now be evident. Wars to spread democracy are, in intent if not in effect, the ultimate kind of preventive war. The very idea is to remake foreign countries into the image of the developed West, so that they lose their distinctiveness and thereby any desire to resist globalization. Just as we must homogenize the First World in the interests of "human rights" and global capital, we must make the Third World more like the First. Localism, distinctiveness, borders, labor, and minding one's own business must give way to homogenization, connectivity, globalism, capital, and intervention.

All this occurred during a quarter century in which Republicans were in power for a grand total of eight years – or nine, if you want to count the tail end of the elder Bush's administration. The pull of the maximalist approach – of the Fukuyama-Krauthammer-Wolfowitz-Bush Doctrine – may in America have first found a political home on the "Right," but its origins and fundamental aims are of the Left.

The complicated story of how liberal doctrine came to form the basis of "conservatism" can be boiled down to the American ruling class's response to World War II. The "Old Right" foreign policy was guided by George Washington's Farewell Address and the writings and deeds of America's most experienced and successful diplomat, John Quincy Adams.[9] It was characterized by noninterventionism and a careful husbanding of American power. It was not opposed to war per se, and was certainly not "isolationist." But it defined America's interests narrowly: the protection of American territory, citizenry, and commerce. It welcomed expansive commercial relationships with other nations while politically holding the rest of the world at arm's length. This outlook had defined American foreign policy from the Founding until the Progressive Era, and it was still widely popular, if not dominant, into the 1930s. But it was denounced by the interventionist Left and declared discredited by the outbreak of that war which, it was alleged, demanded robust American involvement. Thus did the so-called "internationalist wing" of the Republican Party, led by Senator Arthur Vandenberg of Michigan, triumph over the so-called "isolationist wing" led by Senator Robert Taft of Ohio.

In the early days of the Cold War, Republicans tried to outflank the Truman administration from the Right. Hence calls for "rollback" (i.e., "rolling back" Communism from its then-existing borders, by war if necessary), cries of "Who lost China?" and demands for total victory in Korea. Most Americans, however, found the Truman policy neither weak nor pacifistic. Indeed, the American people believed they were consenting to an unprecedentedly activist foreign policy in peacetime, justified by the unprecedented Communist threat. Few had any desire to do more.

The Republicans succeeded in getting to the Democrats' right only after the Democrats' disastrous handling of the Vietnam War and subsequent abandonment of Trumanism, formalized by the 1972 George McGovern nomination. In the space of four years, a Democratic Party that had formulated and launched America's Cold War strategy turned against that strategy and its underlying assumptions. Jimmy Carter lectured Americans on their supposedly "inordinate fear of communism."[10] The Soviet invasion of Afghanistan (which Carter admitted had surprised him), the losses of Nicaragua and Iran, and especially the ensuing hostage crisis all presented to the American people the spectacle of not just an administration, but of a whole political party, naïve and adrift.

It's a chicken-or-egg question whether Ronald Reagan's critique of détente attracted or was inspired by the neocons. Personally, I believe it was a case of parallel discovery and mutual advantage.

In any event, Reagan and the neocons found each other, and their marriage of convenience laid the foundation for the conservative foreign policy of the post-Cold War era: toughness, peace through strength, a willingness to use force, and a wide-angle view of which parts of the world are integral to American interests.

One can even find the germ of the democracy agenda in Reagan's foreign policy, or at least in the neocons' interpretation (and critique) of it. But for that to happen, the meaning of "neoconservative" had to undergo a change.

In foreign as in domestic policy, "neoconservatism" originally signified a rejection of the Democratic Party's drift into softness and wishful thinking – believing, for instance, that the Soviets posed little or no threat and that abandoning allies in the name of "human rights" carried no costs. Essentially, the remaining Trumanite Democrats found they had no choice but to align with the Republicans. Jeane Kirkpatrick, a neocon in this earlier sense, made her name by arguing against the Carter administration's insistence on democratic purity in our allies. To the contrary, she boldly affirmed that, in the struggle against Communism, America was morally justified in supporting undemocratic anti-Communist allies and foolish for abandoning them. From the perspective of hindsight, this looks more like a realist than a neocon position, which perhaps explains why, a dozen years later, the allegedly "neoconservative" Kirkpatrick found herself on the same side as the avowedly "paleoconservative" Buchanan.

But the claim Kirkpatrick was arguing against – that America somehow diminished itself by supporting anti-Communist autocracies – found sympathy with younger neocons, who had some success in making it part of Reagan's, and Republican, foreign policy. What Kirkpatrick defended as hardheaded prudence, they criticized as cynicism – and, worse, as a moral stain on the nation.

Americans at our best, they argued, democratized Germany and Japan. If we could do that in countries which, only years before, had been governed by the most undemocratic systems in history, there was no excuse for not spreading the project elsewhere. Allies such as Taiwan, South Korea, and the Philippines were warned that our continued support required their democratization. The same principle was extended to trading partners, then to the states of the former Soviet Union, and finally to Iraq and Afghanistan (and, at least in aspiration, to the entire Middle East). Indeed, one may say that the architects of the Iraq and Afghan wars justified those interventions to the world, and to themselves, on the grounds of democratization: democratization sanctifies the use of force in a way that no narrow calculation of interests ever could.

The biggest problem with this line of reasoning is that prewar Germany and Japan, while undoubtedly undemocratic, nonetheless boasted well-developed civil societies, mediating institutions, and First World industrial economies. The soil was there to support democracy. The same eventually became true of Taiwan and South Korea, something that cannot be said of Afghanistan or Iraq. A "realist" foreign policy would have begun from a realistic assessment of where democracy had a fighting chance of taking root and where it did not – a warning that the remaining realists in the career ranks of the bureaucracy delivered to the Bush administration decision-makers, only to go unheeded.

It is widely believed, but I think untrue, that neocons burrowed themselves into the permanent government. First of all, there never were that many neocons – certainly far fewer than their outsize influence would suggest. Second, neocons have never been that interested in civil service jobs. For them government service means high-level appointive positions; otherwise, they believe (correctly) that they can be more influential outside government.

Still, neoconservatism's misunderstanding of the idea of individual rights dovetailed neatly with the permanent bureaucracy's social leftism. If all individuals are equal and possess rights, then justice demands a maximalist interpretation of equality and rights. Thus did the two schools blend together. The bureaucracy came to be more open to the use of force, especially for leftist ends, and neocons became adamant that America's invocation of equal natural rights demanded, for instance, placing the homosexual agenda at the center of American foreign policy, as a "non-negotiable demand of human dignity." Those words of George W. Bush's illustrate the dynamic. He was himself (so he said) opposed to homosexual marriage. Yet the drift of his argument, combined with the aggressive interventionism of his policy, resulted almost inevitably in the marriage of social leftism with military adventurism, or military adventurism in service to social leftism. Perhaps the supreme image of neoconservative foreign policy is the rainbow flag flying from our $800 billion embassy in Kabul.

Another hypothesis, which I mention for the sake of completeness, is that the 9/11 wars were, if not started by, at least continued for the sake of the big defense contractors. Certainly this era was lucrative for them; their market capitalizations grew tremendously, as did their ties to the permanent government. Still, I hesitate to put too much stock in this explanation, if for no other reasons than, having myself sat for a total of almost six years near the center of these deliberations, I heard firsthand all the arguments sketched in this chapter. I never heard this one. Perhaps everyone was simply good at talking around it and I was too naïve to pick up on it.

To bring us back to the beginning, thus did liberal internationalism, whose triumph was supposed to be temporary, outlast the problem it was supposed to address by three generations and counting. Arthur Vandenberg, who had been an "isolationist" in his early years – before Tojo, Hitler, and Stalin converted him to internationalism – died in 1951. Which side would he have taken in that all-important early 1990s debate? I suppose we cannot know, but he never justified the doctrine to which he lent the weight of his reputation as a permanent shift in American strategic practice.

WHERE DOES ALL THIS LEAVE US?

We are left, first, with a Republican Party divided – in two senses. It is divided at the top, with Donald Trump leading a smallish band of elected and appointed officials (or appointees-in-waiting) who reject the continued application of liberal internationalism as the solution to every (real or perceived) problem. This wing wants fewer interventions, an end to many underway now, better relations with Russia, a tougher stand on NATO free riding, and less American hectoring of other countries over adherence to woke doctrine.

On the other side is the majority of the party's leadership, which wants the status quo, only more so: more free trade agreements, more confrontation with Russia, more NATO members, more rainbow flags flying over American embassies.

About the only issue over which the two camps agree is China, though that too is complicated by differences over trade (the Trump wing rejects the TPP; the establishment would revive it if it could) and Taiwan (the Trumpists, though not necessarily Trump himself, seem willing to let Beijing have it whereas McConnell et al. seem sometimes to be itching for war).

The other divide is between the party's leadership and its voters. Trumpists may be outnumbered at the top but they dominate the base, which is not only tired of democracy wars but never supported them in the first place. True, they strongly supported George W. Bush in his first term and dragged him (barely) to reelection in 2004. But there was always a disconnect. To them, the 9/11 wars were about Jacksonian punishment. Bush's democracy rhetoric was out there for them to hear, but they chose not to, or at least supported those wars in spite, not because of, it.

For a while. In 2016, Trump was able in win the Republican nomination, and later the presidency, in no small part because the Republican base rejected not just the democracy agenda but had come to repudiate the wars themselves. For a party that had, since the Carter administration at least, made "hawkishness" a centerpiece of its foreign policy, this was a fundamental shift.

WHAT TO DO GOING FORWARD?

Sketching the outlines of a proper Republican foreign policy, fit for these times (i.e., not for 1950, 1980, or 2001) is not difficult. Getting it adopted by the party at large and then implemented as policy – *that's* hard. I take up here only the former task. Moreover, we should question whether a country so divided internally – which quarrels vituperatively over foreign concerns such as one's opinion on Ukraine – can even have a coherent foreign policy. Since the sine qua non of a successful foreign policy is majority domestic support, what follows presumes something we lack: a country united enough to agree on its core interests.

The United States has only a few: protecting the American homeland and people, preserving American sovereignty, safeguarding American commerce, and preventing any hostile power from dominating those few areas in the world vital to our interests: Northwest Europe, Northeast Asia, and the Persian Gulf.

First, we cannot allow any aggressive foreign power to gain a foothold in the Western Hemisphere – especially not in North America. At present, China is the only such power capable of even trying to do so, and its leaders are well aware of American sensitivities on this point, which is why their incursions are more subtle. Massive espionage, debasing our corporations, corrupting our universities with cash and flooding them with spies, buying up strategic assets, even buying our homes – all these not only further China's goal of establishing toeholds throughout our society but can be, and are, defended by well-paid lobbyists and unpaid ideologues. All of it, and more, will have to be creatively checked. We ought to be much more aggressive in countering Chinese espionage and unapologetic in protecting domestic assets, free market ideologues be damned.

As a commercial republic and (for a little while longer) the world's leading economic power, America has a core interest in ensuring that the world's two other leading centers of wealth and innovation – Northwest Europe and the Pacific Rim – remain on friendly terms and don't fall under the sway of a hostile foreign power. The only country with a realistic prospect of threatening that is, again, China, which is doing a very good job of altering the strategic balance in Asia. Helping our Indo-Pacific allies and friends stay out from under China's thumb while not provoking a war should not be too difficult – unless we overreach on Taiwan. I hesitate to say anything seemingly dismissive of the worthy claims of the worthy people of that island. But it's just a fact that Taiwan is more important – much more – to China than it is to us, and that China would sooner force a war than abandon its claims. The best outcome for us is the preservation of the status quo. That requires a careful balance of military preparedness, economic toughness, and diplomatic finesse. As the quarter century after Tiananmen Square showed, overdeference to China is counterproductive. But, as the post-Trump era is demonstrating, it's also possible to be pointlessly confrontational.

One thing that might help would be a new relationship with Russia. Rapprochement with Moscow now seems more impossible than ever after the Russian invasion of Ukraine and the American (and European) response.

This is unfortunate. It's unfortunate for Ukrainians, who will continue to lose lives in a war against a far greater power they likely cannot defeat, cynically egged on by a West that appears to be using them in a (likely futile) attempt to "bleed Russia." And it's unfortunate for us, who share a number of common interests with Russia, including the China threat, on which we could profitably cooperate. But not if Russians perceive that our aim is to "bleed" or even destroy their country. Our foolish actions and rhetoric in Ukraine appear to have guaranteed another generation, at least, of Russian hostility to the West, all for the sake of some nebulous "moral principle" that cuts at the heart of our true interests. Jeane Kirkpatrick would not have made this mistake.

As distant as this possibility now seems, recall that the United States has in the past successfully turned foe into friend – at least for a time. Those who argue that any attempt to reduce temperatures with Russia for the sake of great power relations is inherently immoral and even treasonous should recall the so-called "reset" peddled by Hillary Clinton, or Barack Obama's infamous hot mic gaffe, when he told Russia's then-president Dmitri Medvedev that he'd have "more flexibility" to negotiate a new treaty after the 2012 election. What changed? It wasn't the invasion of Ukraine; Russia was already liberalism's foreign enemy number one by 2015. Was it Moscow's increasing resistance to the West's insistence on social libertinism as the price of good relations?

Whatever the cause, easing tensions and accommodating Russia's desire for a seat at the European, and even Transatlantic, table are in our interest. But we would first have to accept that the Russians will inevitably exercise more latitude in their nation's "near abroad" than our elites would like, and that we lack the power to stop them absent threatening, and risking, a potentially nuclear World War III.

American and European elites would also have to give up their fantastical insistence that Russia "democratize." It's conceivable that Russia could become more moderate. Indeed, compared to its Soviet days, the country has already traveled a great distance in that direction – even factoring in the Ukraine invasion. But Russia will always be, at least compared to what we think of as "democracy," "authoritarian." And corrupt. And not a little bit gangsterish. We also need to realize that the by-product of Washington's lectures to Moscow is not improved Russian behavior but worse Russo-American relations.

Since we're dreaming, we might as well dream big. Russia is part of our civilizational "sect" in ways that China can never be. For a thousand years, Russia has played an integral part in European history, in the history of the West. Tchaikovsky, Rachmaninov, and Rimsky-Korsakov, among many others, are constantly played in our concert halls, just as Chekhov, Tolstoy, and Dostoyevsky are still read (in those corners where they haven't been canceled, and by those in the West who still read). Democratic India might also serve as a plausible hedge against Chinese power, but that would require a less hectoring posture toward Hindu nationalism, something our foreign policy mandarins are at present unwilling to contemplate. Also, as the response to Ukraine has shown, the more we alienate Russia and demand that others do the same as the price of our friendship, the more standoffish India becomes.

The likelihood of greater cooperation seems, at this point,

vanishingly small. But it's at least possible that were we to stop the ceaseless demonization, end the ineffectual moral lectures, accept the inevitability of Russian influence in its border regions, forgo reckless talk of bringing Ukraine and Georgia into NATO, and try in good faith to make real deals that benefit both countries, tensions might ease and new vistas for cooperation open up. At any rate, all those things are worth doing for our own interests, whether or not they improve relations with Moscow.

If they did, however, the Transatlantic Alliance, along with our alliances in the Anglosphere and in the Indo-Pacific, would be immeasurably strengthened against our one common foe. The West itself might gather renewed strength if the one Western and one quasi-Western country among the world's three greatest powers at long last found themselves on the same side. That's probably too much to hope for. But the benefits are so obvious and potentially immense that it's worth a try.

As for the Middle East, our chief interest there – ensuring that oil and gas flow freely out the Strait of Hormuz – will decline in importance if our domestic energy supplies grow, a goal that American policy currently opposes. Reversing that mistake should be a top priority as much of our foreign as of our domestic policy.

America will always have an interest in preventing a hostile power from seizing Gulf oil supplies and using them against us, just as we will always an interest in preventing states or groups motivated by religion or ideology (or both) from doing violence to our homeland or people. But those threats can be deterred – and, if necessary, countered – with a much smaller force presence than we maintain in the region today.

Closer to home, Mexican drug cartels are the gravest danger we face. These heavily armed gangs kill Americans with guns and drugs, and they terrorize large swaths of the Southwest. Some have actually won tactical confrontations with the Mexican military; the Little Rascals they ain't.[11] It's time to consider using our own military – whose ultimate purpose is, after all, to protect the lives of American citizens and the territorial integrity of the United States – to defeat or at least beat back these cartels and secure our border against armed, hostile incursion. Increased drone and other surveillance activity could not only help secure the border but serve as a testing ground for emerging technology. If punitive, cross-border raids are necessary to protect Americans, so be it. If the Mexicans object, they can work with us on a joint solution. If they're incapable of doing so, then they can't reasonably object.

Other than that, America needs to ensure that sea lanes and other transportation routes vital to our commerce remain open and unmolested. It's hard to think of any other urgent interests that require massive American diplomatic or military engagement – which means that something like two-thirds of what we do today on the global stage is at best unnecessary and at worst counterproductive.

NOTES

1   Jeane Kirkpatrick, "A Normal Country in a Normal Time," *National Interest*, Fall 1990; Jeane Kirkpatrick, "Dictatorships & Double Standards," *Commentary*, November 1979, https://www.commentary.org/articles/jeane-kirkpatrick/dictatorships-double-standards/.

2   Francis Fukuyama, "The End of History?" *National Interest*, Summer 1989, 3–18; Charles Krauthammer, "The Unipolar Moment," *Foreign Affairs* 70, no. 1 (1990/1991): 23–33.

3   Wikipedia, s.v., "Wolfowitz Doctrine," last modified March 29, 2022, 11:43, https://en.wikipedia.org/wiki/Wolfowitz_Doctrine#CITEREFTyler1992a.

4   Patrick E. Tyler, "U.S. Strategy Plan Calls For Insuring No Rivals Develop," *New York Times*, March 8, 1992.

5   "The National Security Strategy," National Security Strategy Archive, September 17, 2002, https://nssarchive.us/national-security-strategy-2002/.

6   Thucydides, *The Peloponnesian War*, in Thomas Hobbes, *The English Works of Thomas Hobbes of Malmesbury*, vol 8, ed. Sir William Molesworth (London: John Bohn, 1843), 27.

7   See, for instance, Vice President Dick Cheney's speech at the VFW's 103rd National Convention: "Vice President Speaks at VFW 103rd National Convention," White House Archives, August 26, 2002, https://georgewbush-whitehouse.archives.gov/news/releases/2002/08/20020826.html.

8   "Full text: George Bush's Speech to the American Enterprise Institute,"
    Guardian, February 27, 2003, https://www.theguardian.com/
    world/2003/feb/27/usa.iraq2; George W. Bush, "President Bush Discusses
    Freedom in Iraq and Middle East," White House Archives, November 6,
    2003, https://georgewbush-whitehouse.archives.gov/news/
    releases/2003/11/20031106-2.html; "President Bush's Second Inaugural
    Address," NPR, January 20, 2005, https://www.npr.org/templates/story/
    story.php?storyId=4460172.
9   Angelo M. Codevilla, *America's Rise and Fall among Nations: Lessons in
    Statecraft from John Quincy Adams* (New York: Encounter Books, 2022).
10 Jimmy Carter, "Address at Commencement Exercises at the University of
    Notre Dame," American Presidency Project, May 22, 1977, https://www.
    presidency.ucsb.edu/documents/
    address-commencement-exercises-the-university-notre-dame.
11 John Daniel Davidson, "A Drug Cartel Just Defeated the Mexican Military
    In Battle," *Federalist*, October 21, 2019, https://thefederalist.
    com/2019/10/21/a-drug-cartel-just-defeated-the-mexican-military-in-
    battle/.

THE CIVIL RIGHTS REGIME AND THE FAILURES OF LEGAL CONSERVATISM

Jesse Merriam

Nearly all scholars, on the Left and Right alike, treat the legal branch of the conservative movement – the "legal conservative movement" (LCM) – as triumphant. In one scholar's words, the LCM has mounted a "conservative counterrevolution" against the liberal establishment.[1] But this account is wrong. The LCM has failed to achieve its original goal of restoring the pre-1960s constitutional order – that is, the order that existed before the Warren Court's "rights revolution" subsumed all federal, state, and local power into the Supreme Court's evolving understandings of liberty and equality under the Fourteenth Amendment's Due Process and Equal Protection Clauses.

Below, I will explain *how* the LCM has failed, and then explore *why* it has failed. The overarching theme of my argument is that the civil rights revolution, by reordering our system around the value of diversity and the evil of discrimination, has neutered the LCM of its power to constrain the advances of legal liberalism.

HOW THE LCM HAS FAILED

The most fundamental problem with the conventional "counter-revolution" narrative is its metric for success. Scholars generally point to three factors as evidence of the LCM's triumph: (1) the Republican Party's control of the Supreme Court over the last fifty years; (2) originalism's rise as a mode of constitutional interpretation; and (3) the Federalist Society's growth as an institution.

None of these factors, however, directly relates to the movement's success. In fact, of all the sociolegal movements that scholars study, the LCM is the only one evaluated with criteria that do not directly relate to actual substantive results.

A helpful contrast can be found in the political science scholarship on how liberal activists used courts to advance civil rights in the 1950s and 1960s. Much of this scholarship focuses on how liberal activists successfully completed the following three steps: (1) they identified a goal (to promote racial integration in various areas of American public and private life); (2) they devised a litigation agenda in accord with that goal (first articulated in Nathan Margold's 1930 NAACP memorandum); and (3) they strategically deployed this agenda to achieve the movement's goal (producing *Brown v. Board of Education*, as well as the various judicial decisions and civil rights statutes that effectuated *Brown's* purpose).[2]

To determine the LCM's success, we should use the same criteria. This means that, before we assess its success, we first must identify the movement's goals, agenda, and strategies. This requires dividing the movement into two periods: its formation period, covering roughly 1955 to 1985, and its operation phase, covering roughly 1986 to the present.

THE MOVEMENT'S FORMATION PERIOD:
1955 TO 1985

The formation of the LCM's intellectual roots can be traced to the emergence of postwar conservatism with William F. Buckley's creation of *National Review* in 1955. The publication's legal commentary, led by James Kilpatrick, focused on the constitutional errors and societal harms wrought by the Warren Court's "rights revolution" – particularly in the areas of race relations, school prayer, and the centralization of federal powers. Politically, it was Richard Nixon in 1968 who ushered in a new era of conservative politics by turning these critiques of the Warren Court into a Republican Party platform.

But the full maturity of the agenda and strategy to overturn the Warren Court's legacy crystallized during the course of President Reagan's two terms, punctuated by Attorney General Meese's formal endorsement of originalism as the administration's preferred mode of interpreting the Constitution. This formal endorsement was made most explicit in Meese's 1985 American Bar Association speech, which identified a specific agenda (to challenge "the radical egalitarianism and expansive civil libertarianism of the Warren Court") and a specific strategy to pursue that agenda ("a Jurisprudence of Original Intention").[3] In explaining how this originalist jurisprudence would challenge the Warren Court's "radical egalitarianism and expansive civil libertarianism," Meese placed the greatest emphasis on how originalism would restore federalism by undoing the doctrine of incorporation – that is, the process by which the Supreme Court used the Fourteenth Amendment to subject the states to the most "fundamental liberties" enumerated in the Bill of Rights. In Meese's words, "nowhere else has the principle of federalism been dealt so politically violent and constitutionally suspect a blow as by the theory of incorporation."[4]

The following year, President Reagan appointed William

Rehnquist to chief justice and Antonin Scalia to associate justice. With control over the Supreme Court, an agenda to pursue, and a strategy to pursue that agenda, the movement seemed primed and ready to take on the Warren Court's legacy.

THE MOVEMENT'S OPERATION PERIOD: 1986 TO PRESENT

Yet in nearly forty years of operation, the LCM has failed to reverse or even narrow a single major Warren Court decision. In fact, over this period, the issues that most galvanized legal conservatives between the 1950s and 1980s have essentially been wiped from the movement's agenda. Astonishingly, many legal conservatives have even shifted to adopt what had been the Warren Court's positions, thereby assimilating the Warren Court's "rights revolution" into the constitutional canon.

Even the Supreme Court's 2021–22 term – which many are claiming will go down in history as a revolutionary term in creating a new originalist and conservative regime in American constitutional law – did little by way of threatening the Warren Court's legacy.

On this point, consider the most controversial and transformative decisions of the 2021–22 term: *Dobbs v. Jackson Women's Health Organization* (overruling the right to an abortion created by *Roe v. Wade*), *New York State Rifle & Pistol Association, Inc. v. Bruen* (requiring states to be more permissive in issuing "right to carry" firearm licenses), *Carson v. Makin* (requiring Maine to include religious schools in its private education voucher program), and *Kennedy v. Bremerton School District* (holding that a public school football coach has a religious liberty and free speech right to engage in public prayer after school games). Of these four, only *Dobbs* is a clear victory for the movement in light of its original goals. *Bruen*, *Carson*, and *Kennedy*, by contrast, continue the conservative shift toward centralization by imposing national rights in areas of law on which states vary greatly.[5] This raises the following question: Why is it that, after more than fifty years of Republicans controlling the Court, the success of legal conservatism has been so limited in scope, to the extent that a movement built around resisting the Warren Court's "rights revolution" now operates within the confines of its revolutionary parameters?

WHY THE LCM HAS FAILED

A successful sociolegal movement requires many features that the LCM has possessed, such as funding, organizational support, and intellectual capital. But it also requires three features that the LCM has lacked: (1) a support structure with a concrete and enduring legal agenda to bind and organize its agents; (2) an underlying moral narrative to substantiate this legal agenda; and (3) a nexus to a political movement and electorate to effectuate, solidify, and broaden this agenda through political action.

LACKING A SUPPORT STRUCTURE WITH A CONCRETE AND ENDURING CONSERVATIVE AGENDA

The failures of the LCM are best understood in light of these particular features. A successful sociolegal movement requires a support structure with a concrete and enduring agenda. This agenda is necessary to coalesce the movement's various factions into a binding and unifying litigation strategy. A significant part of the civil rights movement's success, for example, was a result of the way its support structures (namely, the NAACP and ACLU) unified white liberals, labor activists, and blacks around a concrete litigation agenda. The gay rights movement, likewise, has been successful because its support structures (the Lambda Legal Defense Fund and Human Rights Campaign) have effectively unified the movement's various factions around litigation advancing sexual liberation and marriage equality.

By contrast, the LCM has not had a support structure with a

concrete and enduring agenda. The closest thing the movement has had to a support structure is the Federalist Society, which was created in 1982 by three law students seeking to generate greater intellectual diversity on law school campuses.

Importantly, these students did not seek to replicate the liberal support structures. Instead of modeling the Federalist Society after groups like the NAACP and ACLU (i.e., groups that developed legal agendas, devised litigation strategies, and led litigation campaigns), the Federalist Society founders created a debating society.[6] In fact, in its early years the Federalist Society refused to take sides in political and legal battles, even while the Reagan administration centered its legal agenda around limiting the Warren Court's legacy. As Ted Olson (a key participant in the group's creation) recently recounted, "I don't recall *Roe* being an issue in any such conversations I had concerning [the] creation of Fed Soc." Instead, the creation of the organization was "all about creating a forum/venue for debate" and "not taking sides on any particular issue."[7]

The Federalist Society, of course, has shifted over time, so that it is now much more than a debating society. It now has an established affiliation with the Republican Party and is actively involved in aiding Republican presidential administrations in the judicial appointment process. Even with these changes, however, the Federalist Society still does not have a concrete agenda. To be sure, in accord with the Reagan administration's endorsement of originalism, the Federalist Society's commitment to the rule of law as a general principle has evolved into a more particular commitment to originalism. But originalism does not by itself provide such a concrete agenda. Rather, originalism is a mode of constitutional interpretation that can be shaped and adapted for different substantive ends.

Originalism's malleability as a mode of interpretation is highlighted by how judges and academics have changed its methodology and content over the last twenty-five years. Beginning in the late 1990s, several libertarian-leaning constitutional theorists (such as Randy Barnett) developed what is commonly known in the literature as "New Originalism." Whereas the "old" originalists (like Judge Robert Bork, Professor Raoul Berger, and Attorney General Edwin Meese) limited themselves to historical materials in seeking to ascertain the original intent behind a constitutional provision, the new originalists focus on textual meaning and thus rely more on linguistic interpretive techniques.[8]

This is not a mere philosophic disagreement. The more linguistic approach of New Originalism opened up a broader range of arguments that could be made under the banner of originalism. Accordingly, over the last two decades, several libertarian-leaning New Originalist practitioners have availed themselves of this newfound flexibility by invoking the rhetorical power of originalism while embracing the politics surrounding the Warren Court's activism – particularly as it relates to judicial power, unenumerated liberties, and civil rights.[9]

As a result, the arguments and issues that animated originalists in the 1970s and 1980s have been excised from originalism as a theory and the Federalism Society as a support structure.

LACKING A CONSERVATIVE MORAL NARRATIVE

A successful sociolegal movement must be framed as part of a larger moral and cultural narrative. Courts are inherently conservative institutions, in the sense that they operate through institutional mechanisms – such as jurisdictional prerequisites, procedural requirements, and precedent constraints under the doctrine of *stare decisis* – that are designed to prevent rapid and radical change. Overcoming these obstacles to create change through the judiciary requires convincing courts that there is a moral exigency and broader cultural revolution at hand.

This is precisely what legal liberalism has done. The NAACP, for example, was able to persuade courts to overcome various legal obstacles – such as the state action doctrine, standing requirements, and *stare decisis* – only because there was an accompanying moral and cultural narrative substantiating the movement's legal strategy.

Legal conservatism has operated somewhat differently. While the LCM has not ignored the significance of morality and culture, it has made the mistake of mimicking liberalism by seeking to appropriate the moral authority that civil rights have come to occupy in the American ethos. A critical moment in this regard arose in 1979, when the Scaife Foundation commissioned Michael Horowitz, a former civil rights activist and recent convert to "neoconservatism," to draft a report on how to construct a legal strategy for conservative lawyers. This report, distributed informally to conservative donors and activists, is now known as the "Horowitz Report."[10] Clearly reflecting his background as a civil rights activist and life-long liberal, Horowitz prescribed what Steven Teles has dubbed "liberalism light," in that the report's overarching strategy was to take "the side of blacks in conflicts with liberal interests" so that conservatives – not liberals – would be viewed as "the true inheritors of the civil rights struggle."[11]

This report, in turn, shaped the creation of the Federalist Society. In fact, Horowitz provided much of the Federalist Society's early organizational networking, even going so far as to arrange, together with Irving Kristol, for the organization's initial funding and first office in the AEI building. According to Steven Teles, "Horowitz also played a critical role in getting the Society off the ground, no doubt recognizing that [the Federalist Society] was doing what he called for in his report."[12] Indeed, the Federalist Society's structure as a debating society reflected Horowitz's strategy of structuring legal conservatism as a complement to, rather than a direct opponent of, legal liberalism.

The Horowitz strategy has been triumphant within legal conservatism, so that now much of the movement reflects the governing civil rights morality – centered around the federal judiciary's role in promoting racial diversity as our nation's greatest good and banishing private discrimination as our nation's greatest evil. As will be explained in more detail in the final section of this chapter, the LCM, to be more effective, must assert a moral system that challenges diversity and discrimination as the axes around which our constitutional order revolves.

LACKING A NEXUS TO A CONSERVATIVE POLITICAL MOVEMENT

A successful sociolegal movement must connect its legal agenda and underlying moral narrative to a political movement and electoral constituency. This is because courts have limited power to effect change by themselves. While courts can change a legal interpretation, that interpretation will not translate into actual social change without a nexus to a larger political movement – including private actors, legislators, and executive officials.

Just as the LCM has sought to appropriate the legal Left's moral framework, it has also sought to tap into the Democratic Party's political electorate by focusing on how issues like school choice, affirmative action, and economic liberty relate to the interests of nonwhite constituencies.

The Horowitz Report is again relevant to examine here. This was not simply a strategy for how to pursue conservative litigation; the Horowitz Report was also explicitly framed as an electoral strategy for the Republican Party. Indeed, Horowitz explicitly rested his strategy on "five basic tenets" and one of these five tenets was whether a position could "attract ... potential constituencies for conservatism."[13] As Steven Teles explains, the report's underlying rationale was that "only by embracing the moral imperative of the civil rights ideal and the need to appeal directly to the interests of black Americans could conservatives gain a hearing for their ideas."[14]

In addition to Michael Horowitz, another key figure in developing the LCM's political strategy is Clint Bolick, the founder of Institute for Justice, a libertarian-oriented public interest law firm. Through the course of his work at Institute for Justice, and his many books on conservative legal activism, Bolick has worked, probably more than anyone else, on linking a conservative litigation strategy to a broader political movement. And like the Horowitz Report, Bolick's strategy has been to search principally for black plaintiffs and to depict legal conservatism as a movement that has "blacks as its beneficiaries rather than whites."[15] Notably, in accord with the nation's changing demographics, Bolick has extended this reasoning to Hispanics, arguing in *Immigration Wars: Forging an American Solution*, a book he wrote with Jeb Bush, that conservatives should embrace immigration to attract Hispanic voters.[16] In fact, Bolick has explicitly cautioned against the "losing strategy" of making working-class whites the face of legal conservatism.

This political strategy has come to dominate the LCM, which may explain why conservative law professors were some of the most vocal critics of Donald Trump's 2016 presidential campaign. Consider how, a month before the 2016 election, many leading Federalist Society members signed a statement, *Originalists Against Trump*, pledging their opposition to the Republican candidate.[17] Even after Trump's victory, and the Federalist Society's resulting empowerment under the Trump Administration, the organization continued to resist his populist agenda, so that it is now sharply out of step with the direction of the overall conservative movement, which, in accord with the 2016 election, is increasingly coalesced around varieties of right-wing populism and nationalist conservatism.

Until the LCM gets in line with this shift, so that it can create a stronger nexus to the trajectory of American conservatism, any victories in the Supreme Court will be of limited effect, without the power to mobilize a larger political movement and in turn create significant change in American public and private affairs.

A NEW LEGAL CONSERVATISM?

At the moment, there is only one alternative being offered in terms of how to make legal conservatism more successful as a movement. That alternative is the "common good constitutionalism" project, led by the Catholic integralist and Harvard Law School professor Adrian Vermeule.

This project, however, satisfies only one of the three conditions identified above. Common good constitutionalism does provide a moral framework (grounded in natural law and Catholic theology), and it is a moral framework that is averse to legal liberalism on many important issues. But the movement fails to identify a concrete agenda and strategy to implement that framework. This failure seems to be by design; the movement's proponents resolutely refuse to move beyond theoretical abstractions and to provide particular policy prescriptions. This reluctance to engage the practical sphere is at least partly because there is little electoral support for a movement that seeks to subordinate 330 million Americans to a religious authority.

So, is there an alternative to both common good constitutionalism (which is unlikely to succeed as a movement) and the current form of legal conservatism (which is unlikely to secure any meaningful victories in its success)? There is much uncertainty as to what this third way might look like, but three items should frame how this movement is developed.

One, this new movement should frame a concrete agenda around the freedom of association, on the ground that our other fundamental rights depend on this freedom as both a logical and a practical matter. We cannot, for example, exercise our religious liberty, freedom of speech, and property rights, if we cannot determine whom we worship with, whom we speak to, and whom we have as neighbors. It should be emphasized here that framing a concrete agenda around the freedom of association does not require resting arguments fully or even explicitly on that freedom.

Nor does it require directly challenging the Warren Court's landmark civil rights precedents, which, at this point, are deeply entrenched in our legal system. Just as the NAACP pursued its integrationist agenda through a range of proximate legal arguments and without directly attacking precedent, legal conservatives could pursue the freedom of association through litigation on conceptually adjacent areas of the law, such as education, local governance, and religious liberty. Just as integration as a goal framed the way in which the NAACP developed its particular agenda, the freedom of association should frame how legal conservatives develop their agenda.

Two, this new movement will need to ground the freedom of association in a moral framework. That will require two tasks – a negative task of challenging the civil rights morality and a positive task of offering an alternative moral framework.

The civil rights morality revolves around two moral axes, positing racial diversity as our ultimate good and racial discrimination as our ultimate evil. The civil rights morality thus generates the following two principles: (1) diversity is a constitutional good that our system must seek to promote everywhere, no matter the consequences (hence the persistence of affirmative action); and (2) private discrimination is a constitutional evil that our system must seek to extirpate everywhere, no matter the consequences (hence the acceptance of the way civil rights law impinges on various individual rights and structural limitations). Taking on the negative task of challenging the civil rights morality requires demystifying and indeed desacralizing all the discourse surrounding the good of diversity and the evil of discrimination.

The positive task of offering an alternative moral framework requires explaining how the freedom of association relates not simply to the enforcement of other important rights but also, more fundamentally, to the core moral principle in our system – the idea that we have a God-given natural right to constitute "free and independent" political communities through the exercise of self-governance. This natural right does not stop at the level of political participation in national elections. The moral power of the freedom of association lies in how this freedom can be extended as a right of self-governance all the way down to engagement in the successive political communities of states, local governments, and neighborhoods.

Three, legal conservatives will need to link this freedom-of-association agenda and moral framework to a broader political movement. Here it may prove helpful to tap into the underlying concerns driving the 2016 election and the general backlash against establishment conservatism. Even though this backlash has not been framed explicitly around law and civil rights, the concerns driving that backlash undoubtedly relate to the manner in which various elite institutions (both foreign and domestic, public and private) have coalesced around the civil rights agenda – most fundamentally in terms of how we understand our national identity, whose injuries count as legitimate grievances, and whose interests shape public policy.

To tap into this burgeoning but still inchoate political movement, legal conservatives must change the way they operate, so that they are not siloed off in the Mayflower Hotel as a debating society, or in Poland conspiring to restore papal supremacy in Christendom. Rather, legal conservatives must find a way to engage with the mass and welter of American life, so that the agenda and morality driving legal conservatism goes hand in glove with what ordinary Americans see as the problems plaguing our schools, families, and communities.

None of this will be easy. The expansion of the civil rights regime has rendered the freedom of association a taboo concept in American law and politics. Civil rights have, in turn, become our moral system, subsuming the Founding Era's two moral pillars – Christianity and natural rights. And after decades of propaganda, indoctrination, and subordination, Americans have largely lost the discipline, will, and virtue to engage in republican self-governance. Restoring an ethos of self-governance in a nation with a vanishing role for Christian teaching, communal belonging, and familial order may seem an impossible task.

It would, of course, be easier for legal conservatives to continue following the Horowitz strategy of tracking the path set by legal liberalism. While an easier task, this is ultimately a losing strategy, one that will almost certainly make conservatism a narrower and more challenging project for future generations. The only meaningful way forward is for conservatives to gather the moral fortitude, intellectual seriousness, and political will to reject the civil rights regime and to push for something new. The first thing to do is to look to the freedom of association for guidance.

NOTES

1   Amanda Hollis-Brusky, *Ideas with Consequences: The Federalist Society and the Conservative Counterrevolution* (New York: Oxford University Press, 2015). For similar depictions of this "counterrevolution," see Herman Schwartz, *Right-Wing Justice: The Conservative Campaign to Take Over the Courts* (New York: Nation Books, 2004); Steven M. Teles, *The Rise of the Conservative Legal Movement: The Battle for Control of the Law* (Princeton, NJ: Princeton University Press, 2008); Ann Southworth, *Lawyers of the Right: Professionalizing the Conservative Coalition* (Chicago: University of Chicago Press, 2008); Erwin Chemerinsky, *The Conservative Assault on the Constitution* (New York: Simon & Schuster, 2010); Michael Avery and Danielle McLaughlin, *The Federalist Society: How Conservatives Took the Law Back from Liberals* (Nashville, TN: Vanderbilt University Press, 2013); Michael J. Graetz and Linda Greenhouse, *The Burger Court and the Rise of the Judicial Right* (New York: Simon & Schuster, 2016).
2   Mark V. Tushnet, *The NAACP's Legal Strategy against Segregated Education, 1925–1950* (Chapel Hill: University of North Carolina Press, 2005); Bruce Ackerman, *We the People*, vol. 3, *The Civil Rights Revolution* (Cambridge: Belknap Press, 2014); Megan Ming Francis and John Fabian Witt, "Movement Capture or Movement Strategy? A Critical Race History Exchange on the Beginnings of *Brown v. Board*," *Yale Journal of Law & Humanities* 31 (2021): 521–46; John Fabian Witt, "Garland's Million; or, the Tragedy and Triumph of Legal History: American Society for Legal History Plenary Lecture, New Orleans," *Law and History Review* 40, no. 1 (2022): 123–47.
3   Edwin Meese III, "Speech to the American Bar Association," Washington, DC, American Bar Association, 1985, https://www.justice.gov/sites/default/files/ag/legacy/2011/08/23/07-09-1985.pdf.

4   Ibid.
5   That is not to downplay the extent to which conservatives favor gun rights and school choice as policy matters. Nevertheless, it is still the case that the Supreme Court's using the Fourteenth Amendment to construct a uniform national policy on these issues is inconsistent with the movement's original goal to limit federal judicial power over local affairs. In this sense, *Bruen*, *Carson*, and *Kennedy* extend rather than resist the Warren Court's legacy of creating a Supreme Court that oversees and manages how states exercise their police powers.
6   Steven M. Teles, *Rise of the Conservative Legal Movement*, 137–80.
7   Emma Green, "How the Federalist Society Won," *New Yorker*, July 24, 2022, https://www.newyorker.com/news/annals-of-education/how-the-federalist-society-won.
8   Jesse Merriam, "A Sheep in Wolf's Clothing: The Story of Why Conservatives Began to Look Beyond Originalism," *Faulkner Law Review* 11, no. 1 (2021): 121–23.
9   For example, in Randy Barnett's most significant piece of originalist scholarship, *Original Meaning of the Fourteenth Amendment: Its Letter and Spirit* (Cambridge: Belknap Press, 2021) (coauthored with his protege, Evan Bernick), Barnett and Bernick do not identify a single Warren Court decision that would be substantively changed under their proposed originalist framework of interpreting the Fourteenth Amendment. They do concede that the *reasoning* for some of the Warren Court's decisions might have to be altered slightly, but the *actual legal outcomes* would not need to be changed.
10 Teles, *Rise of the Conservative Legal Movement,* 67–73.
11 Steven Teles, "Compassionate Conservatism, Domestic Policy, and the Politics of Ideational Change," in *Crisis of Conservatism? The Republican Party, the Conservative Movement, and American Politics After Bush*, ed. Joel D. Aberback and Gillian Peele (New York: Oxford University Press, 2011), 193.
12 Teles, *Rise of the Conservative Legal Movement,* 141.
13 Ibid., 72.
14 Teles, "Compassionate Conservatism," 193.
15 Ibid., 197.
16 Clint Bolick and Jeb Bush, *Immigration Wars: Forging an American Solution* (New York: Threshold Editions, 2014), 210–25.
17 See 2016 Statement: Originalists against Trump, WordPress, accessed November 21, 2022, https://originalistsagainsttrump.wordpress.com/2016-statement/; Ilya Somin, "Originalists Against Trump," *Washington Post*, October 17, 2016, https://www.washingtonpost.com/news/volokh-conspiracy/wp/2016/10/17/originalists-against-trump/. Likewise, the 2016 National Lawyer's Convention, held just two weeks after the

election, did not have a single panel on immigration. The convention featured speeches by two politicians, then-governor Nikki Haley and Senator Ben Sasse, both at the time vociferous critics of Trump's populism.

THE NUCLEAR OPTION
Transforming America's Failed Immigration Policy

Jeremy Carl

FOR DECADES, Americans on the Right have been arguing for a serious immigration policy that protects our borders and our sovereignty. The consequences of not doing this are clear. As President Theodore Roosevelt argued, "The one absolutely certain way of bringing this nation to ruin, of preventing all possibility of its continuing to be a nation at all, would be to permit it to become a tangle of squabbling nationalities."[1] More than a century has passed since Roosevelt's observation, and his words look increasingly prophetic.

America will not survive in any meaningful sense if we do not get control of our border and develop a will for national life and a unified American identity. And this will be impossible if we do not challenge the open-borders fanatics both intellectually and practically in ways that transcend the narrow policy/bargaining approach of previous administrations.

Elites from both parties, addicted to cheap labor (and Democrats, to easy votes), have refused to do anything meaningful to stop it. Current polling from Gallup suggests that those who want immigration reduced outnumber those who want it increased nearly four to one.[2] Historically, those who have supported general amnesty for illegals have been outnumbered by those who opposed it by nearly ten to one.[3]

We have failed in past opportunities to do just this. During the Clinton administration, at a time when even the Democrats still had to pretend to care about America's borders, a bipartisan commission chaired by civil rights icon and former congresswoman Barbara Jordan produced an entirely sensible blueprint for genuine immigration reform focused on reducing chain migration, focusing on skills-based immigration, getting serious about deportation, and capping the number of legal immigrants at 550,000 per year.[4]

Almost three decades later, we have done none of this, even after the presidency of Donald Trump, who ran on immigration restriction and border control as his central campaign issue. Indeed, after a brief lull under Trump, immigration, and in particular illegal immigration, has continued at a torrid pace with a record number of illegal arrivals during the beginning of the Biden administration, totaling almost five million people in its first eighteen months.[5] The practical arc of US immigration policy is long, but it bends toward continuous invasion and amnesty.

It has not helped that the Right's leading "intellectuals" have often acquiesced in this selling out of the American people. As President Bush was contemplating the Immigration Act of 1990, Ben Wattenberg, the leading scholar of demographics at AEI, wrote "The Case for More Immigration" in *Commentary*. While acknowledging the costs of immigration in terms of social cohesion, Wattenberg claimed that "We are ethnically, religiously, and racially diverse. This does not always make for easy relations, but there is no changing it."[6] But of course something could change it, which would require transforming that unhelpful diversity into a unity, possible only if immigration were massively reduced, and if existing newcomers were made to assimilate to American norms.

NOT A NATION OF IMMIGRANTS

To prepare the ground politically for real policy change, we need to tell Americans the genuine history of American immigration. We must begin this process by rejecting the mid-twentieth century's leftist myth, now accepted by much of the Right, that we are "a nation of immigrants."

The "nation of immigrants" myth contains a political strategy, which is, of course, why the Left adopted it: if we're a nation of immigrants, then it is wrong to meaningfully restrict our border.

In truth, immigrants have never been a dominant group in our population; indeed, as recently as 1970, they made up as little as 4.7 percent of the population. Even then, they were primarily elderly immigrants from Europe. In the 1960 census, the last one conducted before the Hart-Celler immigration act of 1965 (which fundamentally transformed the country by creating our modern immigration system, getting rid of national origins quotas, enabling chain migration, and drastically reshaping American immigration policy) the average age of immigrants was fifty-seven, as opposed to twenty-seven for native-born Americans. Eighty-four percent of these immigrants came from Europe or Canada.[7]

Given life expectancies at the time, we would have expected even this small number to be cut almost in half by 1980 without Hart-Celler. Instead, on an absolute basis we now have more than three times the number of immigrants that we had during previous immigration peaks. This level of immigration eventually leads directly to social instability; it leads to a loss of a cohesive national identity in the shorter term. While social conflict is present in every country, anyone alive during, say, the 1980s (to say nothing of earlier decades) knows that on the most fundamental questions (e.g., should we be tearing down the statues of our countries' founders) our country is far more fragmented today than it was then. Simply put, the current cold civil war we are engaged in would have been unimaginable without the overheated immigration policies of the last several decades.

Ironically, leftists have a better sense of our immigration history than most conservatives. Leftist historian Roxanne Dunbar-Ortiz's bestselling book, titled *Not a Nation of Immigrants*, argues that America was a nation of settlers. Settlers created new communities, a new culture, and a society where no settled society had existed before.[8] Settlers build a society – immigrants inhabit it only after the settlers have done the hard work of creation. As America expanded its frontiers, some people did immigrate into existing cities and towns, yet many more would help redefine America by settling on and developing the frontier, expanding America's culture and people to places it had not existed previously. America was still being created, not simply joined.

Such observations were not once the sole province of radicals. Alexis de Tocqueville, for instance, does not mention the words *immigrant* or *immigration* at all in *Democracy in America*, as immigrants were a tiny percentage of 1830s America. This was true for the first two hundred plus years of American history (a time greater, in total, than all the time that has gone by since). During the revolution, our citizen population was 85 percent British, 9 percent German, and 4 percent Dutch.[9] And, as one commentator on Tocqueville noted about this incongruity, "The initial groups that had come to America two centuries before were conceived of as Pilgrims, colonists, or settlers, but not immigrants per se."[10]

We continued in this vein until around 1890, when the Census Bureau determined that the frontier was closed – everywhere in America now had settlers. Thus, the great American historian Frederick Jackson Turner would famously declare in an 1893 speech that "The frontier has gone, and with its going has closed the first period of American history."[11] Prior to the closure of the frontier, a period encompassing most of the history of nonindigenous settlement in America, we were not a nation of immigrants – we were a nation of settlers *with* immigrants – and that is a core distinction.

BECOMING "A NATION OF IMMIGRANTS"

The phrase, "A Nation of Immigrants," originates from the title of a 1958 book by then senator John F. Kennedy, as he prepared for a presidential run.

Kennedy's book was republished in 1964 after his assassination during the debate over the Hart-Celler act. The first outlined draft was written by a historian hired by the Anti-Defamation League, the premier Jewish NGO in America. That outline was turned into a book by Kennedy staffer Myer Feldman (whose Jewish parents had arrived from Ukraine three years before his birth). The law itself was passed in no small part owing to heavy lobbying from Catholics and Jews, whom Kennedy (a Catholic) had been targeting in his campaign. Many Jews, stung by the many instances of oppression experienced in ethnically unified countries in Europe in which most had formerly resided, were eager not to have an ethnically unified America in which the majority might discriminate against them.[12] Catholics also often felt like second-class citizens; electing one of their own (Kennedy) as president and justifying continued immigration from Catholic-majority countries, therefore, would increase their political power.[13]

A more accurate retelling of America's immigration history would describe America in two distinct phases: during the first half of our history, we were a nation of settlers, largely an outpost of Britain, whose free population was overwhelmingly of British origin. The next period, ending in the nineteenth century, is characterized by a mixture of settlement and immigration from a broader swath of Europe alone. These two trends overwhelmingly defined our history up to the point that we went from a tiny peripheral colony to one of the world's great powers. While twentieth-century patterns of immigration fit more closely with Kennedy's immigration mythos, we didn't become "a nation of immigrants" until the Democratic Party needed it as a voting strategy.

And getting this history right matters: If we're a nation of immigrants, fundamentally, then we are wrong not to just throw open the door. But if we are a nation not of immigrants, but a nation *with* immigrants, this does not apply. This is a crucial distinction. In our settlement phase and later, when we rose as an industrializing power, settlement and then immigration may have served the national interest. America during this period was a largely stable nation. Today, in a postindustrial welfare state, it does not, though it does accelerate balkanization in an already fractious populace.

Because the Republican establishment has, in many ways, embraced the Left's flawed premises on immigration, in some ways it was destined to fail on immigration policy. But there are other, structural reasons why the Republican establishment has failed.

A focus on formal policymaking is necessary for change, but it is not sufficient. But the Right has several serious policy advocacy groups – ranging from the Center for Immigration Studies to the Federation of American Immigration Reform to Numbers USA. We have informational websites like Refugee Resettlement Watch that discuss in detail the Left's immigration scams and blatant violations of both the letter and spirit of the law.[14] We even had a president who wanted to build a border wall, who was joined in that desire by his original attorney general Jeff Sessions and his key policy advisors, and who had serious champions in Congress. Nevertheless, much opposition was encountered by establishment conservatives, who personify the yawning gap between the GOP's working- and middle-class voting base and its historically corporatist power structure, which reliably produced presidents and presidential nominees with dire records on immigration.

The original sin of the GOP was the Immigration Reform and Control Act of 1986, President Reagan's "amnesty in exchange for enforcement" compromise deal, which may have seemed like a reasonable bargain at the time. But ultimately, Americans got all of the amnesty (of nearly three million illegal aliens) promised in the bill and no enforcement. George H. W. Bush, scion of northeastern liberal corporate Republicanism, was a dedicated amnesty supporter, increasing immigration numbers in the Immigration Act of 1990, which he signed into law, adding the diversity visa (fifty thousand annually), and increasing Reagan's immigration amnesty, raising the cap of legal immigrants each year to 675,000 from 290,000, while accomplishing little or nothing on enforcement.

His son George W. Bush, a liberal New England Republican cosplaying as a Texan conservative, repeatedly attempted to enact "comprehensive immigration reform" (i.e., mass amnesty with no enforcement) only to be derailed after an open rebellion by a furious base. In his postpresidency, he's spent his time doing oil paintings of immigrants while continuing to push for amnesty.[15]

The GOP's next nominee, John McCain, was perhaps the party's most notorious amnesty supporter, who fortunately never set immigration policy as president but who attempted to drag the whole party to the left with him. His "gang of eight" immigration compromise, if it had been enacted, would have led to the legalization of up to eleven million illegals. Mitt Romney's immigration policy was better on paper (including self-deportation incentives), but had no credibility, given the incessant pandering to the political Left that has defined his political career. Only Trump stepped into the breach to finally align the GOP's immigration policy with the interests and desires of its voting base. Yet even Trump could not fundamentally alter the tide of US immigration policy. To understand why that is the case, let us look at the Trump administration's actual immigration record.

THE LESSONS OF TRUMP'S
IMMIGRATION FAILURES

Under Trump, immigration, both legal and illegal, was significantly reduced from the Obama years. Deportations increased. The Remain in Mexico policy, which required those seeking asylum in the United States at the Mexican border to remain in Mexico until their court date, worked to discourage hundreds of thousands of bogus asylum claims. Refugee numbers crashed to a low of 15,000 per year from a high of 80,000 or so in the last years of the Obama administration. Some parts of the border wall were built and strengthened. Yet there was little fundamental long-term change – no mass deportations of illegals, no meaningful legislation passed; moreover, most of the Trump administration's accomplishments have been undone by President Biden.

The Trump administration failed to end Obama's blatantly unconstitutional DACA executive order after being thwarted by the left-wing judges and by the Supreme Court's allegedly conservative wing. The absurd diversity visa lottery is still in place.

While Trump was extremely skilled at riling up the Republican base on immigration, his "murderers and rapists" and "shithole countries" language played into the strategies of his opponents to paint his policies as extreme. Simply put, Trump managed to frame the popular narrative on immigration but, as on so many other issues, he failed to successfully move policy elites whom he allowed to exercise veto power over his action – for example, by letting legal advisors dictate who he appointed to run DHS, or by allowing district court judges to stymie his facially legal travel ban on multiple occasions without fundamentally challenging their authority. Meanwhile, on the ground, catch and release is still the standard way of dealing with immigration, a policy that originated in an unsound five to four Supreme Court ruling in *Zadvydas v. Davids*, which arbitrarily limited the ability to detain illegal aliens. Trump's signature

RAISE Act centered on skills-based immigration policy did not even come close to passing (being tabled in 2017 and getting just thirty-nine votes in the Senate in 2019).

These failures can be a blessing – if we choose to learn from them. The principal lesson we can learn from the Trump administration's failures is that there is simply no way to win on the immigration issue, no matter how dedicated the GOP is, if we play under the current rigged system, in which advocacy groups, resettlement agencies, and endless leftist lawfare determine immigration policy.

Another valuable lesson is that a strategy focusing primarily on immigration as a single policy issue, rather than an embedded issue within a broader sociopolitical context of leftist institutional capture of the government, is doomed to fail. The Right lacks the power to enact an effective immigration policy because we lack institutional power within the government more generally. This is a core problem.

If, in attempting to enact immigration policy, we engage in a process of bargaining with the judiciary, the administrative state, and the media mandarins, all of which are captured by the Left, we are doomed to failure. If we do not rout the corporatists in our own party we are doomed to failure. If we do not remove ourselves from international agreements that subject our immigration policies to foreign veto, such as various international migration treaties and compacts, often under the aegis of a corrupt United Nations, we are doomed to failure.[16] If we allow the so-called civil rights bureaucracy – in particular, radical activist civil rights bureaucrats in the Department of Justice – to determine our immigration policy, we are also doomed to failure.

The good news is that we are not, in fact, doomed to failure: we have the power to succeed if we accept that political power is where we say it is rather than where the Left says it is. The conservative political theorist Sam Francis offered a compelling critique of the Right's approach to policymaking decades ago in his essay "Beautiful Losers" in which he wrote:

In the absence of a significant cultural base, such political efforts not only were bound to fail but also had the effect of drawing the right further into the institutional and conceptual framework of the liberal regime. Political maneuver by its nature is a process of bargaining, and the more conservatives have engaged in political action, the more they have found themselves bargaining and compromising with their opponents, who often do not need to bargain at all. Since their opponents on the Left, in Congress or the executive branch, have ready access to and sympathy from the mass media, they are able to discredit the men and measures of the Right that will not bend to their manipulation.

In other words, we cannot win on the Left's battlefield using their tools. Replacing the regime apparatus, rather than bargaining with it, is the first step to achieve victory. This means paying more attention to tactics and execution and less to abstract policy design.

CHANGE FACTS ON THE GROUND

Combined with an educational campaign, we need a campaign of practical steps that will not be constrained by robed activists or engaged in give-and-take with the Left, one that accepts the president's historical and legal role as the primary driver of our immigration policy.[17] This would be done as an adjunct to efforts to reform our legal immigration system through a bill similar to the RAISE Act.

Elements of this could include but should not be limited to:

REMOVING PROTECTIONS AND INCENTIVES FOR ILLEGAL ENTRY

1. Remove Temporary Protected Status completely rather than piecemeal. There are currently more than four hundred thousand otherwise illegal immigrants living in the United

States under TPS. We should end this en masse and repeal the portion of the immigration act of 1990 that authorizes it. We should not negotiate with the bureaucracy, judges, and the media about whether ending TPS is appropriate on a country by country basis.

2. Simultaneously, Congress should also repeal the presential parole authority it granted in 1952 that allowed presidents to circumvent immigration caps by bringing in immigrants for "humanitarian reasons" or significant public benefit, an authority that has been abused under numerous presidential administrations. Current court challenges by Texas to the administration's parole power may accomplish this, and the fifth circuit has already ruled against the Biden administration's illegal "mass parole" activities.

3. Connected to this, we should enter into agreements with other countries that would be willing to accept aliens on a permanent basis who had originally migrated to America because of legitimate fears of political persecution in their home countries... Such agreements would be accompanied by aid necessary to pay for the transfer and the initial maintenance of such immigrants, along with extra financial incentives for these third countries.

   These nations will not likely be among the most desired landing spots for asylum seekers, but for those with legitimate claims they will certainly offer a more attractive alternative than genuine persecution or fear for one's life at home. Without a golden ticket to the United States, bogus asylum claims (that is to say, the overwhelming majority of them) would be dramatically reduced and, after an initial surge of cases, numbers would likely be quite modest.

4. We should challenge birthright citizenship at the Supreme Court. Children born to illegal immigrants should not be

granted citizenship, something that, as it currently stands, is almost unique in the United States among developed nations. This could be done using a model similar to that of Australia, which granted citizenship to the children of citizens or Green Card holders while offering some legal status (not citizenship) to existing illegal immigrants who have lived the majority of their childhoods in the United States (with a zero tolerance policy going forward). While it is not clear that such an effort would be successful with the current court, it is clear that 100 percent of the battles will be lost if they are not fought at all.

TAKING CONCRETE ENFORCEMENT ACTIONS AND DELEGITIMIZING BUREAUCRATIC AND JUDICIAL INTERFERENCE

1. We should immediately deport people presumed to be here illegally and ignore any judicial attempts to thwart the process. This should be particularly true at the border, but also in legally clear cases in the interior (for example, known illegal aliens who are caught in the US interior).

2. We should put the US Army at the border and make it clear in the mission to the soldiers that a primary goal for our armed forces should be protecting our border (in conjunction with frontline work for the border patrol), as nations have understood the role of armies from time immemorial. Rules of engagement should be made clear, but the soldiers should have the right to legally fire, where necessary, on anyone invading US territory.

3. Taking a page from President Lincoln, we should develop a coordinated strategy for thwarting radical judicial decisions, beginning with challenging the alleged powers of district judges to issue nationwide injunctions. Lincoln ignored judicial supremacy in the Dred Scott case before the Civil

War and would later do the same during the war in Ex Parte Maerryman, in which the court attempted to limit his ability to hold prisoners of war. Prestigious legal scholars such as Harvard's Noah Feldman have even argued that the Emancipation Proclamation itself was a constitutional violation. But it was certainly not a moral one. The actions of blue states in attempting to nullify Dobbs or recent firearms cases may suggest possible strategies of resistance.

More fundamentally, we should reassert Congress's plenary power over immigration, which is constitutionally supported and has decades of judicial rulings. The president should issue a legal opinion confirming this power, and Congress should explicitly strip jurisdiction from the courts and make it clear that immigration policy is set by the politically accountable branches of government.

4. We should debureaucratize immigration claims by taking power away from so-called "immigration judges." Policymaking takes place at the executive and legislative level. Bureaucrats are there to implement policy, not to themselves demand policy, and their scope for granting immigration claims should be reduced dramatically. Even doing simple things like requiring multiple judges to approve a claim before it is granted (but only one to deny it) would help dramatically.

5. We should criminally prosecute members of the previous regime who have broken their oath of office and subverted the law. We should use FOIAed communications and a January 6 strategy to build the case. We need to go after big names – Secretary Mayorkas and the senior officials who have enabled him, mayors who enact sanctuary city policies, and so on. Until senior officials flouting the law feel that there is a personal risk to themselves, the Left's approach will not change. Redirect much of the civil rights bureaucracy at the

Department of Justice toward this end, which will strengthen the civil rights of Americans. We need the equivalent of a January 6 commission to prosecute those who have allowed the current invasion.

BEEFING UP EXISTING ENFORCEMENT MECHANISMS

1. We should dramatically increase criminal penalties for those involved in human trafficking or human smuggling.

2. We can dramatically increase the ICE enforcement budget. Much of the alleged "discretion" used by Democrats to ignore immigration laws involves claims that they must prioritize their enforcement using prosecutorial discretion. We can provide enough budget for removal that this excuse is no longer viable. This must specifically be targeted at enforcement and not just customers. Ideally, this should be done in the context of a broader rethinking of asylum policies worldwide, as the current ones are Cold War relics.

3. We should enact mandatory E-verify for employment, and strengthen it with federal enforcement. The government itself should take over checks and approvals, reducing the burden on employers.

4. We should prosecute visa overstayers much more harshly – this is the hidden part of illegal immigration. Make higher-risk visa holders post visa bonds and more carefully track those who come on visas. The substantial majority of illegal immigrants under Trump were those who overstayed their visas. While the outrageous opening of our border under Biden may mean this is no longer true, they are still a huge portion of illegals. We should revive the 2005 proposal that treated a visa overstay of thirty days as legally the same as illegal entry.

ASSERTING NATIONAL AND, WHERE NECESSARY,
STATE IMMIGRATION SOVEREIGNTY

1. We should withdraw from all global conventions on refugees. Whether we will take refugees at all, let alone how many of them we take, should be determined solely by our sovereign interests.

2. When we don't control the White House, we should empower the states to enforce immigration laws. The recent attempts of the state of Arizona and some Texas counties at the border to declare an invasion and demand Federal constitutional protections against invasion (Article IV, section 4) are a welcome start along these lines. Better yet, have states and localities simply start deporting people, since the federal government has refused to take action. Will the Democrats really risk the optics disaster of bringing in the army to keep localities from enforcing the federal laws that they refuse to enforce?

While each element of the nuclear option will generate hysteria from the Left and fury from their propaganda organs in the media, such an approach, which favors execution over abstract policy, is necessary for victory.

Ultimately our immigration aims must be as clear as they are simple: As Winston Churchill said in his inaugural speech as prime minister: "You ask, what is our aim? I can answer in one word. It is victory. Victory at all costs … for without victory there is no survival."[18]

And John Locke, in his *Essay Concerning Human Understanding*, wrote that "The actions of men [are] the best interpreters of their thoughts."[19] And it is only by translating our thinking on immigration into concrete action that we can restore our borders and sovereignty, and simultaneously, secure America's future.

NOTES

1   Theodore Roosevelt, "Address to the Knights of Columbus," transcript of
    speech delivered at Carnegie Hall, New York, October 12, 1915, https://
    en.wikisource.org/wiki/Address_to_the_Knights_of_Columbus.

2   Megan Brenan, "Dissatisfaction With U.S. Immigration Level Rises to
    58%," Gallup, February 14, 2022, https://news.gallup.com/poll/389708/
    dissatisfaction-immigration-level-rises.aspx.

3   Lydia Saad, "Americans Clearly Oppose Amnesty for Illegal Mexican
    Immigrants," Gallup, September 6, 2001, https://news.gallup.com/
    poll/4852/americans-clearly-oppose-amnesty-illegal-mexican-immi-
    grants.aspx. Even today 60 percent or more of Americans are significantly
    worried about illegal immigration. See Andrew R. Arthur, "Gallup: 60
    Percent of Americans Are Concerned About Illegal Immigration," *Center
    for Immigration Studies*, April 21, 2022, https://cis.org/Arthur/Gallup-
    60-Percent-Americans-Are-Concerned-About-Illegal-Immigration.

4   Commission on Immigration Reform, *Becoming an American: Immigration
    & Immigrant Policy* (1997), https://www.numbersusa.com/sites/default/
    files/public/from_drupal5/JordanCommissionfull-report.pdf.

5   "FAIR Analysis: 4.9 Million Illegal Aliens Have Crossed our Borders Since
    President Biden Took Office," Press Releases, Federation for American
    Immigration Reform, August 16, 2022, https://www.fairus.org/press-
    releases/border-security/fair-analysis-49-million-illegal-aliens-have-
    crossed-our-borders.

6   Ben J. Wattenberg, "The Case for More Immigration," *Commentary*, April
    1990, https://www.commentary.org/articles/ben-wattenberg-2/
    the-case-for-more-immigration/.

7   "Chapter 5: U.S. Foreign-Born Population Trends," Pew Research Center,
    May 30, 2020, https://www.pewresearch.org/hispanic/2015/09/28/chap-
    ter-5-u-s-foreign-born-population-trends/.https://www.pewresearch.org/
    hispanic/2015/09/28/chapter-5-u-s-foreign-born-population-trends/

8   Roxanne Dunbar-Ortiz, *Not "A Nation of Immigrants": Settler Colonialism,
    White Supremacy, and a History of Erasure and Exclusion* (Boston: Beacon
    Press, 2022), 37–42.

9   "The Growth of the Colonies," Boundless US History, Course Hero,
    accessed November 21, 2022, https://www.coursehero.com/study-guides/
    boundless-ushistory/the-growth-of-the-colonies/.

10 Nancy L. Green, "Tocqueville, Comparative History, and Immigration in
    Two Democracies," *French Politics, Culture & Society* 26, no. 2 (Summer
    2008): 1.

11 Frederick Jackson Turner, "The Significance of the Frontier in American
    History (1893)," https://nationalhumanitiescenter.org/pds/gilded/empire/
    text1/turner.pdf.

12 See, for example, Otis Graham, *Unguarded Gates: A History of America's Immigration Crisis* (Lanham, MD: Rowan & Littlefield Publishers, 2004), 73–79; Maddelena Marinari, *Unwanted: Italian and Jewish Mobilization Against Restrictive Immigration Laws, 1882–1965* (Chapel Hill: University of North Carolina Press, 2020), 151–74.

13 See Marinari, *Unwanted*; Danielle Battisti, "The End of the National Origins System and the Limits of White Ethnic Liberalism" in *Whom Shall We Welcome: Italian Ameicans and Immigration Reform 1945-1965* (New York: Fordham University Press, 2019); "1965 Legislation," American Catholic History Classroom, The Catholic University of America, accessed November 22, 2022, https://cuomeka.wrlc.org/exhibits/show/immigration/background/1965-intro.

14 For examples, see Refugee Resettlement Watch, https://refugeeresettle-mentwatch.org/.

15 "Out of Many, One," Events and Exhibits, George W. Bush Presidential Center, accessed November 21, 2022, https://www.bushcenter.org/exhibits-and-events/exhibits/2021/out-of-many-one.html.

16 These would include the UN's convention on the status of refugees (to which we are party to an amended protocol) and the Global Compact on Migration, which the Trump administration wisely excluded us from but which the Biden administration would happily join if it could.

17 Congress does have the power to naturalize and to set some broad laws, but the president, as with his role as commander in chief, is in the best position to determine immigration policy. As the chief law enforcement officer, the president is well positioned to immediately direct enforcement of deportation without congressional approval.

18 Winston Churchill, "Blood, Toil, Tears, and Sweat," transcript of a speech delivered to the House of Commons, London, May 13, 1940, https://www.nationalchurchillmuseum.org/blood-toil-tears-and-sweat.html.

19 John Locke, *An Essay Concerning Human Understanding*, chap. 3 (London: T. Tegg and Son, 1836), 22.

DEMOGRAPHIC CHANGE AND AMERICAN INSTABILITY

Eric Kaufmann

DEMOGRAPHIC CHANGES – shifts in the size and composition of the population – affect national identity and effectiveness. Yet this is a policy area in which post-1960s progressive taboos have almost entirely suppressed debate. When it comes to seriously thinking about – not to mention managing – demography there is either silence or only one acceptable viewpoint, strictly enforced, both by those on the Left and the free market Right.

The Hart-Celler Act of 1965 removed cultural criteria from US immigration policy, with its sponsors, like Bobby Kennedy, insisting this would not change the ethnic composition of the country. At the same time, border enforcement was relaxed compared to the 1950s, when President Eisenhower's administration deported large numbers of illegal immigrants. This liberalization occurred following a revolution in public morality when, as Shelby Steele notes in his book *White Guilt*, racism emerged as a public taboo. The result has been a major change in the country's ethnic demographics, from 85 percent non-Hispanic white in 1960 to approximately 60 percent non-Hispanic white in 2020.

In the United States, as in some other Western countries, politicians tend to duck questions such as how to manage ethnic change or whether it is proper to do so, and how to increase fertility rates. Often conservatives simply endorse the progressive consensus on the matter: increase immigration and improve choices for women to manage work and childcare. Progressive views are not necessarily wrong (especially on the link between female choice and higher fertility), but, over the last generation, Republicans have cleaved to a deceptively stylized "pro-growth" dogma, which takes as its core political consideration that of maximizing population size and GDP. They have forgotten that one can have a large GDP but a lower per capita GDP, or that economic growth may be purchased at the cost of widespread national alienation and hollowed-out communities. In the post-1965 period, as in earlier eras in American history, left-liberal activists and big business made common cause against much of the American public.[1]

The enforcement of a tight Overton Window of acceptable debate around demography does not change the reality that problems stemming from population change are increasing, and are vital for the United States to manage well if it is to avoid economic, social, and political conflict.

THE POLITICS OF ETHNIC TRANSFORMATION

The Right rarely considers changes in the ethnic composition of the American population and what this means for voting, national identity, populism, and polarization. Global population change is having a major impact on both international and domestic politics. Why? Because we are living through a period of mass population change. The post-1800 demographic transition from high birth rates to below-replacement birth rates is accelerating and has spread around the world. But the transition is occurring extremely unevenly across the globe, causing imbalances within and between countries, often producing tension and instability. Countries that are early in their transition, such as Mali or Afghanistan, are undergoing population explosion – in part because of the delivery of medicine and technology by the West –

as infant mortality rates have fallen faster than birth rates. On the flipside, countries that have gone through the transition, especially in the West and East Asia, are aging and entering into a period of population decline.

The West had its population explosion in the nineteenth and early twentieth centuries, but this took place when medicine and hygiene were less advanced, so the population increase was much more gradual. For instance, Denmark and Guatemala had similar populations prior to their transition, but Denmark went through it gradually from the late eighteenth century to the mid-twentieth century while Guatemala only did so in the late twentieth and early twenty-first centuries. Because medicine was so superior in the late twentieth century compared to that of earlier periods, Guatemala's population may expand as much as twenty-four times its pretransition level, compared to just five times for Denmark. If one multiplies these stories across the globe, it is easy to understand why there were two Europeans for every African in 1950 but will be four Africans for every European in 2050.[2]

Meanwhile, globalization has encouraged a major increase in long-distance immigration from the Global South, where 97 percent of the world's population growth takes place, to the West. The share of people born outside their country of residence has nearly doubled in the West since 1990 but has remained flat elsewhere in the world.[3] This south-to-north long-distance migration results in uneven population growth between religions and ethnic groups in countries receiving the migrants, altering the social and political balance. Voting in a democracy is based on population ("one person, one vote"), and, where ethnic or religious identity is tightly linked to party, demography clearly affects power.

Sometimes birth rate differences alone cause ethnic change, while in other cases immigration is the driver. Often both are at work. The result can be a shift in political power. In California, the change from nearly 80 percent non-Hispanic white in 1970 to 40 percent in the 2000s helped shift California from a safely Republican to a safely Democratic state.[4]

Even in America or Western Europe, the fact that minorities are more likely to vote for the Left, and are growing, has big political implications. While assimilation may gradually erode the Left's advantage, as occurred with white Catholics in America after 1960 and has begun to take place among nonwhites since 2008, the outcome of this process is not yet certain.[5]

A second component of political demography concerns the reasonable fear of demographic change. Demographic anxieties have been a consistent driver of international and domestic conflict. The French, for example, once feared the British because England's population, which was a third of France's in 1700, had pulled equal by 1900 while exporting 25 million people to Canada, the United States, Australasia, and South Africa. Britain and France reasonably feared Germany, which underwent a population boom starting in the late nineteenth century. Germans in turn feared the Russians, whose population boomed in the interwar period.[6]

Within countries, the United States, Canada, and Scotland, for example, fretted over their growing Catholic populations between 1840 and 1940, leading to immigration restrictionism and anti-Catholic voting. The rise of the populist Right in Europe, and of Trump in America, would be unimaginable without the perception that the immigration issue, as well as its knock-on effects on the decline of the ethnic majority, has gone unaddressed. This also largely explains why there is muted national populism in East Asia's low-immigration democracies. In Eastern Europe, only those countries within the European Union, and thus those potentially exposed to ethnic change, have experienced powerful national populism.

Cultural and psychological disquiet over ethnic change and escalating diversity, not personal economic circumstances, largely accounts for public concern over immigration.[7] When I ask Trump voters how worried they are on a 0–100 scale about urban sprawl, or Brexit voters how concerned they are about pressure on public services, the average answer is under fifty out of a maximum one hundred. By contrast, when I ask how worried these voters are about immigration leading to sprawl or pressure on services, concern jumps to seventy. This can only be explained by psychological and cultural worries about immigration, not by material factors such as sprawl or public services.[8]

NATIONAL IDENTITY, WHITE MAJORITIES, AND ETHNIC DIVERSITY

Governments, whether they intend to or not, control the pace of ethnic change through immigration policy. They also tell a story – in schools, government, and media – about ethnic change and how it fits into the nation's identity. This is arguably as important as how they regulate it. Both sets of policies have contributed to the divisions we see today in America.

Before going further, it's vital to define a few terms. *Ethnic groups* are communities that believe themselves to share ancestry and possess one or more cultural markers, such as language, religion, or physical appearance, which distinguish them from other groups – like the Japanese, for example. In the case of physical appearance, however, boundaries can be fuzzy rather than sharp. *Panethnic* groups are a higher-order aggregation of ethnic groups into larger descent categories. Panethnic groups can be aggregated along the lines of physical appearance into "races" (i.e., whites or blacks), along linguistic lines (i.e., Hispanics), or into superordinate religious groups (i.e., Christians). The term "race" basically refers to panethnic groups aggregated by physical appearance.

Nation-states are territorial-political communities that have a sense of history and are typically connected to dominant ethnic groups who form the bulk of the national population. Nation-states, of which there are nearly two hundred in the United Nations, are political units which control a well-defined territory.

Seven in ten of the world's states have an ethnic majority group. Eighty percent contain a group that makes up at least 40 percent of the population. Deeply diverse nation-states are almost as rare as homogeneous ones. Ethnic majorities are important in anchoring nation-states and ensuring that politics runs more along the lines of issues and ideology than those of ethnicity.

In general, ethnically diverse states have a lower level of economic development than more homogeneous ones.[9] Those with a few large groups tend to have more conflict than others. Voting tends to run along ethnic lines in diverse states such as South Africa, Kenya, or Lebanon, which helps explain why diverse nations find it difficult to agree on where to locate useful public goods like hospitals, and why conflict is higher and development slower.[10] Some highly diverse states are successful, but even in developed societies like Mauritius, Belgium, or Northern Ireland, the question of which group gets what becomes the core of politics.

Most Western elites have taken ethnic majorities for granted. Our traditions of thought were developed in relatively homogeneous Western societies where the congruence between ethnic group, nation, and state could be largely assumed. The American free population at the time of the Revolution, for instance, was 80 percent British and 98 percent Protestant. Only in the 1830s did the Catholic share begin to rise, and only after the Civil War were blacks incorporated into the nation. Meanwhile, the foreign-born share of most Western European countries was just 1 or 2 percent in the early twentieth century. Consequently, writers and statesmen spoke regularly about nations, occasionally about minorities, and almost never about ethnic majorities like WASPs in America or ethnic Germans in Germany. A great deal of that thinking may no longer apply to current circumstances. This is why international law and political theory generally recognize nation-states and ethnic minorities but have no conception of ethnic majority rights or how to justify defending them.[11]

IS DEMOGRAPHY DESTINY?

Demographic change can be overcome in one of two ways: assimilation or through a reframing of ethnic boundaries. Immigrant ethnic minorities can assimilate over time into the laws and culture of the nation-state. Their children, grandchildren, or great-grandchildren can also assimilate, in a deeper way, into the ethnic majority by marrying in. In the United States, intermarriage between WASPs and Protestant groups like Germans and Scandinavians increased from the late nineteenth century onward. Catholic groups, like the Irish and Italians, began mixing with WASPs much later, generally after 1960. Thus the process of melting into the majority group took three to four generations, which is evident also in the breakup of long-standing ethnic neighborhoods.

Change took a long time, but suddenly accelerated. By the 1970s, the ethnic majority was reframed from WASP to "white" or "Judeo-Christian" to include Catholics and Jews. High intermarriage solidified these ties. This deeper assimilation is the main way ethnic diversity declines over time. Ethnic assimilation now means encompassing an important share of mixed-race Hispanics and Asians, especially those whose families have been in America for several generations. There has also been an increased shift to the Republican Party, especially among Hispanics, which is one indicator of assimilation.

The "melting pot" refers not just to ethnic groups adopting the American creed and mass culture, but to the deeper ties of consanguinity that incorporate descendants of immigrants and historic minorities into the ethnic majority. This idea presumes, of course, that there remains an ethnic majority that can act as a pole of attraction for immigrants and their descendants to assimilate into.

This is what the now deeply unfashionable Milton Gordon referred to as "identificational" and "marital" assimilation in 1964.[12] Assimilation is essentially a swearword among American ethnic studies scholars, but it continues to occur, and one or two academics have been brave enough to advocate for it.[13] Assimilation has meant a blurring and an expansion of the boundaries of the white majority over time. This is not limited to nonblacks, as there is now no insuperable legal or social barrier to black assimilation. This majority group, which may one day be referred to simply as "American," is characterized by a collective memory and belief in common ancestry more than outward manifestations of culture, which can change. This of course presumes that there will be many descendants of the earlier ethnic majority in order to render these myths of descent plausible, and that some degree of European phenotypical influence remains.

This ethnic interaction begs the question of how the white ethnic majority thinks of itself. What are this majority's myths, collective memories, habits of character and mind? There are WASP migration stories such as those of the Puritans in New England, the Scotch-Irish in the Appalachian upland South, and the Cavaliers in the coastal South. There is the memory of Western settlement by WASPs and Northwestern Europeans. For many Southern and Eastern Europeans whose forbears arrived in the industrial Northeast and Upper Midwest, there is the story of Ellis Island and factory work. Alongside this we have the creedal memories of the Founding, of Independence, of the Civil War and World War II. One day it may be that African American myths and memories become incorporated as an ingredient into a new majority group, as in Mexico with its 90 percent Mestizo majority.

Progressives and conservatives approach the "facts" of ethnic demography in diametrically opposed ways. Both the white majority and minorities serve as symbols that underpin different national storylines. For the Left, diversity represents progress with the white majority being the chief obstacle to advancement. For most on the Right, the white majority is, like sports or the landscape, a central component of "everyday" American nationhood, connecting present-day America to its past. Many are attached to the historic ethnic composition of the country as a tradition, among others, that they wish to maintain by decreasing the rate of ethnic change. They perceive ethnic diversity to be a less important feature of American nationhood than progressives do. But, it must be said, this describes the sentiments of the conservative populace rather than of Republican elites, who have accepted and cheered on the Left's narrative about America. For example, John McCain, a pro-immigration Republican, argued that the country is built on ideals, "not blood and soil," and is the "immigrant's dream." This partial interpretation of American tradition is not accurate. In fact there has long been an implicit conception of American consanguinity whose expression is traceable to Founders like John Jay or Thomas Jefferson. Jefferson traced Americans' genealogical and political descent to the Anglo-Saxon tribes who were conquered by the Normans, while Jay spoke of the importance of Americans being descended largely from common British ancestors. Its boundaries have widened, but the idea of a melting pot in which people form genealogical attachments to each other, and to past generations, is an important tradition that has only recently been jettisoned.

As Western nation-states become "majority-minority," ethnic majorities are becoming increasingly self-conscious and mobilized. This affects voting behavior among conservative whites who are attached to their group's traditional demographic preponderance locally and nationally. In terms of voting, minorities tend to lean Left while majorities lean Right. Nonwhites furnished around half the Democratic vote in 2020 compared to little more than 10 percent for the Republicans. Though this is breaking down as many native-born minorities assimilate, whites still lean more toward the GOP than Asians and Hispanics do. As the population changes with the arrival of new groups, we could begin to see a more multipolar society of the kind we see in other highly multiethnic societies around the world like Kenya, Dubai, or Guyana. Politics may revolve more on ethnic ties than policy issues.

The American cultural Left defines itself, above all, through its resistance to white-majority Americanism, which they dub "white supremacy," nativism, or racism. But the distinction between affection for one's in-group and hatred of out-groups, which is an established finding in psychology, is collapsed into a simplistic, Manichean worldview.[14] The line between a white nationalist ethnostate and a regulated assimilationist melting pot is blurred. The idea of controlling the flow of immigration to balance increases in diversity with decreases in diversity brought about by assimilation is treated as every bit as racist as ethnic exclusion. Sacred values, as Atran notes, are not up for nuance and negotiation.[15]

The Left's binary mode of processing the world allows space for only two types of people, the open and the closed, liberals and racists, good and bad – with no sense that there is a continuum running from those who want faster change to those who prefer slower change. Lacking this more nuanced perspective, the Left is unable to compromise on questions such as the pace of immigration and ethnic change, for to do so is to profane the sacred value of diversity and not offending the sensibilities of totemic racial groups.

The Left is sometimes considered antinationalist, but it isn't. It just rejects traditional interpretations of nationhood. This moral-perfectionist nationalism is demonstrated by self-flagellation of the kind exhibited by US ambassador to the United Nations Linda Thomas-Greenfield, who called on her country to dismantle its legacy of white supremacy. Hatred of one's past becomes a sign of national virtue, a prop of nationhood.

To understand why, consider that there are two variants of nationhood, particularist and universalist. Particularist forms define a nation by ascriptive characteristics such as language, culture, landscape, history, and ethnic composition. Universalist versions focus on a nation's performance against the yardstick of its defining creed. Where a number of nations have the same creed, national identity emerges through competition, as each creedal nation struggles to be judged "first among equals." Saudi

Arabia, Iran, and Pakistan jockey to be the most pious Muslim nation. The United States, France, and Britain, among others, fight for the crown of most liberal nation. Since the 1960s, the shift in public morality means that this competition is about which country can signal the most antiracism, antisexism, and antihomophobia. The winner will lead the world in self-abasement, to produce a new nation, the core of which is protecting racial and sexual minorities from psychological harm, and closing gaps in income, self-esteem, and power among racial groups.

Fulfilling its national destiny means exporting these ideas abroad, though with a bizarre twist. The Liberal Progressive movement of the first decade of the 1900s held that WASP Americans would, like the Jews in Reform Jewish theology, fulfil their creedal mission and then, in John Dewey's words, "universalize themselves out of existence."[16] Leading the world toward the identitarian utopia of equity and diversity, America fulfils its anointed mission and, when that work is done, will no longer need to exist. A liberal worldwide competition exists among Western nations for who can erase themselves more quickly. Until the utopia arrives, however, conservative enemies abound.

WHAT IS TO BE DONE?

There are three paths forward: educational, economic, and bureaucratic.

First, conservatives need to push back far more strenuously against the hegemonic diversity narrative, making the case that a healthy ethnic majority, augmented by assimilation and blurred boundaries, is a vital component for building a more cohesive nation. This would permit space for cosmopolitanism and diversity to flourish, as well as for people who wish to remain attached to their minority ethnicity. But it would also emphasize that there is a historic and evolving American ethnic majority that, alongside minority groups with long settlement histories, lends distinctiveness and identity to the nation – a self-conception that all citizens can participate in. This means celebrating historical rootedness as well as immigration, the WASP-influenced white majority as well as diversity. The current high culture centers diversity in an attempt to expunge the country's ethno-traditions. Not being ashamed of our national past and its clear contributions is key.

As such, conservatives must seek a recentering of the positive contribution of the ethnic majority – in their advertising, history teaching, political speeches, school curricula, culture, and media – not to a position of dominance that excludes others, but to a place proportional to its share of the population and contribution to American society. For example, the WASP narratives of Jamestown and Plymouth rock, and the largely Northwestern European-origin settlement of the West, should serve as important national touchstones. So too should traditions that flow from these eras such as country music or vernacular housing styles. This doesn't mean that all ethnic or ideological groups must be attached to these symbols, but the high culture should accept that these are important parts of the national fabric. By extension, any official portrayals of the nation should accurately and proportionately reflect the different political perspectives that exist in the country.

Conservative voters are especially sensitive to rapid ethnic change. But there is a traditionally liberal constituency for this too. It is incumbent on Republican politicians to make a principled and intelligent case for the legitimacy of these cultural concerns in the public square, and to contest the Left's control over the bounds of acceptable debate. Pretending that the desire for slower immigration is mainly about jobs, pressure on the welfare state, or crime, while accepting the contention that openly discussing ethnic change is racist is to bend the knee to the ideological regime.

Second, an illusion in which the Right deeply wants to believe is that immigration is a solution to population aging. As any decent demographer knows, immigrants, though usually younger, age alongside the rest of the population. In order to maintain its age structure, the United States would have to import perhaps ten million immigrants a year, and be willing to escalate the number even further, in an exponentially rising curve. One EU study found that in order to maintain the dependency ratio between those of working age (fifteen to sixty-four) and those over sixty-five, 13.5 million immigrants would be needed each year – *twenty times the current influx*.[17] A better solution for the aging problem, mooted by Norwegian demographer Vegard Skirbekk, is to make the workplace more flexible for older workers to work part-time or less intensively while investing in preventive medicine and lifelong education to allow workers to remain productive for longer.

It is nearly impossible to preserve a cohesive nation with high rates of immigration. Europe, like America, is embarking on this experiment: in the end, they will lose social cohesion while making no substantial dent in their aging problem. Moderating the rate of immigration, especially illegal immigration, is needed to produce a more cohesive society. This means slowing the rate of change to pre-1970s rates to permit assimilation to reduce diversity to a level that makes cohesive nationhood possible.

Third, elected Republican governments need to take culture more seriously than in the past. They must raise the profile of culture war issues and force the Left to sideline wokeness if they hope to prevail. The Right needs to move beyond soundbites such as budget cuts or abolishing academic tenure: these do nothing to change the culture and can even be counterproductive. Instead, conservative governments at the federal and state levels must get into the details of law and policy guidance, crafting new legislation and forming new bureaucratic offices to execute it. Political appointees who believe in the mission of pursuing impartiality must be appointed to the new offices, while the power of agencies captured by the left should be reduced.

This means developing guidance, backed up by carrots and sticks, to institute political neutrality and ideological nondiscrimination in hiring and promotion across all publicly funded institutions – including those accessing federal funds such as private universities. It means requiring institutions receiving federal or state funds to devote as many resources to *political* diversity as they do to race and gender diversity, a position that commands bipartisan support in surveys. One example that might be salient for the United States in this regard is Britain's academic freedom directorate, established by the Conservative government, which has the power to issue guidance with tight definitions, fining universities that breach academic freedom to pursue equity goals.

Legal and bureaucratic change can, as Cass Sunstein notes, change culture. Seatbelt and smoking laws created new norms, as, unfortunately, did civil rights regulations on disparate impact and preventing hostile environments.[18] At present, the Left has succeeded in creating an elite culture based on anticonservative prejudice. Norms that promote and protect conservatives in elite institutions, and guard against anticonservative statements and environments, are a way of using the tools of equity and diversity to rebalance the system. An example would be for universities to adopt and enforce the 1967 Kalven Report which states that university officials cannot take political positions. Political belief should be added to the characteristics in all Equity, Diversity and Inclusion policies and documentation, and performance on this measure monitored accordingly. Protected characteristics are not going to disappear, so the best way to pare them back is to compel institutions to equalize action between race/gender diversity and political/ideological diversity. Most will probably elect to cut back on the former to avoid having to do the latter. In order to staff these organizations, conservatives will need to develop more intensive policy networks, a kind of Federalist Society for the bureaucracy, to create a database of talented individuals that can be trained and called upon to fill key positions and apply to key agencies.

In a world where the Left controls the elite institutions, the Right needs to centralize control over these institutions through regulation, and, like appointments to the Supreme Court, open secretive institutions up to political contestation. That way, if the Left wins power, the outcome is no worse than what already exists. A return to progressive illiberalism under the Democrats – as with Title IX guidance or Critical Race Theory under Biden – will come under fire from opposition media and politicians, exposing the illiberal business-as-usual practices of these institutions, which have heretofore been conducted behind closed doors.

These new legal and bureaucratic reforms will produce an ethic of fair political representation and ideological nondiscrimination. This will diminish anticonservative bias in elite institutions, generating a receptivity to the rebalancing of American national identity. This can transform the way the American ethnic majority and its history are represented, as well as the question of how that ethnic majority's identity is treated in relation to that of other groups. It can help to raise the legitimacy of conservative concerns over the pace of immigration and ethnic change, bringing about a less fractured society.

NOTES

1   Brian Gratton, "Demography and Immigration Restriction in United States History," in *Political Demography: Identity, Conflict and Institutions*, ed. J. A. Goldstone, Eric Kaufmann, and Monica Duffy Toft (Oxford: Oxford University Press, 2012), 159–75; E. Kaufmann, *The Rise and Fall of Anglo-America: The Decline of Dominant Ethnicity in the United States* (Cambridge, MA: Harvard University Press, 2004).
2   Paul Demeny, and Geoffrey McNicoll, eds., *The Political Economy of Global Population Change, 1950–2050* (New York: Population Council, 2006).
3   Eduardo Porter and Karl Russell, "Migrants Are on the Rise Around the World, and Myths About Them Are Shaping Attitudes," *New York Times*, June 20, 2018.
4   John L. Korey and Edward L. Lascher Jr., "Macropartisanship in California," *Public Opinion Quarterly* 70, no. 1 (2006): 48–65.
5   Eric Kaufmann, "Hispanic Americans Are No Longer 'Minority Voters,'" Unherd, December 9, 2021, https://unherd.com/thepost/hispanic-americans-are-no-longer-minority-voters/.

6   Paul Morland, *The Human Tide: How Population Shaped the Modern World* (New York: PublicAffairs, 2019).

7   Jens Hainmueller and Daniel J. Hopkins, "Public Attitudes Toward Immigration," *Annual Review of Political Science* 17 (2014): 225–49.

8   Eric Kaufmann, *Whiteshift: Populism, Immigration, and the Future of White Majorities* (New York: Abrams Press, 2019).

9   William Easterly and Ross Levine, "Africa's Growth Tragedy: Policies and Ethnic Divisions," *Quarterly Journal of Economics* 111, no. 4 (1997): 1203–50.

10 Alberto Alesina et al., "Public Goods and Ethnic Divisions," *Quarterly Journal of Economics* 114 (November 1999): 1243–84.

11 Liav Orgad, *The Cultural Defense of Nations: A Liberal Theory of Majority Rights* (Oxford: Oxford University Press, 2015).

12 Milton M. Gordon, *Assimilation in American Life: The Role of Race, Religion and National Origins* (Oxford: Oxford University Press, 1964).

13 Richard Alba, *The Great Demographic Illusion: Majority, Minority, and the Expanding American Mainstream* (Princeton, NJ: Princeton University Press, 2020).

14 Marilynn B. Brewer, "The Psychology of Prejudice: Ingroup Love and Outgroup Hate?" *Journal of Social Issues* 55, no. 3 (1999): 429–44.

15 Scott Atran and Robert Axelrod, "Reframing Sacred Values," *Negotiation Journal* 24, no. 3 (2008): 221–46.

16 Eric Kaufmann, *The Rise and Fall of Anglo-America: The Decline of Dominant Ethnicity in the United States* (Cambridge, MA: Harvard University Press, 2004).

17 Craig Parsons and Timothy M. Smeeding, "What's Unique about Immigration in Europe," in *Immigration and the Transformation of Europe*, eds. C. Parsons and T. M. Smeeding (Cambridge: Cambridge University Press), 16.

18 Cass R. Sunstein, *Conformity: The Power of Social Influences* (New York: NYU Press, 2019).

WHAT THE RIGHT GETS WRONG ABOUT ART

Roger Kimball

> Nice things are nicer than nasty ones.
> KINGSLEY AMIS

CONSERVATIVES IN THE WEST long ago ceded culture to the Left. Culture, they felt, was not really serious. You cannot eat Rembrandt or the Ninth Symphony or *Paradise Lost*. You cannot make the payroll writing poetry or studying Botticelli or Herodotus. True, in 1780, John Adams wrote that "I must study politics and war that my sons may have liberty to study mathematics and philosophy. My sons ought to study mathematics and philosophy . . . in order to give their children a right to study painting, poetry, music, architecture, statuary, tapestry, and porcelain." That sounds noble, but who still believes it? Not paid-up members of establishment conservatism. Quote that passage to them. Then watch them smile.

It is the same smile they display when you quote Andrew Breitbart's observation that "politics is downstream from culture." They might nod. They might say they agree. But how do they act? More or less like Medea in Ovid's *Metamorphoses*: "I see the better path and approve: I follow the worse."

Back in 1973, Irving Kristol wrote an essay called "On Capitalism and the Democratic Idea." In the course of that essay, Kristol touched upon the conservative indifference to the claims of culture. "For two centuries," he wrote, the very important people who managed the affairs of this society could not believe in the importance of ideas – until one day they were shocked to discover that their children, having been captured and shaped by certain ideas, were either rebelling against their authority or seceding from their society. The truth is that ideas are all-important. The massive and seemingly solid institutions of any society – the economic institutions, the political institutions, the religious institutions – are always at the mercy of the ideas in the heads of the people who populate these institutions. The leverage of ideas is so immense that a slight change in the intellectual climate can and will – perhaps slowly but nevertheless inexorably – twist a familiar institution into an unrecognizable shape.[1]

Kristol was talking more about the humanities than about art. But his point applies equally to the attitude of "the very important people" who manage the affairs of our society regarding art. They did not think or care much about art – it was something that went on, as it were, behind their backs. But then one day, they woke up and found the art world, and even the formerly staid world of museums, was awash in sexualized garbage, postmodern inanity, and race worship. Their indifference mutated first into outrage. Then, as they took note of the prices fetched by the garbage, it mutated into capitulation.

This process did not take place in a vacuum. It was part and parcel of a larger culture rebellion against bourgeois values that got going in earnest with the advent of modernism. In art, as the Australian philosopher David Stove observed,

Western Europe found that its anti-academy had become its academy "even in the twinkling of an eye." The galleries were suddenly full of the art of African societies formerly the most despised. Victorian architecture was all at once the object of a universal detestation, or rather horror.

Black music began its long and excruciating revenge on the white man. The Jazz Age, in short, had arrived.[2]

Today, we are living in the aftermath of that avant-garde: all those "adversarial" gestures, poses, ambitions, and tactics that emerged and were legitimized in the 1880s and 1890s, flowered in the first half of the last century, and that live a sort of posthumous existence now in the frantic twilight of postmodernism. Establishment conservatives have done nothing effective to challenge this. On the contrary, despite little whimpers here and there, they have capitulated to it.

In part, our present situation, like the avant-garde itself, is a complication (not to say a perversion) of our Romantic inheritance. The elevation of art from a didactic pastime to a prime spiritual resource; the self-conscious probing of inherited forms and artistic strictures; the image of the artist as a tortured, oppositional figure: all achieve a first maturity in Romanticism. These themes were exacerbated as the avant-garde developed from an impulse to a movement and finally into a tradition of its own.

The avant-garde genre gradually transformed a recalcitrant bourgeois culture into a willing collaborator in its raids on established taste. But in this victory were the seeds of its own irrelevance, for without credible resistance, its oppositional gestures degenerated into a kind of aesthetic buffoonery. In this sense, the institutionalization of the avant-garde spells the death or at least the senility of the avant-garde.[3]

What can be done? For one thing, it is time that we recognized that art need not be adversarial or "transgressive" in order to be good or important. Until the advent of modernism, art aimed to please by allowing us to experience beauty, and to also force us to reflect on ourselves. A lot of ink has been spilled trying to explain the nature of art because our fascination with beauty is perennial. Much of the Western tradition of thought has eulogized beauty as providing intimations of spiritual wholeness and lost unity. Rightly understood, aesthetic experience is not a matter of merely private delectation; it has a civilizing function as well. It is part of the human condition that we find ourselves torn between conflicting impulses, between reason and desire, duty and inclination, our purposes as individuals and as members of a community. Depictions of such conflicts or their resolution bring us closer to understanding ourselves and the world.

Moreover, there is much about the modern world that exacerbates those conflicts. The progress of science has yielded rich dividends for our understanding of the world, but it has also encouraged our analytical powers at the expense of our sensuous powers. The demands of specialization make it increasingly difficult to achieve a sense of wholeness in life. This is where the aesthetic for us moderns is so important. By encouraging the "enlarged mode of thought" that Kant spoke of, aesthetic experience promises to heal these rifts and provide a vision of wholeness.

We must bear in mind that art satisfies no practical need; it is not useful in the sense in which a law court or a hospital, a farm or a machinist's shop is useful. But utility is not, and should not be, our only criterion of value. We care about many things that are not in any normal sense useful. Indeed, for many of the things we care about most the whole question of use seems peculiarly out of place, a kind of existential category mistake.

In this context, it is worth noting that great damage has been done – above all, to artists but also to public taste – by romanticizing the tribulations of the nineteenth-century avant-garde. Everyone is brought up on stories of how an obtuse public scorned Manet, censored Gauguin, and drove poor Van Gogh to madness and suicide. But the fact that these great talents went unappreciated has had the undesirable effect of encouraging the thought that because one is unappreciated one is therefore a genius. It has also made it extremely difficult to expose fraudulent work as such. For any frank dismissal of art – especially art that cloaks itself in the mantle of the avant-garde – is immediately met by the rejoinder: "Ah, but they made fun of Cézanne, too: they thought that Stravinsky was a charlatan."

This is the easiest and also the most shallow response to criticism. It has been adopted as much by the Right as the Left. To quote David Stove again, it is yet another version of what he called "The 'They All Laughed at Christopher Columbus' Argument."[4] The idea is that we ought to welcome all innovators (moral, social, artistic, whatever) because all improvements in human life have come about as the result of some such "new beginning." The rub, of course, is that it works the other way, too. As Stove observed, "someone first had to make a new departure for any change for the worse ever to have taken place." This is perfectly obvious, and it is reason enough to regard innovators with caution, to say the least.

If the Columbus Argument is puerile when applied to politics and morals, it is equally puerile when applied to art. In the first place, most artists whom we now associate with the nineteenth-century avant-garde did not set out to shock or "transgress" moral boundaries: they set out to make art that was a true articulation the world. Today, the primary – often, it seems, the only – goal of many so-called "cutting-edge" artists is to shock and transgress. The art is secondary, a license for bad behavior.

There is also the uncomfortable and inegalitarian truth that in any age most art is bad or failed art. And in our time, most art is not only bad but also dishonest: a form of therapy or political grumbling masquerading as art. Like everything important in human life, art must be judged on the basis of first-hand experience: no formula can be devised to prescribe its assessment, including the formula that what is despised today will be championed as great work tomorrow. The art world today retains little of the idealism that permeated Romanticism, but it remains Romantic in its moralism and hubris about the salvific properties of art.

The road to our current impasse began with the "anti-art" movement of Dadaism in the early twentieth century. For with Dada the brash energy of the avant-garde was short-circuited, flipped on its head. Dada did not seek to provide yet another fresh answer to the question "What's new?" On the contrary, Dada sought to subvert the entire context in which the question gained urgency. Then the extreme strategies of Dada, too, were quickly incorporated as part of the metabolism of art.

From this perspective, Dada, and every subsequent innovation, by definition appears as a variation on an already defined theme: an anti-theme, really, whose very negativity provides a foil for the ceaseless play of novelty. But the incorporation of Dada into the fabric of the avant-garde did have consequences. For one thing, Dada altered the tenor of the avant-garde. Dada might seek to occupy extreme points, but it did so out of a systematic contrariness: it had no ambition "to attain for an hour that crest of the wave in a tossing sea," as the French critic Albert Thibaudet put it, because it had given up on the whole idea of art as a spiritual quest.[5] Indeed, Dada was an art form that had given up on art.

Consider: in 1914, Marcel Duchamp dusted off a commercial bottle rack and offered it, tongue firmly in cheek, to the public as art. The public (at least the taste-making part of it) swooned with delighted outrage. In 1917, Duchamp upped the ante. He scrawled the name "R. Mutt" on a urinal, baptized it *Fountain*, and said (in effect) "How about it?" What a delicious scandal ensured. How original! How innovative! But also how destructive of the essential protocols and metabolism of art.

But not, it soon became clear, as destructive as Duchamp had wished. "I threw the bottle rack and the urinal into their faces as a challenge," Duchamp noted contemptuously some years later, "and now they admire them for their aesthetic beauty." Oh dear.

Duchamp had wished not to extend but to subvert, to destroy, the whole category of art and aesthetic delectation. Instead, his antics polluted and trivialized it. How much of contemporary art is essentially tired repetition of gestures inaugurated by Duchamp and his immediate successors? Damien Hirst? Been there. Tracy Emin? Ditto. Jeff Koons, Barbara Kruger? Ditto, ditto. As the sage of Ecclesiastes put it, there is nothing new under the sun.

The ironies abound. Today, *Fountain* is (in the words of one reverential commentator) widely considered "a recognizable icon in the history of modern art." Given Duchamp's iconoclastic intentions, what do you suppose he would have thought of Pierre Pinoncelli, the chap who has so far availed himself of at least two opportunities to attack this treasure with a hammer?

Now you might be tempted (I certainly was) to applaud this exercise of creativity and innovation as an exemplary instance of emperor's-new-clothes vandalism. It is part of Duchamp's legacy, however, that Mr. Pinoncelli should (surprise, surprise) style himself an artist, be accepted by the public as an artist, and denominate his little acts of "philosophizing with a hammer" (as Nietzsche said of his own efforts at creative destruction) as signal instances of "performance art."

Well, whatever the presiding judge thought of Mr. Pinoncelli's artistic efforts, he grasped the principles of private property with sufficient clarity to understand that chipping away without leave at a piece of plumbing valued at $3.4 million (and this, incidentally, for a late version of the blessed pissoir that Duchamp signed in 1964) just wasn't on. The judge indulged his own innovative creativity and fined Mr. Pinoncelli some £140,000.

These familiar but exemplary episodes from the annals of contemporary art illustrate Marx's one indisputable contribution to civilization – namely, his observation that important historical events tend to occur twice: the first time as tragedy, the second as farce.

They also illustrate the cynical truth of Andy Warhol's observation that that "Art is what you can get away with." Warhol's own career and, indeed, a large part of the contemporary art world testify to the power – if not the truth – of that observation. The sad fact is that today, anything can be not only be put forward but also and accepted and celebrated as a work of art.

HOW DID WE GET HERE

What had to happen such that a bisected cow in a tank of formaldehyde is accounted an important work of art? That is a complicated question to which there is no short answer. But if one had to sum up volumes in a single word, a good candidate would be the word "beauty": What the art world is lacking today is an allegiance to beauty.

I know that this is both vague and portentous. But surely we are in a very curious situation. Traditionally, the goal or end of fine art was to make beautiful objects. Beauty itself came with a lot of Platonic and Christian metaphysical baggage, some of it indifferent or even positively hostile to art. But art without beauty was, if not exactly a contradiction in terms, at least a description of failed art.

But if large precincts of the art world have jettisoned the traditional link between art and beauty, they have done nothing to disown the social prerogatives of art. Indeed, we suffer today from a peculiar form of moral anesthesia: an anesthesia based on the delusion that by calling something "art" we thereby purchase for it a blanket exemption from moral criticism – as if being art automatically rendered all moral considerations beside the point.

George Orwell gave classic expression to this point in "Benefit of Clergy: Some Notes on Salvador Dalí."[6] Acknowledging the deficiency of the philistine response to Dalí's work – categorical rejection along with denial that Dalí possessed any talent whatever – Orwell goes on to note that the response of the cultural elites was just as impoverished. Essentially, the elite response to Dalí was the response of *l'art pour l'art*, of extreme aestheticism. "The artist," Orwell writes,

is to be exempt from the moral laws that are binding on ordinary people. Just pronounce the magic word "Art," and everything is O.K. Rotting corpses with snails crawling over them are O.K.; kicking little girls in the head is O.K.; even a film like *L'Age d'Or* [which shows, among other things, detailed shots of a woman defecating] is O.K.

A juror in the obscenity trial in Cincinnati in 1990 over Robert Mapplethorpe's notorious photographs of the S and M homosexual underworld memorably summed up the paralyzed attitude Orwell described. Acknowledging that he did not like Mapplethorpe's rebarbative photographs, the juror nonetheless concluded that "if people say it's art, then I have to go along with it."

"If people say it's art, then I have to go along with it." It is worth pausing to digest that comment. It is also worth confronting it with a question: Why do so many people feel that if something is regarded as art, they "have to go along with it," no matter how offensive, foolish, or corrosive it might be? Part of the answer has to do with the confusion of art with "free speech." Another part of the answer has to do with the evolution, and what we might call the institutionalization, of the avant-garde and its posture of defiance.

You know the drill: black-tie dinners at major museums, *tout le monde* in attendance, celebrating the latest art world freak: maybe it's the Chapman brothers with their pubescent female mannequins festooned with erect penises; maybe it's Mike Kelley with his mutilated dolls, or Jeff Koons with his pornographic sculptures depicting him and his now-former wife having sex, or Cindy Sherman with her narcissistic feminism, or Jenny Holzer with her political slogans. The list is endless. And so is the tedium. Today in the art world, anything goes but almost nothing happens. As with any collusion of snobbery and artistic nullity, such spectacles have their amusing aspects, as Tom Wolfe, for example, has brilliantly shown.[7] In the end, though, the aftermath of the avant-garde has been the opposite of amusing. It has been a cultural disaster. For one thing, by universalizing the spirit of opposition, it has threatened to transform the practice of art into a purely negative enterprise. In large precincts of the art world today, art is oppositional or it is nothing. Celebrity replaces aesthetic achievement as the goal of art.

The Right, especially the libertarian Right, has been complicit in this development, first in its indifference, second in its capitulation, third by its embrace of kitsch.

What is kitsch? A lot of ink has been expended in the effort to define this amphibious aesthetic-moral term. Kitsch flirts with idealism, but it is a rancid idealism. It is a version of sentimentality, which is to say manufactured sentiment in the face of a failure of genuine feeling. The novelist Milan Kundera, who devoted many pages to the subject, noted that "Kitsch is the translation of the stupidity of received ideas into the language of beauty and feeling."[8] Kitsch is histrionic, self-dramatizing. Its confections can be sweet: think, for example, of John Currin's diabetic fantasies. They can also be sour: I would include some of the grimmer fabulations of Odd Nerdrum in this category.

It is worth noting that technical command is no barrier to – it might even be a facilitator of – kitsch. At its core it is a failure of nerve that is also a rejection of truth. Kitsch describes one variety of failed art. But – another thing worth noting – it is also the case that the most ambitious art must have the courage to flirt with kitsch, to negotiate that passage between the Scylla of sterility and the Charybdis of sentimentality. There are no formulas, no dependable navigational aids, for this voyage. The sine qua non is that most demanding but also least definable of gifts – that is, taste. The exercise of taste is what elevates a traditional artistic practice from the quaintly antiquarian to the inescapably pertinent. Success in this realm is not only something that must be won anew daily; it is something about which judgment will often vary or be withheld indefinitely.

That said, it is no secret that much, if not most, art in recent decades since has abandoned beauty, abandoned the ambition to please the viewer aesthetically. Instead, it seeks to shock, discommode, repulse, proselytize, or startle. Beauty is out of place in any art that systematically discounts the aesthetic.

But "beauty" is by no means an unambiguous term. In degenerate or diluted form, it can mean the merely pretty, and in this sense beauty really is an enemy of authentic artistic expression. But beauty is not always the "merely pretty" or agreeable. One thinks, for example, of Dostoyevsky's observation, in *The Brothers Karamazov*, that "beauty is the battlefield on which God and the devil war for man's soul."

The point is that, in its highest sense, beauty speaks with such great immediacy because it touches something deep within us. Understood in this way, beauty is something that absorbs our attention and delivers us, if but momentarily, from the poverty and incompleteness of everyday life. At its most intense, beauty invites us to forget our subjection to time and imparts an intoxicating sense of self-sufficiency. Our art closes us to the experience of the beautiful.

Art that loses touch with the resources of beauty is bound to be sterile. But it is also true that striving self-consciously to embody beauty is a prescription for artistic failure. This may seem paradoxical. But, like many of the most important things in life, genuine beauty is achieved mainly by indirection. In this sense, beauty resembles happiness as it was described by Aristotle: it is not a possible goal of our actions, but rather the natural accompaniment of actions rightly performed. Striving for happiness in life all but guarantees unhappiness; striving for beauty in art is likely to result in kitsch or some other artistic counterfeit.

The trick, for viewers as well as artists, is not to lose sight of beauty but to concentrate primarily on something seemingly more pedestrian – the making of good works of art. The best guides to this task are to be found not in the work of this season's art world darlings but in the great models furnished by the past.

In the introduction to my book *Art's Prospect: The Challenge of Tradition in an Age of Celebrity* (2003), I noted that most of the really good contemporary art was taking place "out of the limelight."[9] You didn't see it in the trendy art emporia. It was not, usually, reviewed by the *New York Times* or other such organs colluding in the degradation of culture. Serious art today has tended to be a quiet affair, proceeding in an obscure studio in midtown or even out of town. "Tradition" was for its practitioners an enabling, not a dirty word. Real art tends to involve not the latest thing, but permanent things. Permanent things can be presented anew; they can be old; but their relevance is measured less by the buzz they create than by the silences they inspire. In other words, the future of our artistic culture is not in the hands of today's taste makers, but those whose talent, patience, and perseverance will ultimately render them the taste makers of tomorrow.

Art today is enlisted in all manner of extra-artistic projects, from gender politics to the grim linguistic leftism of neo-Marxists, post-structuralists, gender theorists, and all the other exotic fauna who are congregating in and about the art world and the academy. The subjugation of art – and of cultural life generally – to political ends has been one of the great spiritual tragedies of our age. Among much else, it has made it increasingly difficult to appreciate art on its own terms, as affording its own kinds of insights and satisfactions. This situation has made it imperative for critics who care about art to champion its distinctively aesthetic qualities against attempts to reduce art to a species of propaganda.

At the same time, however, I believe that we lose something important when our conception of art does not have room for an ethical dimension. That is to say, if the politicization of art is constricting, so, too, in a different way is a purely aesthetic conception of art. By the nineteenth century, art had long been free from serving the ideological needs of religion; and yet the spiritual crisis of the age tended to invest art with ever greater existential burdens – burdens that continue, in various ways, to be felt down to this day. The poet Wallace Stevens articulated one important strand of this phenomenon when he observed that "after one has abandoned a belief in God, poetry is that essence which takes its place as life's redemption."[10] The idea that poetry –

that art generally – should serve as a source – perhaps the primary source – of spiritual sustenance in a secular age is a Romantic notion that continues to resonate powerfully.

We have come a long way since the time when Dostoyevsky could declare that "Incredible as it may seem, the day will come when man will quarrel more fiercely about art than about God." Whether that trek has described a journey of progress is perhaps an open question. This much, I think, is clear: without an allegiance to beauty, art degenerates into a caricature of itself; it is beauty that animates aesthetic experience, making it so seductive; but aesthetic experience itself degenerates into a kind of fetish or idol if it is held up as an end in itself, untested by the rest of life. As I have put it elsewhere, the trivialization of outrage leads to a kind of moral and aesthetic anesthesia not the least of whose symptoms is the outrage of trivialization.

NOTES

1   Irving Kristol, *Neoconservatism: The Autobiography of an Idea* (New York: Free Press, 1995), 198.

2   David Stove, "Cole Porter and Karl Popper: The Jazz Age in the Philosophy of Science," in David Stove, *Against the Idols of the Age*, ed. Roger Kimball (New Brunswick: Transaction: 1999), 3–32.

3   Clement Greenberg, *Art and Culture: Critical Essays* (Boston: Beacon Press, 1961).

4   David Stove, "The Columbus Argument," *Commentary*, December 1987, https://www.commentary.org/articles/david-stove/the-columbus-argument/.

5   Albert Thibaudet, *Histoire de la littérature française de 1789 à no jours* (Paris: Stock, 1936), quoted in Hilton Kramer, *The Triumph of Modernism: The Art World, 1987-2005* (Lanham, MD: Rowman & Littlefield, 2013), 294.

6   George Orwell, "Benefit of Clergy: Some Notes on Salvador Dali," Orwell Foundation, https://www.orwellfoundation.com/the-orwell-foundation/orwell/essays-and-other-works/benefit-of-clergy-some-notes-on-salvador-dali/.

7   Tom Wolfe, *The Painted Word* (New York: Farrar, Straus, and Giroux, 1975).

8   Milan Kundera, *The Art of the Novel* (New York: Grove Press, 1988), 163.

9   Roger Kimball, *Art's Prospect: The Challenge of Tradition in an Age of Celebrity* (Chicago: Ivan R. Dee, 2007).

10 Wallace Stevens, *Opus Posthumous*, ed. Milton J. Bates (1957; repr., London: Faber and Faber, 1990), 185.

MICHAEL ANTON is a lecturer and research fellow at Hillsdale College, a senior fellow at the Claremont Institute, and a former national security official in the Trump administration. He has published in numerous outlets, and is the author of *The Stakes* (Regnery, 2020).

RICHARD HANANIA is a research fellow at the Salem Center for Public Policy at the University of Texas, and the president and founder of the Center for the Study of Partisanship and Ideology. He writes about geopolitics and the future of technology. He is the author of *Public Choice Theory and the Illusion of Grand Strategy* and *The Origins of Woke*.

CARSON HOLLOWAY is a Washington Fellow at The Claremont Institute's Center for the American Way of Life. He is also the Ralph Wardle Diamond Professor of Arts and Sciences and Professor of Political Science at University of Nebraska, Omaha. Carson is co-editor, with Bradford P. Wilson, of the two-volume work *The Political Writings of Alexander Hamilton* (Cambridge University Press, 2017). He is also the author of *Hamilton versus Jefferson in the Washington Administration: Completing the Founding or Betraying the Founding?* (Cambridge University Press, 2015). Professor Holloway received his B.A. from the University of Northern Iowa and his Ph.D. from Northern Illinois University.

JOHN FONTE is a senior fellow and director of the Center for American Common Culture at Hudson Institute. Fonte is the author of *Sovereignty or Submission: Will Americans Rule Them-*

selves or be Ruled by Others?, winner of the Intercollegiate Studies Institute's Paolucci-Bagehot book award for 2012 and a number-one rated Amazon best-seller in international law. He is co-editor of *Education for America's Role in World Affairs*, a book on civic and world affairs education used in universities and teacher training institutes.

DAVID AZERRAD is an Assistant Professor and Research Fellow at Hillsdale College's Van Andel Graduate School of Government in Washington, D.C. Prior to joining Hillsdale, Azerrad was the Director of the B. Kenneth Simon Center for Principles and Politics at The Heritage Foundation.

HELEN ANDREWS is a senior editor at *The American Conservative* and author of *Boomers: The Men and Women Who Promised Freedom and Delivered Disaster* (January 2021). She has worked at the *Washington Examiner* and *National Review*. Her work has appeared in *The New York Times*, *The Wall Street Journal*, *First Things*, and *The Claremont Review of Books*.

SCOTT YENOR is a Washington Fellow at The Claremont Institute's Center for the American Way of Life. Yenor is the author of *Family Politics: The Idea of Marriage in Modern Political Thought* (Baylor, 2011). His latest book is *The Recovery of Family Life: Exposing the Limits of Modern Ideologies* (Baylor 2020). In addition, his academic publications have appeared in *Law & Liberty*, *The Federalist*, *City Journal*, and *The Claremont Review of Books*. He is a political science professor at Boise State University.

JOSHUA MITCHELL is a Washington Fellow at The Claremont Institute's Center for the American Way of Life. His current research focuses on identity politics and the tradition of Western political thought. Mitchell is currently professor of political theory at Georgetown University. From 2002–05, he was the Chairman of the Government Department. In 2005, he was on the start-team for Georgetown's School of Foreign Service in Doha Qatar, and has taught courses there periodically for the past fifteen years. During the 2008–10 academic years, Mitchell took leave from Georgetown and became the Acting Chancellor of The American University of Iraq - Sulaimani. He has been a Visiting Fellow in American Political Thought at The Heritage Foundation. He is the author numerous books, including: *Not by Reason Alone: Religion, History, and Identity in Early Modern Political Thought* (University of Chicago Press, 1993), *The Fragility of Freedom: Tocqueville on Religion, Democracy, and the American Future* (University of Chicago Press, 1995), *Plato's Fable: On the Mortal Condition in Shadowy Times* (Princeton University Press, 2006), *Tocqueville in Arabia: Dilemmas in the Democratic Age* (University of Chicago Press, 2013). His most recent book is *American Awakening: Identity Politics and Other Afflictions of Our Time* (Encounter Books, 2020). His next book project is entitled *The Gentle Seduction of Tyranny*. In addition, Mitchell is an avid conservationist, working to restore his small forest on the Eastern Shore, and working to develop the next generation of solar-electric sailboats.

AARON RENN is a Cofounder and Senior Fellow at American Reformer. He also writes on cultural topics at Substack. Renn was previously an urban policy researcher, writer, and consultant. He was a senior fellow at the Manhattan Institute for Policy Research for five years. His work has been featured in leading publications such as *The New York Times*, *The Guardian*, and *The Atlantic*. Prior to public policy, Renn spent fifteen years in the technology and management consulting industry, mostly at Accenture, where he was a partner. He lives with his wife and son in Indianapolis.

ARTHUR MILIKH is the executive director of The Claremont Institute's Center for the American Way of Life. Previously, he was the Associate Director of the Center for American Studies and AWC Family Foundation Fellow at The Heritage Foundation.

Prior to Heritage, he worked at the House Committee on Armed Services and at The Hudson Institute. Milikh's writings have appeared in *The Claremont Review of Books*, *National Affairs*, *City Journal*, Real Clear Politics, *Law & Liberty*, and *American Greatness*.

DAVID P. GOLDMAN is a Washington Fellow at The Claremont Institute's Center for the American Way of Life. Goldman is Deputy Editor of *Asia Times*, where he has written the "Spengler" column since 2001. He is also a Senior Fellow of the London Institute for Policy Research. He previously was a partner at Reorient Group (Hong Kong), and global head of fixed income research at Bank of America and Cantor Fitzgerald. He was also a Managing Director at Credit Suisse and Bear Stearns, a member of Institutional Investor's All-America Fixed Income Team. His books include *You Will Be Assimilated: China's Plan to Sino-Form the World* (2020), *How Civilizations Die* (2011), and *It's Not the End of the World – It's Just the End of You* (2011). Goldman writes frequently for *The Claremont Review of Books*, *The Wall Street Journal*, *First Things*, *Newsweek*, *Law & Liberty* and *Tablet Magazine*. He has published numerous scholarly articles on economics, finance, and intellectual history.

MATTHEW PETERSON is cofounder of New Founding, a venture firm dedicated to creating a commercial and cultural union that connects, curates, and advocates for the American people. He is Publisher of RETURN – a publication and community that brings together all those who want to harness technology for the sake of human flourishing. Peterson is also President of the Firebrand Super PAC. Peterson founded *The American Mind*, a publication of The Claremont Institute.

JAMES POULOS is the Executive Editor of *The American Mind*, the Claremont Institute's online publication devoted to driving the conversation about the ideas and principles that drive American political life. The author of *The Art of Being Free* (St. Martin's Press, 2017), a study of Tocqueville's Democracy in America, he is also the contributing editor of *American Affairs* and a fellow at the Center for the Study of Digital Life. A frequent commentator on technology and the American character, his writing has been featured in publications from *National Affairs* to *National Review* and *Foreign Affairs* to *Foreign Policy*, and praised at *The New York Times*, *The Washington Post*, *The New Yorker*, and many more. Poulos has appeared on numerous television and radio programs and delivered remarks before audiences at organizations and campuses across the country.

THEODORE WOLD is a Washington Fellow at the Claremont Institute's Center for the American Way of Life. He is also the Solicitor General of Idaho. Previously, he was the Acting-Assistant Attorney General in the Office of Legal Policy at the Department of Justice and Deputy Assistant to the President for Domestic Policy during the Trump Administration. He also served as Deputy Chief Counsel to United States Senator Mike Lee on the Senate Judiciary Committee. Mr. Wold clerked at the United States Court of Appeals for the District of Columbia Circuit for Judge Janice Rogers Brown and the United States District Court for the District of Puerto Rico for Judge José Antonio Fusté.

ROBERT DELAHUNTY is a Washington Fellow at The Claremont Institute's Center for the American Way of Life. He was LeJeune Chair and Professor of Law at the University of St. Thomas School of Law in Minneapolis, Minnesota. Prior to this, he was in the Senior Executive Service at the Office of Legal Counsel in the U.S. Department of Justice. He also served as Deputy General Counsel at the White House Office of Homeland Security, as special advisor to the Solicitor of Labor at the U.S. Department of Labor, and as special advisor to the Assistant Attorney General in the Civil Rights Division of the U.S. Department of Justice. He was an Associate at Sullivan & Cromwell in the litigating division.

Delahunty has written numerous articles on constitutional law, international law, and Shakespeare and the law. He has published in *The Wall Street Journal*, *The Federalist*, *Law & Liberty*, *National Review Online*, and elsewhere. He co-authored a book on war with Antonio F. Perez and authored a book on the 17th century philosopher Baruch Spinoza.

JESSE MERRIAM is a Washington Fellow at The Claremont Institute's Center for the American Way of Life. His research focuses on the constitutional difficulties presented by the civil rights movement, including anti-discrimination and affirmative-action law. He is currently an Associate Professor of Government at Patrick Henry College in Purcellville, Virginia. Prior to that, he served for six years as an Assistant Professor of Political Science at Loyola University, Maryland. He has worked as an appellate litigator at a D.C. constitutional law firm, and has been a research associate at the Pew Research Center's Forum on Religion & Public Life. Merriam has published over a dozen academic print articles in top law-review and peer-reviewed journals, covering such diverse topics as legal conservatism, the meaning of the rule of law, church-state relations, and the theory and practice of originalist constitutional interpretation. In addition, his other publications have appeared in *Law & Liberty*, *National Review Online*, *The American Conservative*, *American Greatness*, and *The Claremont Review of Books*.

JEREMY CARL is a Senior Fellow at the Claremont Institute. Prior to joining Claremont, Carl worked for a decade as a research fellow at the Hoover Institution at Stanford University, serving as a policy advisor to many national political figures. Carl is the author and editor of several books on energy policy, most recently, *Keeping the Lights on at America's Nuclear Power Plants*. His political writing and commentary has been featured in *The New York Times*, *The Wall Street Journal*, *Time Magazine*, *National Review*, Politico, and *The Economist*, along with other leading newspapers and magazines. His academic writing has appeared in numerous professional journals.

ERIC KAUFMANN is Professor of Politics at Birkbeck, University of London, and author of *Whiteshift: Immigration, Populism and the Future of White Majorities*. He is a Senior Fellow at Policy Exchange. He has also written *Changing Places: Mapping the White British Response to Ethnic Change* (Demos, 2014), *Shall the Religious Inherit the Earth: Demography and Politics in the Twenty-First Century* (Profile, 2010), *The Rise and Fall of Anglo-America: The Decline of Dominant Ethnicity in the United States* (Harvard, 2004) and two other books.

ROGER KIMBALL is Editor and Publisher of *The New Criterion* and President and Publisher of Encounter Books. He writes regular columns for *American Greatness*, *The Epoch Times*, and *The Spectator*, US edition. Mr. Kimball lectures widely and has appeared on national radio and television programs as well as the BBC. Among other writings, Mr. Kimball is the author of *The Fortunes of Permanence: Culture and Anarchy in an Age of Amnesia* (St. Augustine's Press, 2012), *The Rape of the Masters: How Political Correctness Sabotages Art* (Encounter Books), *Lives of the Mind: The Use and Abuse of Intelligence from Hegel to Wodehouse* (Ivan R. Dee), and *Art's Prospect: The Challenge of Tradition in an Age of Celebrity* (Ivan R. Dee). Mr. Kimball has served on the Board of Advisors of the Gilder-Lehrman Institute of American History, the Board of Visitors and Governors of St. John's College, Annapolis and Santa Fe, and Transaction Publishers. He currently serves on the board of the Manhattan Institute for Policy Research and is Chairman of the William F. Buckley Jr. Program at Yale. He is the recipient of a Bradley Prize from the Lynde and Harry Bradley Foundation and the Thomas L. Phillips Career Achievement Award from the Fund for American Studies, both in 2019.

| INDEX |

The letter *t* following a page number denotes a table or graph.

Disney (Walt Disney Company), 141, 145

diversity: American Founders and, 36–37; American nationhood and, 267–68; civil rights morality and, 238; fear of ethnic change, 263–64; justice and meritocracy and, 64–65; prioritizing over performance, 6

Diversity, Equity, and Inclusion (DEI), 52, 54, 111, 116, 118

divorce, 8–9, 80, 82

Dobbs v. Jackson Women's Health Organization, 230, 255

Domestic Investigations and Operations Guide, 197–98

domestic security. *See* Deep State

Dorsey, Jack, 142

Douglass, Frederick, 64

drug and alcohol abuse, 13, 70, 87, 134, 224

drug problem, US, 5–6

Duchamp, Marcel, 281–82

Dunbar-Ortiz, Roxanne, 246

Durbin, Dick, 196

economic nationalism: Founder's nationalism and, 35–36; revenue of Fortune 500 companies, 128

economics. *See also* manufacturing; wages: business and economy, neutrality of, 139–41; conservatism and, 122–37; culture and, 133–34; entrepreneurship, 122–23, 128–33; as fake, 11–12; federal R&D budget, 125, 126; free markets, 101, 142, 143, 145, 154, 161, 171, 221, 260; free-trade, 39–40, 42, 220; GDP, 1–2, 11, 123, 125–29 (passim), 134–36, 149, 261; Great Recession of 2008-9, 129–30; growth of, working women and, 70; Hamiltonian economics, rein-

vention of, 124–27; income and wealth inequality, 10; internet and, 134 (*See also* internet); moralizing, viii; prosperity, ix, 9, 35, 49, 107, 179; stagflation, 2, 124; supply-side economics, 124, 128, 133–34; tax cuts, 122–23, 123, 124, 134; trade deficits, 123, 128, 133; transfer payments, 125, 126, 127t, 130t; voo-doo economics, 125; woke capital, 138; woke economics, development of, 139–41

education. *See also* higher education; high schools; K-12 education; teachers: anti-racism doctrines, 107; charter schools, 110; curriculum priorities, 136; defunding DEI projects and divisive concepts, 54, 113, 118, 273; Department of Education, 22, 30, 54, 108, 113, 169, 175; educational choice programs, 110, 111–12; elimination of admissions tests, 67; ESAs (education savings accounts), 110, 111; HBCUs (historically black colleges or universities), 66; homeschooling, 109–10; KIPP, 110; Left control of, viii, 108, 109; magnet schools, 110; mediocrity of, 107–8; merit-based pay, 109; patriotism in, 115–16; physical fitness programs, 115–16; propositional-nation conservatives and, 41; racism as curriculum, 63; roadmap for reforming, 113–16; school prayer, 229; sex education programs, 91, 107, 108, 112; standardized testing, 26, 27, 109; state teacher certification standards, 114; student loan system, 77, 111, 116, 117, 118; working women and, 77

education savings accounts (ESAs), 110, 111

First Great Awakening, 94, 102–3

First Step Act, 65

Floyd, George, 59, 67, 96, 160

foreign nationals, vetting of, 169

foreign ownership of US assets, 10–11

foreign policy: American history of, 215–16; Bush and, 219–20; current state of, 219–20; Deep State and, 184–85; Founder's nationalism and, 35; future of, 220–25; neoconservatism, evolution of, 209–19; realist foreign policy, 218; Truman and, 215–16; Trump and, 219–20

Fortune 500 companies, revenue of, 128

Founding, American. *See* American Founding

Fountain (Duchamp), 281–82

Fourteenth Amendment, 227, 229

freedom of association, gay rights and, 25

free markets, 101, 142, 143, 145, 154, 161, 171, 221, 260

free speech: art and, 284; Big Tech and media, 2–3, 11; digital technology and, 165; gay rights and, 25; *vs.* hate speech, 67; living constitutionalists and, 24; online free speech, 162

free-trade, 39–40, 42, 220

French Revolution, 100–101

FTAA, 214

Fukuyama-Krauthammer-Wolfowitz-Bush Doctrine, 215

gang of eight immigration compromise, 249

Garland, Merrick, 195

Gay Pride, 82, 90. *See also* LGBTQ+ individuals

gay rights. *See* LGBTQ+ individuals

GDP, 1–2, 11, 123, 125–29 (passim), 134–36, 149, 261

gender. *See also* LGBTQ+ individuals; male-dominated industries; women: art and gender politics, 287; political/cultural issues of, 46–47, 77–78; psychological differences of, 88–89

gender reassignment, 13, 15, 87, 90, 150, 175

Germany, 133, 217, 218, 263, 265

Ginsburg, Ruth Bader, 70

globalization, 129, 140, 157, 160, 214–15, 262

global warming, 5, 67

Goldwater insurgency of 1964, ix–x

Google, 122, 128, 132, 141, 143–44, 161, 162

GOP, Hispanic shift toward, 25

Gordon, Milton, 266

governance: public-private partnerships in, 181–82; self-governance, 12, 167–70, 173, 239–40

government institutions, redeemability of, 24–25

grammar schools. *See* K-12 education

Grassley, Chuck, 196

Great Awokening, 66

Great Recession of 2008–9, 129–30

guns, 22, 30, 175, 230, 255

Hamilton, Alexander, 124–27, 139–40

Hamiltonian economics, reinvention of, 124–27

Hart-Celler Act of 1965, 245, 247, 260

hate speech *vs.* free speech, 67

HBCUs (historically black colleges or universities), 66

Health Care Exchange, 28, 182

Herz, John, 185

higher education. *See also* education: defunding bureaucracies of, 30; educational choice programs, 111;

INDEX

A NOTE ON THE TYPE

UP FROM CONSERVATISM *has been set in Fernando Mello's Brabo types, which he first developed during a typographic workshop at the Plantin-Moretus Museum in Antwerp and named in honor of Silvius Brabo, the mythic Roman savior of the ancient port city. As legend has it, Brabo defeated the giant Druon Antigoon, who terrorized the city by extorting taxes on shipping and demanding payment to cross the bridge over the river Scheldt, cutting off the hands of those who refused to pay. Brabo defeated the giant and paid him back in kind, tossing his severed hand into the Scheldt, an act that (so the legend tells us) is commemorated in the the city's name: the Dutch for "hand-throw" is* hand werpen, *hence, Antwerpen.* ◆ *A distinctly modern type, Brabo acknowledges the proportions and crisp drawing of sixteenth-century faces like Garamond and Plantin, making it a fine choice for literary texts.*

DESIGN & COMPOSITION BY CARL W. SCARBROUGH